THE FABER LIBRARY—No. 26

THE PROGRESS OF A PLOUGH-BOY TO A SEAT IN PARLIAMENT

WILLIAM COBBETT

A WOOD-ENGRAVING BY JOHN FARLEIGH

THE
PROGRESS OF A PLOUGH-BOY
TO A
SEAT IN PARLIAMENT

AS EXEMPLIFIED IN
THE HISTORY OF THE LIFE
OF
WILLIAM COBBETT
MEMBER FOR OLDHAM

EDITED BY
WILLIAM REITZEL

LONDON
FABER AND FABER LIMITED
24 RUSSELL SQUARE

FIRST PUBLISHED IN JUNE MCMXXXIII
BY FABER & FABER LIMITED
24 RUSSELL SQUARE LONDON W.C. 1
REPRINTED OCTOBER MCMXXXV
BY KIMBLE & BRADFORD LONDON W. 1
ALL RIGHTS RESERVED

EDITOR'S NOTE

IN 1834, COBBETT ANNOUNCED THAT IT WAS his intention to close the *Political Register* and to publish, "as the work of another year", the history of his life. He later expands this idea. "I shall entitle my book 'The Progress of a Plough-boy to a seat in Parliament, as exemplified in the History of the Life of William Cobbett, Member for Oldham'; and, I intend that the frontispiece to the book shall represent me, first in a smock-frock, driving the rooks from the corn; and, in the lower compartment of the picture, standing in the House of Commons, addressing the Speaker." This intention was never carried out.

The present work was prepared with Cobbett's plan in the editor's mind. The method, that of using the autobiographical parts of Cobbett's writings, was suggested by the anonymous *Life* of 1835 and by the more fully developed work of E. I. Carlyle in 1904. In the present book the method has been used to its fullest extent, and all but a few linking passages are of Cobbett's own composition.

All editorial insertions have been enclosed in square brackets. The exact source of all the material used has been indicated in the Sources of the Text. Any reader who wishes to see exactly what has been done in the way of combining

[v]

separated passages, or what changes in grammatical construction have been made for the sake of continuity, will find it easy to refer to the original passages. The latter changes have not been indicated in the notes, except when the source is still unpublished, and then the passage has been printed for convenience of reference.

The editor wishes to thank H. W. Cobbett, Esq., of Manchester, for his courtesy in permitting the *Cobbett Papers* in his possession to be examined, and for his kindness in permitting them to be examined frequently.

CONTENTS

[vii]

CHAPTER I

1763–1782

*   *   *   *   *

I WAS BRED AT THE PLOUGH-TAIL, AND IN the Hop-Gardens of Farnham in Surrey, my native place, and which spot, as it so happened, is the neatest in England, and, I believe, in the whole world. All there is a garden. The neat culture of the hop extends its influence to the round about. Hedges cut with shears and every other mark of skill strike the eye at Farnham, and become fainter and fainter as you go from it in every direction. Arthur Young calls the vale between Farnham and Alton the finest ten miles in England.

To [a taste for farming], produced in me by a desire to imitate a father whom I ardently loved, and to whose every word I listened with admiration, I owe no small part of my happiness, for a greater proportion of which very few men ever had to be grateful to God. These pursuits, innocent in themselves, instructive in their very nature, and always tending to preserve health, have been a constant, a never-failing source, of recreation to me.

Early habits and affections seldom quit us while we have vigour of mind left. I was brought up under a father, whose talk was chiefly about his garden and his fields, with regard to which he was

The Progress of a Plough-boy

famed for his skill and his exemplary neatness. From my very infancy, from the age of six years, when I climbed up the side of a steep sand rock, and there scooped me out a plot four feet square to make me a garden, and the soil for which I carried up in the bosom of my little blue smock-frock, I have never lost one particle of my passion for these healthy and rational and heart-cheering pursuits, in which every day presents something new, in which the spirits are never suffered to flag, and in which industry, skill, and care are sure to meet with their due reward. I have never, for any eight months together, during my whole life, been without a garden. So sure are we to overcome difficulties where the heart and mind are bent on the thing to be obtained!

All that I can boast of in my birth is that I was born in old England. With respect to my ancestors, I shall go no further back than my grandfather, and for this very plain reason, that I never heard talk of any prior to him. He was a day-labourer, and I have heard my father say, that he worked for one farmer from the day of his marriage to that of his death, upwards of forty years. He died before I was born, but I have often slept beneath the same roof that had sheltered him, and where his widow dwelt for seven years after his death. It was a little thatched cottage with a garden before the door. It had but two windows; a damson tree shaded one, and a clump of filberts the other. Here I and my brothers went every Christmas and

Whitsuntide, to spend a week or two, and torment the poor old woman with our noise and dilapidations. She used to give us milk and bread for breakfast, an apple pudding for our dinner, and a piece of bread and cheese for supper. Her fire was made of turf cut from the neighbouring heath and her evening light was a rush dipped in grease.

My father, from the poverty of his parents, had received no very brilliant education; he was, however, learned for a man in his rank of life. When a little boy, he drove the plough for two pence a day and these his earnings were appropriated to the expenses of an evening school. What a village schoolmaster could be expected to teach he had learnt, and had besides considerably improved himself in several branches of the mathematicks. He understood land-surveying well, and was often chosen to draw the plans of disputed territory; in short, he had the reputation of possessing experience and understanding, which never fails in England, to give a man in a country place, some little weight with his neighbours. He was honest, industrious, and frugal; it was not, therefore, wonderful, that he should be situated in a good farm, and happy in a wife of his own rank, like him, beloved and respected.

I was born in the month of March, 1766:[1] the exact age of my [three] brothers I have forgotten, but I remember having heard my mother say, that there was but three years and three quarters difference between the age of the eldest and that of the youngest.

I do not remember the time when I did not earn my living. My first occupation was, driving the small birds from the turnip seed, and the rooks from the peas. When I trudged afield, with my wooden bottle and my satchel over my shoulders, I was hardly able to climb the gates and stiles, and, at the close of day, to reach home was a task of infinite labour. My next employment was weeding wheat, and leading a single horse at harrowing barley. Hoeing peas followed, and hence I arrived at the honour of joining the reapers in harvest, driving the team and holding the plough. We were all of us strong and laborious, and my father used to boast, that he had four boys, the eldest of whom was but fifteen years old, who did as much work as any three men in the parish of Farnham.

I have some faint recollection of going to school to an old woman who, I believe did not succeed in teaching me my letters. In the winter evenings my father taught me to read and write, and gave me a pretty tolerable knowledge of arithmetic. Grammar he did not perfectly understand himself, and therefore his endeavours to teach that, necessarily failed; for, though he thought he understood it, and though he made us get the rules by heart, we learnt nothing at all of the principles.

As to politics, we were like the rest of the country people in England; that is to say, we neither knew nor thought anything about the matter. The shouts of victory or the murmur at a defeat, would now-and-then break in upon our tranquillity for a moment; but I do not remember ever having seen a newspaper in the house, and most certainly that privation did not render us less free, happy, or industrious.

After, however, the American War had continued for some time, and the cause and nature of it began to be understood, or rather misunderstood, by the lower classes of people in England, we became a little better acquainted with subjects of this kind. My father was a partisan of the Americans: he used frequently to dispute on the subject with the gardener of a nobleman who lived near us. This was generally done with good humour, over a pot of our best ale; yet the disputants sometimes grew warm, and gave way to language that could not fail to attract our attention. My father was worsted without a doubt, as he had for antagonist, a shrewd and sensible old Scotchman, far his superior in political knowledge; but he pleaded before a partial audience: we thought there was but one wise man in the world, and that one was our father.

My father used to take one of us with him every year to the great hop fair at Weyhill. The fair was held at Old Michaelmastide, and the journey was to us, a sort of reward for the labours of the summer. It happened to be my turn to go thither the very year that Long Island was taken by the British.[2] I rode a little pony, and remember how

[5]

1763
to
1782

proud I was on the occasion; but, I also remember, that my brothers, two out of three of whom were older than I, thought it unfair that my father selected me; my own reflections upon the occasion have never been forgotten by me.

A great company of hop-merchants and farmers were just sitting down to supper as the post arrived, bringing in the extraordinary Gazette which announced the victory. A hop-factor from London took the paper, placed his chair upon the table, and began to read in an audible voice. He was opposed, a dispute ensued, and my father retired taking me by the hand, to another apartment where we supped with about a dozen others of the same sentiments. Here Washington's health and success to the Americans were repeatedly toasted, and this was the first time, as far as I can recollect, that I ever heard that General's name mentioned.

It would be [as] useless as unentertaining to dwell on the occupations and sports of a country boy; to lead the reader to fairs, cricket-matches, and hare-hunts; [but one occasion I must recount.] A huntsman, named George Bradley, who was huntsman to Mr Smither, of Hale, very wantonly gave me a cut with his whip, because I jumped in amongst the dogs, pulled a hare from them, and got her scut, upon a little common, called Seal Common, near Waverley Abbey. I was only about eight years old; but my mind was so strongly imbued with the principles of natural justice, that I did

not rest satisfied with the mere calling of names, 1763
of which, however, I gave Mr George Bradley a *to*
plenty. I sought to inflict a just punishment upon 1782
him.

Hounds (hare-hounds, at least) will follow the
trail of a red herring as eagerly as that of a hare,
and rather more so, the scent being stronger and
more unbroken. I waited till Bradley and his pack
were trailing for a hare in the neighbourhood of
that same Seal Common. They were pretty sure to
find in the space of half an hour, and the hare was
pretty sure to go up the Common and over the hill
to the south. I placed myself ready with a red
herring at the end of a string, in a dry field, and
near a hard path, along which, or near to which, I
was pretty sure the hare would go. I waited a long
while; the sun was getting high; the scent bad;
but, by and by, I heard the view-halloo and full
cry. I squatted down in the fern, and my heart
bounded with the prospect of inflicting justice,
when I saw my lady come skipping by, going off
towards Pepper Harrow; that is to say, towards
the south. In a moment, I clapped down my
herring, went off at a right angle towards the west,
climbed up a steep bank very soon, where the
horsemen, such as they were, could not follow;
then on I went over the roughest part of the common that I could find, till I got to the pales of
Moor Park, over which I went, there being holes at
the bottom for the letting in of hares. That part of
the park was covered with short heath; and I gave

[7]

some twirls about to amuse Mr Bradley for half an hour. Then off I went, and down a hanger at last, to the bottom of which no horseman could get without riding round a quarter of a mile. At the bottom of the hanger was an aldermoor, in a swamp. There my herring ceased to perform its service. The river was pretty rapid: I tossed it in, that it might go back to the sea and relate to its brethren the exploits of the land. I washed my hands in the water of the moor; and took a turn, and stood at the top of the hanger to witness the winding-up of the day's sport, which terminated a little before dusk in one of the dark days of November. After over-running the scent a hundred times; after an hour's puzzling in the dry field, after all the doubles and all the turns that the sea-born hare had given them, down came the whole posse to the swamp; the huntsman went round a millhead, not far off, and tried the other side of the river: "No! damn her, where can she be?" And thus, amidst conjectures, disputations, mutual blamings, and swearings a plenty they concluded, some of them half-leg deep in dirt, and going soaking home.

In those "dark ages" that the impudent Scotch economists talk about, we had a great many holidays. There were all the fairs of our own place, and all the fairs of the places just round about. There were several days at Christmas, at Easter, at Whitsuntide; and we had a day or two at Hollantide, as we used to call it, which came in

November, I believe, and at Candlemass. Besides
these, there were cricket-matches, and single-stick
matches; and all these were not thought too much.
I verily believe, that if I had been born in these
[present] days of slavery, of rags, and of hunger, I
should never have been any more known in the
world, than the chap I, this very moment, see slink-
ing by the side of a road-waggon, with scarcely a
shoe on his foot, and with a smock-frock that none
but actual beggars wore in the " dark ages ", when
I was a boy. I never knew a labouring man, in
those " dark ages ", go out to his work in the morning without a bottle of beer and a satchel of
victuals, containing cheese, if not bacon, hung
upon his crook. A bottle-crook made as usual a
part of the equipage of a labourer, as his smock-
frock, or his hat did. Except in about five or six
instances, in Essex, I have not seen a bottle-crook
these twenty years.

In the " dark ages ", when I was a boy, country
labourers' wives used to spin the wool, and knit
the stockings and gloves that were wanted in
the family. My grandmother knit stockings for
me after she was blind. Farmers' wives, and
daughters, and servant maids, were spinning, reel-
ing, carding, knitting, or at something or other of
that sort, whenever the work of the farm-house
did not demand them.

Accordingly, be it observed, that there wanted
no schools, no Lancastrian or Bell work, no Tracts,
no circulation of Bibles, to make the common

1763
to
1782

people generally honest and obedient. I remember a little sort of fair that used to be held at a village in Surrey. I remember the white smock-frocks and red handkerchiefs, and nice clean clothes of the girls, that used to ornament that fair. By accident, I stumbled upon it in a rural ride [in 1822]. Not a tenth part of the people, and these, in general ragged and dirty, with some few girls drawn off in tawdry cottons, looking more like town prostitutes than country girls; and this was a pretty fair sample of the whole country.

The truth is, that the system which has been pursued in England from the time of the Revolution [of 1680], the system of government debt, is a system which begins by totally debasing the labouring classes, and that ends by producing its own overthrow, and, generally, that of the state along with it. It draws property into great masses; it gives to cunning the superiority over industry; it makes agriculture a subject of adventure; it puts down all small cultivators; it encloses every inch of that land which God himself seems to have intended for the poor.

[There is] a place called the Bourne, which lies in the heath at about a mile from Farnham. It is a winding narrow valley, down which, during the wet season of the year, there runs a stream beginning at the Holt Forest, and emptying itself into the Wey just below Moor Park, which was the seat of Sir William Temple, when Swift was residing with him. There is a little hop-garden in which

I used to work from eight to ten years old; from which I have scores of times run in order to follow the hounds, leaving the hoe to do the best that it could to destroy the weeds; but the most interesting thing was a sandhill, which goes from a part of the heath down to the rivulet.

As a due mixture of pleasure with toil, I with my two brothers, used occasionally to disport ourselves, as the lawyers call it, at this sandhill. Our diversion was this: one used to draw his arms out of the sleeves of his smock-frock, and lay himself down with his arms by his sides; and then the others, one at head and the other at feet, sent him rolling down the hill like a barrel or a log of wood. By the time he got to the bottom, his hair, eyes, ears, nose and mouth, were all full of this loose sand; then the others took their turn, and at every roll, there was a monstrous spell of laughter. I often told my sons of this while they were very little, and [in 1822] I took one of them to see the spot. But that was not all. This was the spot where I was receiving my education; and this was the sort of education; and I am perfectly satisfied that if I had not received such an education, or something very much like it; that, if I had been brought up a milksop, with a nursery-maid everlastingly at my heels, I should have been at this day as great a fool, as inefficient a mortal, as any of those frivolous idiots that are turned out from Winchester or Westminster School or from any of those dens of dunces called Colleges and Univer-

1763
to
1782

sities. It is impossible to say how much I owe to that sandhill; and I went to return it my thanks.

[At this time] when my chief occupation was to hobble over the clods by the side of the plough-horses, I remember, that I used to wonder how it happened, that the land produced enough, and only enough for all the animals that fed on its produce. My mind did not penetrate so far as the human species: it found quite sufficient to be astonished at in perceiving, that there was always just horses enough to eat the hay, and just hay enough for the horses; just meadows enough for the cattle, and cattle for the meadows; sheep enough for the downs, and downs enough for the sheep. If I rambled into the forest or over the common, I never found a blade of grass to spare, and yet there was always enough to maintain all the various kinds of animals that fed on it, though they belonged, perhaps, to a thousand different persons, every one of whom wished to feed thereon as many animals as he could, and though there was no active law to regulate the conduct of these persons. Such astonishment was natural enough in a boy nine or ten years old.

At eleven years of age my employment was clipping of box-edgings and weeding beds of flowers in the garden of the Bishop of Winchester, at the Castle of Farnham. I had always been fond of beautiful gardens; and, a gardener, who had just come from the King's gardens at Kew, gave such a description of them as made me instantly resolve to work in these gardens. The next morning, with-out saying a word to anybody, off I set, with no clothes, except those upon my back, and thirteen halfpence in my pocket. I found that I must go to Richmond, and I, accordingly, went on, from place to place, inquiring my way thither. A long day (it was in June) brought me to Richmond in the afternoon. Two pennyworth of bread and cheese and a pennyworth of small beer, which I had on the road, and one halfpenny that I had lost somehow or other, left three pence in my pocket. With this for my whole fortune, I was trudging through Richmond in my blue smock-frock and my red garters tied under my knees, when, staring about me, my eye fell upon a little book, in a bookseller's window: "Tale of a Tub; price 3*d.*" The title was so odd, that my curiosity was excited. I had the 3*d.*, but, then, I could have no supper. In I went and got the little book, which I was so impatient to read, that I got over into a field, at the upper corner of Kew Gardens, where there stood a haystack. On the shady side of this, I sat down to read. The book was so different from anything that I had ever read before: it was some-thing so new to my mind, that, though I could not at all understand some of it, it delighted me be-yond description; and it produced what I have always considered a sort of birth of intellect. I read on till it was dark, without any thought about supper or bed. When I could see no longer, I put my little book in my pocket, and tumbled down

1763
to
1782

by the side of the stack, where I slept till the birds in Kew Garden awaked me in the morning; when off I started to Kew, reading my little book. The singularity of my dress, the simplicity of my manner, my confident and lively air, induced the gardener, who was a Scotchman, I remember, to give me victuals, find me lodging, and set me to work. And, it was during the period that I was at Kew, that the King[3] and two of his brothers laughed at the oddness of my dress, while I was sweeping the grass plat round the foot of the Pagoda. The gardener, seeing me fond of books, lent me some gardening books to read; but, these I could not relish after my Tale of a Tub, which I carried about with me wherever I went, and when I, at about twenty years old, lost it in a box that fell overboard in the Bay of Funday in North America, the loss gave me greater pain than I have ever felt at losing thousands of pounds.

Towards the autumn of 1782, I went to visit a relation who lived in the neighbourhood of Portsmouth. From the top of Portsdown, I, for the first time, beheld the sea, and no sooner did I behold it than I wished to be a sailor. I could never account for this sudden impulse, nor can I now. Almost all English boys feel the same inclination: it would seem that, like ducks, instinct leads them to rush on the bosom of the water.

But it was not the sea alone that I saw: the grand fleet was riding at anchor at Spithead. I had heard of the wooden walls of Old England: I had

formed my idea of a ship and of a fleet; but what I
now beheld so far surpassed what I had ever been
able to form a conception of, that I stood lost
between astonishment and admiration.

I arrived at my uncle's late in the evening, with
my mind full of my seafaring project. Though I
had walked thirty miles during the day, and consequently was well wearied, I slept not a moment.
It was no sooner daylight than I arose and walked
down toward the old castle on the beach at Spithead. For a sixpence given to an invalid I got
permission to go upon the battlements: here I had
a closer view of the fleet, and at every look my impatience to be on board increased. In short, I
went from the castle to Portsmouth, got into a
boat, and was in a few minutes on board the
Pegasus man-of-war, commanded by the Right
Honourable George Berkley, brother to the Earl
of Berkley.

The Captain had more compassion than is
generally met with in a man of his profession: he
represented to me the toils I must undergo, and
the punishment that the least disobedience or
neglect would subject me to. He persuaded me to
return home, and I remember he concluded his
advice with telling me, that it was better to be led
to church in a halter to be tied to a girl that I did
not like, than to be tied to the gang-way or, as
the sailors call it, married to Miss Roper. From
the conclusion of this wholesome counsel, I perceived that the Captain thought I had eloped on

[15]

1763
to
1782

account of a bastard. I blushed, and that confirmed him in his opinion.

I in vain attempted to convince Captain Berkley, that choice alone led me to the sea; he sent me on shore, and I at last quitted Portsmouth; but not before I had applied to the Port Admiral, Evans, to get my name enrolled among those who were destined for the service. I was, in some sort, obliged to acquaint the Admiral with what had passed on board the Pegasus, in consequence of which my request was refused, and I happily escaped, sorely against my will, from the most toilsome and perilous profession in the world.

I returned once more to the plough, but I was spoiled for a farmer. I had, before my Portsmouth adventure, never known any other ambition than that of surpassing my brothers in the different labours of the field; but it was quite otherwise now; I sighed for a sight of the world; the little island of Britain seemed too small a compass for me. The things in which I had taken the most delight were neglected; the singing of the birds grew insipid, and the heart-cheering cry of the hounds, after which I formerly used to fly from my work, was heard with the most torpid indifference. Still, however, I remained at home till the following spring, when I quitted it for ever.

CHAPTER II

1783–1784

*   *   *   *   *

IT WAS ON THE SIXTH OF MAY, 1783, THAT I, like Don Quixote, sallied forth to seek adventures. I was dressed in my holiday clothes, in order to accompany two or three lasses to Guildford Fair. They were to assemble at a house about three miles from my home, where I was to attend them; but unfortunately for me, I had to cross the London turnpike road. The stage-coach had just turned the summit of a hill, and was rattling down towards me at a merry rate. The notion of going to London never entered my mind till this very moment, yet the step was completely determined on, before the coach came to the spot where I stood.

It was by mere accident that I had money enough to defray the expenses of this day. Being rigged out for the fair, I had three or four crown and half-crown pieces (which most certainly I did not intend to spend) besides a few shillings and halfpence. This my little all, which I had been years in amassing, wilted away like snow before the sun, when touched by the fingers of the innkeepers and their waiters. In short, when I arrived at Ludgate Hill, and had paid my fare, I had but about half a crown in my pocket.

1783
to
1784

By a commencement of that good luck, which has attended me in all the situations in which fortune has placed me, I was preserved from ruin. A gentleman, who was one of the passengers in the stage, fell into conversation with me at dinner, and he soon learnt that I was going I knew not whither or for what. This gentleman was a hop-merchant in the borough of Southwark and, upon closer inquiry, it appeared that he had often dealt with my father at Weyhill. He knew the danger I was in; he was himself a parent, and he felt for my parents. His house became my home, he wrote to my father, and endeavoured to prevail on me to obey his orders, which were to return immediately home. I am ashamed to say that I was disobedient. Willingly would I have returned, but pride would not suffer me to do it. I feared the scoffs of my acquaintances more than the real evils that threatened me.

My generous preserver, finding my obstinacy not to be overcome, began to look out for an employment for me, when an acquaintance of his, an attorney, called in to see him. He related my adventure to this gentleman, whose name was Holland, and who, happening to want an under-strapping quill driver, did me the honour to take me into his service, and the next day saw me perched upon a great high stool, in an obscure chamber in Gray's Inn, endeavouring to decipher the crabbed draughts of my employer.

I could write a good plain hand, but I could not

read the pothooks and hangers of Mr Holland. He 1783
was a month in learning me to copy without almost *to*
continual assistance, and even then I was of but 1784
little use to him; for, besides that I wrote at a
snail's pace, my want of knowledge in orthography
gave him infinite trouble: so that for the first two
months I was a dead weight upon his hands. Time,
however, rendered me useful, and Mr Holland was
pleased to tell me that he was very well satisfied
with me, just at the very moment when I began to
grow extremely dissatisfied with him.

No part of my life has been totally unattended
with pleasure, except the eight or nine months I
passed in Gray's Inn. The office (for so the dungeon
where I wrote was called) was so dark, that, on
cloudy days, we were obliged to burn candle. I
worked like a galley-slave from five in the morning
till eight or nine at night, and sometimes all night
long. I never quitted this gloomy recess except on
Sundays, when I usually took a walk to St James's
Park, to feast my eyes with the sight of the trees,
the grass, and the water. In one of these walks I
happened to cast my eye on an advertisement,
inviting all loyal young men, who had a mind to
gain riches and glory, to repair to a certain ren-
dezvous, where they might enter into His Majesty's
Marine Service, and have the peculiar happiness
and honour of being enrolled in the Chatham di-
vision. I was not ignorant enough to be the dupe of
this morsel of military bombast; but a change was
what I wanted; besides, I knew that marines went

2-2

to sea, and my desire to be on that element had
rather increased than diminished by my being
penned up in London. In short, I resolved to join
this glorious corps; and, to avoid all possibility
of being discovered by my friends, I went down
to Chatham, and enlisted into the marines as I
thought, but the next morning I found myself
before a Captain of a marching regiment.[1] There
was no retreating: I had taken a shilling to drink
His Majesty's health, and his further bounty was
ready for my reception.

When I told the Captain that I thought myself
engaged in the marines "By Jasus my lad", said
he, "and you have had a narrow escape". He told
me, that the regiment into which I had been so
happy as to enlist was one of the oldest and boldest
in the whole army, and that it was at that time
serving in that fine, flourishing and plentiful
country, Nova Scotia. He dwelt long on the
beauties and riches of this terrestrial paradise,
and dismissed me, perfectly enchanted with the
prospect of a voyage thither.

I enlisted in 1784, and, as peace had then taken
place, no great haste was made to send recruits off
to their regiments. I remember well what sixpence a day was, recollecting the pangs of hunger
felt by me, during the thirteen months that I was
a private soldier at Chatham, previous to my embarkation for Nova Scotia. Of my sixpence, nothing
like fivepence was left to purchase food for the
day. Indeed, not fourpence. For there was wash-

ing, mending, soap, flour for hair-powder, shoes,
stockings, shirts, stocks and gaiters, pipe-clay and
several other things to come out of the miserable
sixpence! Judge then of the quantity of food to
sustain life in a lad of sixteen, and to enable him
to exercise with a musket (weighing fourteen
pounds) six or eight hours every day. The best
battalion I ever saw in my life was composed of
men, the far greater part of whom were enlisted
before they were sixteen, and who, when they
were first brought up to the regiment, were clothed
in coats made much too long and too large, in
order to leave room for growing.

We had several recruits from Norfolk (our regiment was the West Norfolk); and many of them
deserted from sheer hunger. They were lads from
the plough-tail. All of them tall, for no short men
were then taken. I remember two that went into
a decline and died during the year, though when
they joined us, they were fine hearty young men.
I have seen them lay in their berths, many and
many a time, actually crying on account of hunger.
The whole week's food was not a bit too much for
one day.

My leisure time was spent, not in the dissipa-
tions common to such a way of life, but in reading
and study. In the course of this year I learnt
more than I had ever done before. I subscribed to
a circulating library at Brompton, the greatest
part of the books in which I read more than once
over. The library was not very considerable, it is

true, nor in my reading was I directed by any
degree of taste or choice. Novels, plays, history,
poetry, all were read, and nearly with equal
avidity.

Such a course of reading could be attended with
but little profit: it was skimming over the surface
of everything. One branch of learning, however,
I went to the bottom with, and that the most
essential too, the grammar of my mother tongue.
I had experienced the want of knowledge of
grammar during my stay with Mr Holland; but it
is very probable that I never should have thought
of encountering the study of it, had not accident
placed me under a man whose friendship extended
beyond his interest. Writing a fair hand procured
me the honour of being copyist to Colonel Debieg,
the commandant of the garrison. I transcribed
the famous correspondence between him and the
Duke of Richmond. The Colonel saw my defici-
ency, and strongly recommended study. He en-
forced his advice with a sort of injunction, and
with a promise of reward in case of success. I
procured me a Lowth's grammar,[2] and applied
myself to the study of it with unceasing assiduity.

The edge of my berth, or that of the guard-bed,
was my seat to study in; my knapsack was my
bookcase; a bit of board lying on my lap was my
writing desk; and the task did not demand anything like a year of my life. I had no money to
purchase candle or oil; in winter time it was rarely
that I could get any evening light but that of the

fire, and only my turn even of that. To buy a pen 1783
or a sheet of paper I was compelled to forgo some *to*
portion of food, though in a state of half-starva- 1784
tion; I had no moment of time that I could call
my own; and I had to read and to write amidst the
talking, laughing, singing, whistling and brawling
of at least half a score of the most thoughtless of
men, and that, too, in the hours of their freedom
from all control. Think not lightly of the farthing
that I had to give, now and then, for ink, pen, or
paper. That farthing was. alas! a great sum to me!
I was as tall as I am now; I had great health and
great exercise. I remember, and well I may! that,
upon one occasion, I, after all absolutely necessary
expenses, had, on a Friday, made shift to have a
halfpenny in reserve, which I had destined for the
purchase of a red herring in the morning; but,
when I pulled off my clothes at night, so hungry
then as to be hardly able to endure life, I found that
I had lost my halfpenny! I buried my head under
the miserable sheet and rag, and cried like a child.

[But this labour was] not without some profit;
for, though it was a considerable time before I
fully comprehended all that I read, still I read and
studied with such unremitted attention, that, at
last, I could write without falling into any very
gross errors. The pains I took cannot be described:
I wrote the whole grammar out two or three times;
I got it by heart. I repeated it every morning and
every evening, and, when on guard, I imposed on
myself the task of saying it all over once every

time I was posted sentinel. To this exercise of my memory I ascribe the retentiveness of which I have since found it capable, and to the success with which it was attended, I ascribe the perseverance that has led to the acquirement of the little learning of which I am master.

I was soon raised to the rank of Corporal, a rank, which, however contemptible it may appear in some people's eyes, brought me in a clear twopence per diem, and put a very clever worsted knot upon my shoulder too. As promotion began to dawn, I grew impatient to get to my regiment, where I expected soon to bask under the rays of royal favour. The happy days of departure at last came: we set sail from Gravesend, and, after a short and pleasant passage, arrived at Halifax in Nova Scotia.

When I first beheld the barren, not to say hideous, rocks at the entrance of the harbour, I began to fear that the master of the vessel had mistaken his way; for I could perceive nothing of that fertility that my good recruiting captain had dwelt on with so much delight. Nova Scotia had no other charm for me than that of novelty. Everything I saw was new: bogs, rocks, and mosquitoes and bull-frogs. Thousands of Captains and Colonels without soldiers, and of 'Squires without stockings or shoes. In England, I had never thought of approaching a 'Squire without a most respectful bow; but, in this new world, though I was but a corporal, I often ordered a 'Squire to bring me a glass of grog, and even to take care of my knapsack. We staid but a few weeks in Nova Scotia, being ordered to St Johns in the Province of New Brunswick. Here, and at other places in the same province, we remained till the month of September, 1791, when the regiment was relieved and sent home. 1783 *to* 1784

Nova Scotia, New Brunswick, and Canada, are the horns, the head, the neck, the shins, and the hoof of the ox, and the United States are the ribs, the sirloin, the kidneys, and the rest of the body. Nova Scotia and New Brunswick were one great heap of rocks, covered with fir trees, with here and there a little strip of land capable of cultivation, by the sides of the rivers. What these countries are, you may judge from the following facts; that almost all the meat and all the flour consumed in them, is carried from the United States, and even cabbages; that, as to fruits, cherries, apples, pears, all go from the United States. In short, the most barren, the most villainous piece of waste land; the thin shell upon the top of a gravel pit in England compared with the fat meadows and gardens in the Medway, or the beautiful valleys in Wiltshire, is precisely what Nova Scotia and New Brunswick are to the United States of America.

Then the horrible climate; the land covered with snow seven months of the year; the danger of death if any man be lost in the snow for only ten minutes. Thousands of deaths took place every year from people being what is called frost-bitten. The men going on guard were wrapped up in great cloth coats lined with flannel, their head covered with caps of the same sort, leaving only an opening for the eyes and the nose. I have seen half a dozen men at a time with their noses frost-bitten, which you perceive the moment you see them, by their having become white. The remedy is instantly to rub with snow the part affected; but, very frequently, if this be delayed only for half an hour, mortification takes place; and there are thousands of men in those countries with their hands or feet cut off in order to save their lives.

I was stationed on the banks of the great and beautiful river St John, which was more than a mile wide at a hundred miles from the sea. That river, as well as all the creeks running into it on both sides, were so completely frozen over every year by the seventh of November, or thereabouts, that we could skate across it and up and down it, the next morning after the frost began, while we could see the fish swimming under the ice upon which we were skating. In about ten days the snow came; until storm after storm, coming at intervals of a week or a fortnight, made the mass, upon an average, ten feet deep; and there we were, nine days out of ten, with a bright sun over our heads, and with snow, dry as hair powder, screeching under our feet. In the month of April, in the last week of that month, the meltings of the snow turned the river into ice again. Soon after this, symptoms of breaking-up began to appear, the immense mass of ice was first loosened near the banks of the river; the creeks where the masses were not so large, and the lakes where the freezing had not been so severe, began to give way, and you every now and then heard a crack at many miles distance, like the falling of fifty or a hundred or a thousand very lofty timber trees coming down all together, from the axes and saws of the fellers. These cracks indicated that the ice had bursted asunder, and was beginning to roll down the great streams made by the melting of the snow: day after day, the cracks became louder and more frequent; till by and by, the ice came tumbling out of the mouths of the creeks into the main river, which, by this time, began to give way itself, till, on some days, toward the latter end of May, the whole surface of the river moved downwards with accelerating rapidity towards the sea, rising up into piles twice as high as [the Duke of Wellington's] great fine house at Hyde Park Corner, wherever the ice came in contact with an island, of which there were many in the river, until the sun and the tide had carried the whole away, and made the river clear for us to sail upon again to the next month of November; during which time, the sun gave us melons in the natural ground, and fine crops of corn and grass. [It is impossible not to be] revisited by the feelings which I participated with others, when the sun began to bless our eyes with the sight of grass, to make us cast off our furs, and to resume our dresses as men, instead of those of bears.

CHAPTER III

1784–1791

$*$ $*$ $*$ $*$ $*$

WHILE I WAS CORPORAL I WAS MADE CLERK
to the regiment. In a very short time, the whole
of the business in that way fell into my hands;
and, at the end of about a year, neither adjutant,
paymaster, or quarter-master, could move an inch
without my assistance. The accounts and letters
of the paymaster went through my hands; or,
rather, I was the maker of them. All the returns,
reports, and other official papers were of my
drawing-up.

Then I became Sergeant-Major to the regiment,
which brought me in close contact at every hour,
with the whole of the epaulet gentry, whose profound and surprising ignorance I discovered in
a twinkling. The military part of the regiment's
affairs fell under my care. In early life, [I] contracted the blessed habit of husbanding well my
time. To this more than to any other thing, I owed
my very extraordinary promotion in the army. I
was always ready: never did any man, or anything, wait one moment for me. Being raised
from corporal to sergeant-major at once, over the
heads of thirty sergeants, I naturally should have
been an object of envy and hatred; but this habit

of early rising really subdued these passions; because everyone felt that what I did he had never
done, and never could do. Long before any other
man was dressed for parade, my work for the
morning was well done, and I myself was on
parade walking, in fine weather, for an hour perhaps. My custom was this: to get up, in summer,
at daylight, and in winter at four o'clock; shave,
dress, even to the putting of my sword belt over
my shoulder, and having my sword lying on the
table before me, ready to hang by my side. Then
I ate a bit of cheese, or pork, and bread. Then I
prepared my report, which was filled up as fast as
the companies brought me in the materials. After
this I had an hour or two to read, before the time
came for any duty out of doors, unless when the
regiment or part of it went out to exercise in the
morning. When this was the case, and the matter
was left to me, I always had it on the ground in
such time as that the bayonets glistened in the
rising sun, a sight which gave me delight, of which
I often think, but which I should in vain endeavour to describe. If the officers were to go out,
eight or ten o'clock was the hour, sweating the men
in the heat of the day, breaking in upon the time
for cooking their dinner, putting all things out of
order and all men out of humour. When I was
commander, the men had a long day of leisure
before them: they could ramble into the town or
into the woods; go to get raspberries, to catch
birds, to catch fish, or to pursue any other recrea-

[29]

tion, and such of them as chose, and were quali-
fied, to work at their trades. So that here, arising
solely from the early habits of one very young
man, were pleasant and happy days given to
hundreds.

About this time, the new discipline,[1] as it was
called, was sent out to us in little books, which
were to be studied by the officers of each regiment,
and the rules of which were to be immediately con-
formed to. Though any old woman might have
written such a book; though it was excessively
foolish from beginning to end; still, it was to be
complied with, it ordered and commanded a total
change.

To make this change was left to me, while not
a single officer in the regiment paid the least attention to the matter; so that, when the time came
for the annual review, I had to give lectures of in-
struction to the officers themselves, the Colonel
not excepted; and, for several of them, I had to
make out, upon large cards, which they bought
for the purpose, little plans of the position of the
regiment, together with lists of the words of command, which they had to give in the field. There
was I, at the review, upon the flank of the grenadier
company, with my worsted shoulder-knot, and my
great high, coarse, hairy cap; confounded in the
ranks amongst other men, while those who were
commanding me to move my hands or my feet,
thus or thus, were, in fact, uttering words, which
I had taught them; and were, in everything except

[30]

mere authority, my inferiors; and ought to have
been commanded by me. It was impossible for
reflections of this sort not to intrude themselves;
and, as I advanced in experience, I felt less and less
respect for those, whom I was compelled to obey.

1784
to
1791

But, I had a very delicate part to act with those
gentry; for, while I despised them for their gross
ignorance and their vanity, and hated them for
their drunkenness and rapacity, I was fully sensible of their power. My path was full of rocks and
pitfalls; and, as I never disguised my dislikes, or
restrained my tongue, I should have been broken
and flogged for fifty different offences, had they
not been kept in awe by my inflexible sobriety,
impartiality, and integrity, by the consciousness
of their inferiority to me, and by the real and
almost indispensable necessity of the use of my
talents. They, in fact, resigned all the discipline
of the regiment to me, and I very freely left them
to swagger about and to get roaring drunk.

To describe the various instances of their ignorance, and the various tricks they played to disguise it from me, would fill a volume. It is the
custom in regiments to give out orders every day
from the officer commanding. These are written by
the Adjutant, to whom the Sergeant-Major is a
sort of deputy. The man, whom I had to do with
was a keen fellow, but wholly illiterate. The orders,
which he wrote, most cruelly murdered our mother-
tongue. But, in his absence, or, during a severe
drunken fit, it fell to my lot to write orders. As we

1784
to
1791

both wrote in the same book, he used to look at these. He saw commas, semi-colons, colons, full points, and paragraphs. The questions he used to put to me, in an obscure sort of way, in order to know why I made these divisions, and yet, at the same time, his attempts to disguise his object, have made me laugh a thousand times. He, at last, fell upon this device: he made me write, while he pretended to dictate! Imagine to yourself, me sitting, pen in hand, to put upon paper the precious offspring of the mind of this stupid curmudgeon! But, here, a greater difficulty than any former arose. He that could not write good grammar, could not, of course, dictate good grammar. Out would come some gross error, such as I was ashamed to see in my handwriting. I would stop; suggest another arrangement; but, this I was, at first, obliged to do in a very indirect and delicate manner. But, this course could not continue long; and he put an end to it in this way; he used to tell me his story, and leave me to put it upon paper; and this we continued to the end of our connection.

He played me a trick upon one occasion, which was more ridiculous than anything else, but will serve to show how his ignorance placed him at my mercy. There were three or four commissioners sent out to examine into the state of the provinces of Nova Scotia and New Brunswick. They closed their work at Fredericton, in New Brunswick, where I was with my regiment. As the arrival of every stranger was an excuse for a roaring drunk

with our heroes, so this ceremony now took place. 1784
But, the Commissioners had their report to make. *to*
And, what did my ass of an Adjutant do, but offer 1791
to do it for them! They took him at his word; and,
there was he in the sweetest mess that ever vain
pretender was placed in. He wanted to get some
favour from these Commissioners, and relied upon
me, not only to perform the task, but to keep the
secret. The report of these fellows was no concern
of mine. It could not, by any contrivance, be
hooked in among my duties. He, therefore, talked
to me at first in a sort of ambiguous manner. He
said, that the Commissioners wanted him to do it,
and, d-n them, he would not do it for them. Then,
when I saw him again, he asked me something
about it, showing me their rude mass of papers, at
the same time. I now began to find what he would
be at; but, I affected not to understand him, turned
the matter as soon as I could, and so we parted.
At this time, I had been long wanting to go and
see an old farmer and his family and to shoot wild
pigeons in his woods; and, as the distance was
great, and a companion on the journey necessary,
I wanted a sergeant to go with me. The leave to do
this had been put off for a good while, and the
Adjutant knew that I had the thing at heart. What
does he now do, but come to me and after talking
about the report again, affect to lament that he
should be so much engaged with it, that there was
no hope of my being permitted to go on my frolic,
till he had finished the report. I, who knew very

well what this meant, began to be very anxious for this finishing, to effect which I knew that there was but one way. Tacked onto the pigeon-shooting, the report became an object of importance, and I said, "perhaps I could do something, Sir, in putting the papers in order for you." That was enough. Away he went, brought me the whole mass, and, tossing them down on the table: "There", said he, "do what you like with them; for, d-n the rubbish, I have no patience with it".

Rubbish it really was, if we looked only at the rude manner of the papers; but the matter would to me, at this day, have been very interesting. I d-d the papers as heartily as he did, and with better reason; but, they were to bring me my week's frolic, and, as I entered into everything with ardour, this pigeon-shooting frolic, at the age of about 23, was more than a compensation for all the toil of this report and its appendix. To work I went, and with the assistance of my shooting companion sergeant, who called over the figures to me, I had the appendix completed in rough draft in two days and one night. Having the detail before me the report was a short work, and the whole was soon completed. But, before a neat copy was made out, the thing had to be shown to the Commissioners. It would not do to show it them in my handwriting. The Adjutant got over this difficulty by copying the report; and, having shown it, and had it highly applauded, "Well, then," said he, "here, Sergeant-Major, go and make a fair copy".

This was the most shameless thing that I ever witnessed.

A copy, which I made for the purpose, was deposited with the Governor at Halifax, which copy the Duke of Kent had, in the year 1800, when he was commander-in-chief in [the] province. He showed it to me in Halifax, when I was there, in the year 1800. When I told him the whole story, he asked me how much the Commissioners gave me; and, when I told him not a farthing, he exclaimed most bitterly, and said that thousands of pounds had, first and last, been paid by the country for what I had done.

I first saw my wife [in New Brunswick]. She was thirteen years old, and I was within about a month of twenty-one. She was the daughter of a sergeant of artillery.[2] I sat in the same room with her for about an hour, in company with others, and I made up my mind that she was the very girl for me. That I thought her beautiful was certain, for that I had always said should be an indispensable qualification; but I saw in her what I deemed marks of that sobriety of conduct, which has been by far the greatest blessing of my life. It was dead of winter, and, of course, the snow several feet deep on the ground, and the weather piercing cold. In about three mornings after I had first seen her, I had got two young men to join me in my walk; and our road lay by the house of her father and mother. It was hardly light, but she was out on the snow, scrubbing out a washing-tub. "That's

[35]

1784
to
1791

the girl for me ", I said, when we had got out of her hearing.*

From the day that I first spoke to her, I never had a thought of her being the wife of any other man, more than I had a thought of her being transformed into a chest of drawers; and I formed my resolution at once, to marry her as soon as we could get permission, and to get out of the army as soon as I could. So that this matter was at once settled as firmly as if written in the book of my fate.

At the end of about six months, my regiment, and I along with it, were removed to Fredericton, a distance of a hundred miles up the river; and, which was worse, the artillery was expected to go off to England a year or two before our regiment! The artillery went, and she along with them; and now it was that I acted a part becoming a real and sensible lover. I was aware that, when she got to that gay place Woolwich, the house of her father and mother, necessarily visited by numerous persons not the most select, might become unpleasant to her, and I did not like, besides, that she should

* One of these young men came to England soon afterwards; and he, who keeps an inn in Yorkshire, came over to Preston, at the time of the elections, to verify whether I were the same man. When he found that I was, he appeared surprised; but what was his surprise when I told him that those tall young men he saw around me were the sons of that pretty little girl that he and I saw scrubbing out the washing-tub on the snow at New Brunswick at daybreak in the morning.

[36]

continue to work hard. I had saved a hundred and fifty guineas. I sent her all my money before she sailed; and wrote to her, to beg of her, if she found her home uncomfortable, to hire a lodging with respectable people: and, at any rate, not to spare the money, by any means, but to buy herself good clothes, and to live without hard work, until I arrived in England; and I, in order to induce her to lay out the money, told her that I should get plenty more before I came home.

At the end of four years, home I came. I found my little girl a servant of all work (and hard work it was) at five pounds a year, in the house of a Captain Brissac; and without hardly saying a word about the matter, she put into my hands the whole of my hundred and fifty guineas unbroken.

[But before I came home] I did a wrong, [of which] I will here give a history. [It was one of those cases] in which you are, by degrees and by circumstances, deluded into something very nearly resembling sincere love for a second object, the first still, however, maintaining her ground in your heart; cases in which you are not actuated by vanity, in which you are not guilty of injustice and cruelty; but cases in which you, nevertheless, do wrong.

In one of my rambles I came to a spot at a very short distance from the source of one of the innumerable small rivers, called creeks. Here was everything to delight the eye, and especially of one like me, who seems to have been born to love

rural life, and trees and plants of all sorts. Here
were about two hundred acres of natural meadow,
interspersed with patches of maple trees in various
forms and of various extent; the creek ran down
the middle of the spot, which formed a sort of dish,
the high and rocky hills rising all round it, except
at the outlet of the creek, and these hills crowned
with lofty pines: in the hills were the sources of
the creek, the waters of which came down in cascades, for any one of which a nobleman in England
would, if he could transfer it, give a good slice of
his fertile estate; and in the creek at the foot of
the cascades, there were, in season, salmon, the
finest in the world, and so abundant, and so easily
taken, as to be used for manuring the land.

If nature, in her very best humour, had made a
spot for the express purpose of captivating me,
she could not have exceeded the efforts which she
there made. But I found something here besides
these rude works of nature; I found something in
the fashioning of which man had had something
to do. I found a large and well-built log dwelling-
house, standing (in the month of September) on
the edge of a very good field of Indian corn, by the
side of which there was a piece of buckwheat just
then mowed. I found a homestead and some very
pretty cows. I found all the things by which an
easy and happy farmer is surrounded; and I found
still something besides all these, something that
was destined to give me a great deal of pleasure
and a great deal of pain, both in their extreme

degree; and both of which, in spite of the lapse of forty years, now make an attempt to rush back into my heart. 1784 to 1791

I had lost my way; and, quite alone, but armed with my sword and a brace of pistols, to defend myself against the bears, I arrived at the log house in the middle of a moonlight night, the hoar frost covering the trees and the grass. I, being very tired, had tried to pass the night in the woods, between the trunks of two large trees, which had fallen side by side, and within a yard of each other. I had made a nest for myself of dried fern, and had made a covering by laying boughs of spruce across the trunks of the trees. But unable to sleep on account of the cold; becoming sick from the great quantity of water that I had drunk during the heat of the day, and being, moreover, alarmed at the noise of the bears, and lest one of them should find me in a defenseless state, I had roused myself up, and had crept along as well as I could.

A stout and clamourous dog, kept off by the gleaming of my sword, waked the master of the house, who got up, received me with great hospitality, got me something to eat, and put me into a feather-bed, a thing that I had been a stranger to for some years. So that no hero of Eastern romance ever experienced a more enchanting change.

I had got into the house of one of those Yankee loyalists, who, at the close of the Revolutionary War (which, until it had succeeded, was called a

1784
to
1791

rebellion), had accepted of grants of land in the King's province of New Brunswick; and who, to the great honour of England, had been furnished with all the means of making new and comfortable settlements. I was suffered to sleep till breakfast time, when I found a table, the like of which I [later saw] so many in the United States, loaded with good things. The master and mistress of the house, aged about fifty, were like what an English farmer and his wife were half a century ago. There were two sons, tall and stout, who appeared to have come in from work, and the youngest of whom was about my age. But there was another member of the family, aged nineteen, who (dressed according to the neat and simple fashion of New England, whence she had come with her parents five or six years before) had her long light-brown hair twisted nicely up, and fastened on the top of her head, in which head were a pair of lively blue eyes, associated with the features of which, that softness and that sweetness so characteristic of American girls, were the predominant expressions; the whole being set off by a complexion indicative of glowing health and forming, figure, movements, and all taken together, an assemblage of beauties, far surpassing any that I had ever seen but once in my life. That once was, too, two years agone; and in such a case and at such an age, two years, two whole years, is a long, long while! It was a space as long as the eleventh part of my then life. Here was the present against the

absent: here was the power of the eyes pitted 1784
against that of the memory: here were all the *to*
senses up in arms to subdue the influence of the 1791
thoughts: here was vanity, here was passion, here
was the spot of all spots in the world, and here
were also the life, and the manners and the habits
and the pursuits that I delighted in: here was
everything that imagination can conceive, united
in a conspiracy against the poor little brunette in
England! What, then, did I fall in love at once
with this bouquet of lilies and roses? Oh! by no
means. I was, however, so enchanted with the
place; I so much enjoyed its tranquillity, the shade
of the maple trees, the business of the farm, the
sports of the water and of the woods, that I stayed
at it to the last possible minute, promising, at my
departure, to come again as often as I possibly
could; a promise which I most punctually ful-
filled.

Winter is the great season for jaunting and
dancing (called frolicking) in America. In this province, the rivers and the creeks were the only
roads from settlement to settlement. In summer
we travelled in canoes; in winter in sleighs on the
ice or snow. During more than two years I spent
all the time I could with my Yankee friends; they
were all fond of me: I talked to them about country
affairs, my evident delight in which they took as a
compliment to themselves: the father and mother
treated me as one of their children; the sons as a
brother; and the daughter, who was as modest and

1784
to
1791

as full of sensibility as she was beautiful, in a way to which a chap much less sanguine than I was would have given the tenderest interpretation; which treatment, I, especially in the last-mentioned case, most cordially repaid.

It is when you meet in the company with others of your own age that you are, in love matters, put most frequently to the test, and exposed to detection. The next-door neighbour might, in that country, be ten miles off. We used to have a frolic, sometimes at one house and sometimes at another. Here, where female eyes are very much on the alert, no secret can long be kept; and very soon, father, mother, brothers, and the whole neighbourhood looked upon the thing as certain, not excepting herself, to whom I, however, had never once even talked of marriage, and had never even told her that I loved her. But I had a thousand times done these by implication, taking into view the interpretation that she would naturally put upon my looks, appelations and acts; and it was of this that I had to accuse myself. Yet I was not a deceiver; for my affection for her was very great: I spent no really pleasant hours but with her; I was uneasy if she showed the slightest regard for any other young man; I was unhappy if the smallest matter affected her health or spirits: I quitted her with dejection and returned to her with eager delight: many a time when I could get leave but for a day, I paddled in a canoe two whole succeeding nights, in order to pass that day with her. If this

was not love, it was first cousin to it; for as to any 1784
criminal intention, I had no more thought of it in *to*
her case, than if she had been my sister. Many 1791
times I put to myself the questions: "What am I
at? Is not this wrong? Why do I go?" But still I
went.

Then, further in my excuse, my prior engage-
ment, though carefully left unalluded to by both
parties, was, in that thin population, and owing
to the singular circumstances of it, perfectly well
known to her and all her family. It was a matter
of so much notoriety, that General Carleton, who
was the Governor when I was there, when he,
about fifteen years ago, did me the honour, on his
return to England, to come and see me, asked,
before he went away, to see my wife, of whom he
had heard so much before her marriage. So that
here was no deception on my part; but still I
ought not to have suffered even the most distant
hopes to be entertained by a person so innocent,
so amiable, for whom I had so much affection, and
to whose heart I had no right to give a single
twinge. I ought, from the very first, to have prevented the possibility of her ever feeling pain on
my account. I was young, to be sure; but I was
old enough to know what was my duty in this
case, and I ought, dismissing my own feelings, to
have had the resolution to perform it.

The last parting came; and now came my just
punishment! The time was known to everybody,
and was irrevocably fixed; for I had to move with

1784
to
1791

a regiment, and the embarkation of a regiment is an epoch in a thinly settled province. To describe this parting would be too painful even at this distant day, and with this frost of age upon my head. The kind and virtuous father came forty miles to see me, just as I was going on board in the river. His looks and words I have never forgotten. As the vessel descended, she passed the mouth of that creek, which I had so often entered with delight; and though England, and all that England contained, were before me, I lost sight of this creek with an aching heart.

On what trifles turn the great events in the life of a man! If I had received a cool letter from my intended wife; if I had only heard a rumour of anything from which fickleness in her might have been inferred; if I had but found in her any, even the smallest, abatement of affection: if she had but let go any one of the hundred strings by which she held my heart: if any of these, never would the world have heard of me. On the lonely banks of this branch-covered creek, which contained (she out of the question) everything congenial to my taste and dear to my heart, I, unapplauded, unfeared, unenvied and uncalumniated, should have lived and died.

Late in the year 1791, I returned to England with my regiment. We landed at Portsmouth on the 3rd of November, and on the 19th of the next month I obtained my discharge, after having served not quite eight years, and having, in that short space, passed through every rank, from that of private sentinel to that of Sergeant-Major, without ever once being disgraced, confined, or even reprimanded. I obtained my discharge after many efforts on the part of the commanding officer, Major Lord Edward Fitzgerald,[3] and of General Frederick, the Colonel of the regiment, to prevail on me to remain (upon a promise of being specially recommended to the King, as worthy of being immediately promoted to the rank of Ensign).

1784
to
1791

CHAPTER IV

1784–1791

*   *   *   *   *

1784
to
1791
SUCH WAS MY CONDUCT DURING THE TIME
that I had the honour (and I shall always think it
a high honour) to wear a red coat, and such was
the character, with which that coat was laid by.
To the army, to every soldier in it, I have a bond
of attachment quite independent of any political
reasonings. I [was] a soldier at that time of life
when the feelings are most ardent and when the
strongest attachments are formed. "Once a soldier,
always a soldier," is a maxim, the truth of which I
need not insist on to anyone who has ever served
in the army for any length of time, and especially,
if the service he has seen has embraced those
scenes and occasions where every man, first or
last, from one cause or another, owes the preser-
vation of his all, health and life not excepted, to
the kindness, the generosity, the fellow-feeling of
his comrades.

There was one of our sergeants, whose name was
Smaller, and who was a Yorkshire man, who began
learning his ABC (under my direction), and who,
at the end of the year, was as correct a writer as I
ever saw in my life. He was about my own age;
he was promoted as soon as he could write and

read; and he well deserved it, for he was more fit to command a regiment than any Colonel or Major that I ever saw. He was strong in body, but still stronger in mind. He had a capacity to dive into all subjects. Clean in his person, an early riser, punctual in all his duties, sober, good-tempered, honest, brave, and generous to the last degree. He was once with me in the dreary woods, amongst the melting snows, when I was exhausted at night-fall, and fell down, unable to go farther, just as a torrent of rain began to pour upon us. Having first torn off his shirt and rent it in the vain hope of kindling fire by the help of his pistol, he took me upon his back, carried me five miles to the first dwelling of human being, and, at the end of his journey, having previously pulled off his coat and thrown it away, he had neither shoe, nor stocking, nor gaiter left; his feet and legs were cut to pieces, and covered with blood; and the moment he had put me down and saw that I was still alive, he bursted into a flood of tears that probably saved his own life; which, however, was there saved only to be lost in Holland, under the Duke of York.[1]

Of this military feeling, I do not believe that any man ever possessed greater portion than myself. I like soldiers, as a class in life, better than any other description of men. Their conversation is more pleasing to me; they have generally seen more than other men; they have less of vulgar prejudice about them. Amongst soldiers, less than

1784
to
1791

amongst any other description of men, have I observed the vices of lying and hypocrisy.

The object of my quitting the army, to which I was attached, was to bring certain officers to justice for having, in various ways, wronged both the public and the soldier. I was so situated as to save England thousands and thousands of pounds during the time that my regiment was stationed in New Brunswick. My vigilance was incessant; and I pursued the interest of the government at home, with as much zeal as if my life depended on the result. I would take my oath that I never saw any other man that did the same, while I was in that country, with the exception of General Carleton the Governor, and the unfortunate Lord Edward Fitzgerald, who was a really honest, conscientious, and humane man.

If my officers had been men of manifest superiority of mind, I should, perhaps, not have so soon conceived the project of bringing them, or some of them, at least, to shame and punishment for the divers flagrant breaches of the law, committed by them. The circumstance which first disgusted me, and that finally made me resolve to tear myself from a service, to which my whole mind and heart were devoted, was, the abuses, the shocking abuses as to money matters, the peculation, in short, which I witnessed, and which I had, in vain, endeavoured to correct.

This project was conceived so early as the year 1787, when an affair happened, that first gave me

a full insight into regimental justice. It was shortly 1784
this: that the Quarter-Master, who had the issuing *to*
of the men's provisions to them, kept about a 1791
fourth part of it to himself. This, the old sergeants
told me, had been the case for many years; and,
they were quite astonished and terrified at the idea
of my complaining of it. This I did, however; but,
the reception I met with convinced me, that I
must never make another complaint, till I got safe
to England, and safe out of the reach of that most
curious of courts, a court-martial.

From this time forward, I began to collect
materials for an exposure, upon my return to
England. I had ample opportunities for this, being
the keeper of all the books, of every sort, in the
regiment, and knowing the whole of its affairs
better than any other man. But, the winter previous to our return to England, I thought it necessary to make extracts from the books, lest the
books themselves should be destroyed. In order
to be able to prove that these extracts were correct,
it was necessary that I should have a witness as to
their being true copies. This was a very ticklish
point. One foolish step here, could have sent me
down to the ranks with a pair of bloody shoulders.
I hesitated many months. At one time I had given
the thing up. I dreamt twenty times, I daresay,
of my papers being discovered, and of my being
tried and flogged half to death. At last, however,
some fresh act of injustice towards us made me set
all danger at defiance. I opened my project to a

1784
to
1791

corporal, whose name was William Bestland, who wrote in the office under me, [and] who was very much bound to me, for my goodness to him. To work we went, and during a long winter, while the rest were boozing and snoring, we gutted no small part of the regimental books, rolls, and other documents. Our way was this: to take a copy, sign it with our names, and clap the regimental seal to it, so that we might be able to swear to it, when produced in court.

All these papers were put into a little box, which I myself had made for the purpose. When we came to Portsmouth, there was a talk of searching all the boxes, etc., which gave us great alarm; and induced us to take all the papers, put them in a bag, and trust them to a custom-house officer, who conveyed them on shore to his own house, when I removed them in a few days after.

Thus prepared, I, [after securing my discharge], went to London, and, on the 14th of January, 1792, I wrote to the then Secretary of War, Sir George Yonge, stating my situation, my business with him, and my intentions; enclosing him a letter or petition from myself to the King. I waited from the 14th to the 24th of January, without receiving any answer at all, and then all I heard was, that he wished to see me at the War Office. At the War Office I was shown into an antechamber amongst numerous anxious-looking men, who, every time the door which led to the great man was opened, turned their heads that way

with a motion as regular and as uniform as if they
had been drilled to it. These people eyed me from
head to foot, and, I shall never forget their look,
when they saw, that I was admitted into Paradise
without being detained a single moment in Pur-
gatory. Sir George Yonge heard my story; and
that was apparently all he wanted of me. I was to
hear from him again in a day or two; and, after
waiting for fifteen days, without hearing from
him, or anyone else, upon the subject, I wrote him
again, reminding him, that I had, from the first,
told him, that I had no other business in London;
that my stock of money was necessarily scanty;
and, that to detain me in London was to ruin me.
I, therefore, began to be very impatient, and,
indeed, to be very suspicious, that military justice
in England was pretty nearly akin to military
justice in Nova Scotia and New Brunswick. The
letter I now wrote was dated the 10th of February,
to which I got an answer on the 15th, though the
answer might have been written in a moment. I
was informed, that it was the intention to try the
accused upon only a part of the charges which I
had preferred, [and,] even on those charges that
were suffered to remain, the parts the most material
were omitted. But, this was not all. I had all along
insisted, that, unless the court-martial were held
in London, I could not think of appearing at it;
because, if held in a quarrelsome place like Portsmouth, the thing must be a mere mockery. In
spite of this, the Judge-Advocate's letter of the

[51]   4-2

23rd of February informed me, that the court was to be held at Portsmouth, or Hilsea. I remonstrated against this, and demanded that my remonstrance should be laid before the King, which, on the 29th, the Judge-Advocate promised should be done by himself; but, on the 5th of March, [he] informed me, that he had laid my remonstrance before—whom, think you? Not the King, but the accused parties; who, of course, thought the court ought to assemble at Portsmouth.

Plainly seeing what was going forward, I, on the 7th of March, made, in a letter to Mr Pitt, a representation of the whole case. This letter had the effect of changing the place of the court-martial, which was now to be held in London; but, as to my other great ground of complaint, the leaving of the regimental books unsecured, it had no effect at all; and, it will be recollected, that without those books, there could be no proof produced, without bringing forward Corporal Bęstland, and the danger of doing that will presently be seen. Without these written documents nothing of importance could be proved, unless the non-commissioned officers and men of the regiment could get the better of their dread of the lash; and, even then, they could only speak from memory. As the court-martial was to assemble on the 24th of March, I went down to Portsmouth on the 20th, in order to know for certain what was become of the books; and, I found, that they had never been secured at all; that they had been left in the hands of the accused from the 14th of January to the very hour of trial.

There remained, then, nothing to rest upon with safety but our extracts, confirmed by the evidence of Bestland, and this I had solemnly engaged with him not to have recourse to, unless he was first out of the army; that is to say, out of the reach of the vindictive and bloody lash. There was a suspicion of his connection with me, and, therefore, they resolved to keep him.

I resolved not to appear at the court-martial, unless the discharge of Bestland was first granted. Accordingly, on the 20th of March, I wrote from Fratton, a village near Portsmouth, to the Judge-Advocate, stating over again all the obstacles that had been thrown in my way, and concluding by demanding the discharge of a man, whom I should name, as the only condition upon which I would attend the court-martial. I requested him to send me an answer by the next day, and told him, that, unless such an answer was received, he and those to whom my repeated applications had been made, might do what they pleased with their court-martial; for, that I confidently trusted, that a few days would place me beyond the scope of their power. No answer came, and, as I had learned in the meanwhile, that there was a design to prosecute me for sedition, that was an additional motive to be quick in my movements.

As I was going down to Portsmouth, I met several of the sergeants coming up, together with

1784
to
1791

the music-master; and, as they had none of them
been in America, I wondered what they could be
going to London for; but, upon my return, I was
told by a Captain Lane, who had been in the regiment, that they had been brought up to swear,
that, at an entertainment given to them by me,
before my departure from the regiment, I had
drunk "the destruction of the House of Brunswick". This was false; but, I knew that that was
no reason why it should not be sworn by such
persons and in such a case. I had talked pretty
freely upon the occasion alluded to; but I had
neither said, nor thought anything against the
King, and, as to the House of Brunswick, I hardly
knew what it meant. My head was filled with the
corruptions and baseness in the army. I knew
nothing at all about politics. Nor would any threat
of this sort have induced me to get out of the way
for a moment; though it certainly would if I had
known my danger; for glorious "Jacobinical"
times were just then beginning. Of this, however,
I knew nothing at all. [I was] told they would
send me to Botany Bay; and, I now verily believe, that, if I had remained, I should have furnished a pretty good example to those, who wished
to correct military abuses. I did not, however,
leave England from this motive. I could not obtain a chance of success, without exposing the
back of my poor faithful friend Bestland. It was
useless to appear, unless I could have tolerable
fair play; and, besides, it seemed better to leave

the whole set to do as they pleased, than to be made a mortified witness of what it was quite evident they had resolved to do.

I have good reason to believe, that my failure upon [this] occasion was, in no way, to be ascribed to Mr Pitt, who, as far as a person in so obscure and perfectly friendless a situation as I then was, could judge, was the friend of fair inquiry and of justice. [Yet] I remember, that in dining with Mr Pitt at Mr Windham's in August, 1800, the former asked me about Lord Edward Fitzgerald. We talked about him a great deal. I gave the company present (of which Mr Canning was one) an account of his conduct, while at the regiment; I spoke in very high terms of his zeal for the service, and I told Mr Pitt, that Lord Edward was the only sober and the only honest officer, I had ever known in the army. I did this for the express purpose of leading him on to talk about the court-martial; but, it was avoided. In fact, they all knew well that what I had complained of was true, and that I had been baffled in my attempts to obtain justice, only because I had neither money nor friends.

During the [same] interval of my discharge and of my departure for France, a proposition, preceded by a speech of the Secretary of War, was made, in Parliament, to augment the pay of the army. Some parts of the speech contained matter which a person, with whom I was acquainted, and to whom I had communicated my information upon such subjects, thought worthy of remark in print. Hence arose a little pamphlet, entitled the "Soldier's Friend".[2] As to the matter of the pamphlet, I cannot now speak in very positive terms, not having read it these fifteen years; but, I can say that, then, I most heartily approved of every word of it, and that, as well as my recollections will enable me to speak, there were some parts of it, of the publication of which I should disapprove now.

But, the reader will have the justice to recollect, that this [was] in 1792; a time when the principles of demolishing governments were little known and little dreaded. Let it be considered that I had just arrived in England; that I was a perfect novice in politics, never having, to my recollection, read even a newspaper while abroad; and, let it be considered, too, that I took up the book of Paine[3] (just then published) with my mind full of indignation at the abuses which I myself had witnessed. Under such circumstances, it would have argued not only want of zeal, but a want of sincerity, and even a want of honesty, not to have entertained sentiments like those expressed in the "Soldier's Friend".

Previous to my leaving England for France, previous to my seeing what republicanism was, I had not only imbibed its principles, I had not only been a republican, but an admirer of the writings of Paine. I will not be much blamed by those who duly reflect. Instead of blame, I am not without hope, that the reader will find something to commend, in a person, who, having imbibed erroneous opinions, was so soon taught, by experience, to correct them.

By way of episode, I had now married.[4] I had, in the whole world, but about 200 guineas, which was a very great deal for a person in my situation. From the moment that I had resolved to quit the army, I had also resolved to go to the United States of America, the fascinating and delusive description of which I had read in the works of Raynal.[5] To France I went [first] for the purpose of learning to speak the French language, having, because it was the language of the military art, studied it by book in America. To see fortified towns was another object; and how natural this was to a young man who had been studying fortification, and who had been laying down Lisle and Brissac[6] upon paper, need not be explained to those who have burnt with the desire of beholding in practice that which they have been enamoured of in theory. I went to France in the spring of 1792.

CHAPTER V

1792–1795

*　　*　　*　　*　　*

I ARRIVED IN FRANCE IN MARCH, 1792, AND continued there till the beginning of September following, the six happiest months of my life. I went to that country full of all those prejudices, that Englishmen suck in with their mother's milk, against the French and against their religion: a few weeks convinced me that I had been deceived with respect to both. I met everywhere with civility, and even hospitality, in a degree that I had never been accustomed to.

I did intend to stay in France till the Spring of 1793, as well to perfect myself in the language, as to pass the winter at Paris; but I perceived the storm gathering; I saw that a war with England was inevitable, and it was not difficult to foresee what would be the fate of Englishmen in that country. I wished, however, to see Paris, and had actually hired a coach to go thither. I was even on the way, when I heard, at Abbeville, that the King was dethroned and his guards murdered. This intelligence made me turn off towards Havre de Grace, whence I embarked for America.*

* Mrs Cobbett had memories of these events, which she communicated to her daughter Susan, who recorded

[58]

The Progress of a Plough-boy

I lived at Wilmington, a town about 20 miles from [Philadelphia]. It is generally said, and

them in a letter to her brother John, dated from Brighton, 30 September, 1835.

"...At one place, which they arrived at on a Sunday, they were very closely examined and made to unpack everything and show all papers, and, as the man could not understand English, he made Papa read the contents of them to him in French...the reason the man...was so particular in his examinations, was because Mama had no passport...this man chose to suspect that she was a Frenchwoman, and she would not give him an opportunity of being undeceived by speaking, for she was so insulted at his behaviour that she would not answer him when he spoke to her, and this confirmed him in his suspicions.... They then went on and were not threatened, or molested much, but there was, of course, a good deal of parleying wherever they stopped. When they got to Havre de Grace, however, things seemed to have assumed a warmer appearance; the people in the streets came running to the carriage and climbed up to look in at the windows, the coachman being much frightened thereat; he begged them to put the windows down, and drove very slowly through the streets till they came to the "Municipality", where Papa was closely questioned as to what and who he was, and where he was going and what for; but they were polite here. They stayed, Mama thinks, a fortnight at Havre de Grace, waiting for a vessel....The passage, she thinks, was eight weeks long, the name of the captain was Grenouille, the passage was very dangerous and the Captain very diligent and skillful. The name of the vessel she does not remember, but it was on board of her that Papa looked at a map and fixed upon Wilmington as the place where he would go and settle and keep school. They went to Wilmington, but they did not keep school because they found a great many Frenchmen there...who wanted to be taught English. Papa then went regularly to the

The Progress of a Plough-boy

often with much justice, that a rolling stone never
gathers moss; this, however, was not the case
with me; for though my rambles in France cost
me above a hundred and ninety guineas, and
though I was reduced to about eighteen at my
arrival at Wilmington, I was [soon] better off than
ever, notwithstanding my expenses in my family
had been enormous. I must not take the merit for
this entirely upon myself: my dear [wife] is entitled to her share of it; it was perhaps owing
entirely to her care, industry, and sweetness of
temper.

The country was good for getting money: that
is to say, if a person was industrious and enter-
prising. Exactly the contrary of what I expected
it. The land was bad—rocky—houses wretched—
roads impassable after the least rain. Fruit in
quantity, but good for nothing. One apple or
peach in England or France was worth a bushel

boarding-house where they lived, and taught them, and
they gave him a great deal of money....They went to
Philadelphia in the February of '94....Mr Matthew was
one of those French gentlemen, but he was so pleased with
Papa's company that he would insist on living in his
house, as well as being taught by him, and they used to go
on together, Mama says, like you and the likes of you,
stealing each other's bread at supper, and so on.... They
continued to receive boarders for some months, but Mama
found them disagreeable and got to dislike Wilmington,
and Mr Matthew thought Papa might do much better...
in Philadelphia,....so to Philadelphia they went in the
Spring."

The Cobbett Papers; cf. Notes.

of them [there]. The seasons were detestable. All
burning or freezing. There was no Spring or
Autumn. The weather was so very inconstant that
you were never sure for a single hour at a time.
The whole month of March was so hot that we
could hardly bear our clothes, and three parts of
the month of June there was a frost every night,
and so cold in the daytime, that we were obliged
to wear great-coats. The people were worthy of
the country—a cheating, sly, roguish gang. Yet
strangers made fortunes in spite of all this,
particularly the English. The natives were by
nature idle, and sought to live by cheating, while
foreigners, being industrious, sought no other
means than those dictated by integrity, and were
sure to meet with encouragement even from the
idle and roguish themselves; for, however roguish
a man may be, he always loves to deal with an
honest man. [The plague was at Philadelphia that
year.] It was no plague: it was a fever of the
country, and was by no means extraordinary
among the Americans. In the fall of the year,
almost every person has a spell of the fever, and
the only way to avoid it is to quit the country.
But this fever was not all—every month had its
particular malady. In July, for example, at least
one half of the people are taken with vomitings for
several days at a time; often carrying off the
patient and almost always children.

I began my young married days in and near
Philadelphia. I had business to occupy the whole

of my time, Sundays and week-days, except sleep-
ing hours; but I used to make time to assist [my
wife] in taking care of her baby,[1] and in all sorts
of things: get up, light her fire, boil her teakettle;
carry her up warm water in cold weather, take the
child while she dressed herself and got the breakfast ready, then breakfast, get her in water and
wood for the day, then dress myself neatly, and
sally forth to my business. The moment that was
over I used to hasten back to her again; and I no
more thought of spending a moment away from
her, unless business compelled me, than I thought
of quitting the country and going to sea. The
thunder and lightning are tremendous in America,
compared with what they are in England. My
wife was, at one time, very much afraid of thunder
and lightning; and, as is the feeling of all such
women, and, indeed, all men too, she wanted company, and particularly her husband, in those
times of danger. I knew well, of course, that my
presence would not diminish the danger; but, be
I at what I might, if within reach of home, I used
to quit my business and hasten to her the moment
I perceived a thunder storm approaching. Scores
of miles [did] I, first and last, run on this errand in
the streets of Philadelphia! I followed the profession of teacher of the English language to
Frenchmen. The Frenchmen who were my scholars
used to laugh at me exceedingly on this account;
and sometimes, when I was making an appoint-
ment with them, they would say, with a smile

and a bow, "Sauve la tonnerre toujours, Monsieur Cobbett".

For about two or three years after I was married, I, retaining some of my military manners, used, both in France and America, to romp most famously with the girls that came in my way. In France, there happened to be amongst our acquaintance a gay, sprightly girl, of about seventeen. I was remonstrating with her, one day, on the facility with which she seemed to shift her smiles from object to object, and she, stretching one arm out in an upward direction, the other in a downward direction, raising herself upon one foot, leaning her body on one side, and thus throwing herself into a flying attitude, answered my grave lecture by singing, in a very sweet voice (significantly bowing her head, and smiling at the same time), the following lines from the vaudeville, in the play of "Figaro":

"Si l'amour a des ailles,
    N'est-ce pas pour voltiger?"

The wit, argument, and manner altogether silenced me. She, after I left France, married a very worthy man, had a large family, and has been, and is, a most excellent wife and mother. But that which does sometimes well in France [would] not do [in America]. Not only could no mistress pass for a wife; but no woman would find admission [in] any circle if she had had the misfortune to have been connected by anticipation with her

1792
to
1795

husband, which I used to think was being starched overmuch.

One day, at Philadelphia, [when I was romping,] my wife said to me, in a very gentle manner, "Don't do that: I do not like it." That was quite enough: I had never thought on the subject before: one hair of her head was more dear to me than all the other women in the world, and this I knew that she knew; but I now saw that this was not all that she had a right to from me; I saw that she had the further claim upon me that I should abstain from everything that might induce others to believe that there was any other woman for whom, even if I were at liberty, I had any affection.

If prudery mean false modesty, it is to be despised; but if it mean modesty pushed to the utmost extent, I confess that I like it. Your "free and hearty" girls I liked very well to talk and laugh with; but never, for one moment, did it enter my mind that I could have endured a "free and hearty" girl for a wife. Skipping, capering, romping, rattling girls are very amusing, where all costs and other consequences are out of the question; and they may become sober in the Somersetshire sense of the word. But while you have no certainty of this, you have a presumptive argument on the other side. If I could not have had a young woman (and I am sure I never should have married an old one) who I was not sure possessed all the qualities expressed by the word

sobriety, I should have remained a bachelor to the
end of life. This sobriety was a title to trustworthi-
ness. I have had all the numerous and indescrib-
able delights of home and children and at the same
time all the bachelor's freedom from domestic
cares; and to this cause, far more than to any
other, my readers owe those labours, which I
never could have performed, if even the slightest
want of confidence at home had ever once entered
into my mind.

Till I had a second child, no servant ever
entered my house, though well able to keep one;
and never, in my whole life did I live in a house so
clean, in such trim order, and never have I eaten
or drunk, or slept, or dressed, in a manner so perfectly to my fancy, as I did then. I had a great
deal of business to attend to, that took me a great
part of the day from home; but whenever I could
spare a minute from business, a child was in my
arms. I rendered the mother's labour as light as I
could; any bit of food satisfied me; when watching
was necessary we shared it between us. We had
a cradle, and I rocked the cradle in great part,
during the time that I was writing my first work,
that famous "Maître d'Anglois,"[2] which has long
been the first book in Europe, as well as in
America, for teaching of French people the English language.

[This] work was written by me in hours not
employed in business, and, in great part during
my share of the night watchings over a sick, and

The Progress of a Plough-boy

then only child, who, after lingering many months
died in my arms. [For,] on the 3rd of June,
[1794, the] dear little fellow was snatched from us.
He was just beginning to prattle and to chase the
flies about the floor with a fan. During a month,
I seldom had my clothes off, being occupied with
the hope of saving his life, and having to assuage
the grief of his young and most affectionate
mother. There were these anxieties at home, while
my scholars were importuning me, the bookseller
and printer bothering me, and their devils haunt-
ing me.

[My wife having been brought to bed of a still-
born child a short time before,] I was greatly
afraid of fatal consequences, she not having, after
[all] was over, had any sleep for forty-eight hours.
All great cities, in hot countries, are, I believe, full
of dogs; and they, in the very hot weather, keep
up during the night, a horrible barking and fighting and howling. Upon the particular occasion to
which I am adverting, they made a noise so terrible
and so unremitted, that it was next to impossible
that even a person in full health should obtain a
minute's sleep. I was, about nine in the evening,
sitting by the bed: "I do think", said she, "that
I could go to sleep now, if it were not for the dogs".
Downstairs I went, and out I sallied, in my shirt
and trousers, and without shoes and stockings;
and, going to a heap of stones lying beside the
road, set to work upon the dogs, going backward
and forward, and keeping them at two or three

hundred yards distance from the house. I walked thus the whole night, bare-footed, lest the noise of my shoes might possibly reach her ears; and I remember that the bricks of the causeway were, even in the night, so hot as to be disagreeable to my feet. My exertions produced the desired effect: a sleep of several hours was the consequence; and, at eight o'clock in the morning, off I went to a day's business which was to end at six in the evening. Women are all patriots of the soil; and when her neighbours used to ask my wife whether all English husbands were like hers, she boldly answered in the affirmative.

Soon after, I translated for a bookseller in Philadelphia, a book on the law of nations.[3] A member of Congress had given the original to the bookseller, wishing for him to publish a translation. The book was the work of a Mr Martens, a German jurist, though it was written in French. I called it "Martens' Law of Nations". The President, the Vice-President, and every member of Congress had a copy of the work, which is now to be found in most of the law-libraries in the United States. I translated it for a quarter of a dollar (thirteen pence halfpenny) a page; and, I made it a rule to earn a dollar while my wife was getting breakfast in the morning, and another dollar after I came home at night, be the hour what it might; and I earned many a dollar in this way, sitting writing in the same room where my wife and child were in bed and asleep.

The Progress of a Plough-boy

This was the way we went on: this was the way that we began the married life; and that which we did with pleasure, no young couple, unendowed with fortune, ought to be ashamed to do.

When I first came to Philadelphia,[4] I was charmed with the liberty which its inhabitants seemed to enjoy. I saw pamphlets in every window, and newspapers in every hand. I was, indeed, rather surprised to find, that these pamphlets, and these newspapers, were all on one side: but, said I to myself, this must be the fault of the authors and editors. Long did I hope and expect to see something like a manly and effectual opposition, but I hoped and expected in vain. At last, it was my fate to enter the field. It is now [a long time] since I first took up the pen with an intention to write for the press on political subjects; and the occasion of my doing so is too curious in itself, as well as of too much importance as to the sequel, not to be described somewhat in detail.

[It was] at the memorable epoch of Dr Priestley's emigration to America. Newspapers were a luxury for which I had little relish, and which, if I had been ever so fond of, I had not time to enjoy. The manifestoes, therefore, of the Doctor, upon his landing in that country, and the malicious attacks upon the monarchy and the monarch of England which certain societies in America thereupon issued from the press, would, had it not been for a circumstance purely accidental, have escaped, probably forever, not only my animadversions, but my knowledge of their existence.

One of my scholars, who was a person that we call in England a Coffee-House Politician, chose, for once, to read his newspaper by way of lesson; and, it happened to be the very paper which contained the addresses presented to Dr Priestley at New York, together with his replies. My scholar, who was a sort of republican, or, at best, but half a monarchist, appeared delighted with the invectives against England, to which he was very much disposed to add. Those Englishmen who have been abroad, particularly if they have had time to make a comparison between the country they are in and that which they have left, well know how difficult it is, upon occasions such as I have been describing, to refrain from expressing their indignation and resentment; and there is not, I trust, much reason to suppose, that I should, in this respect, experience less difficulty than another. The dispute was as warm as might reasonably be expected between a Frenchman, uncommonly violent even for a Frenchman, and an Englishman not remarkable for *sang froid*; and, the result was, a declared resolution, on my part, to write and publish a pamphlet in defence of my country, which pamphlet he pledged himself to answer: his pledge was forfeited: it is known that mine was not. Thus it was that, whether for good or otherwise, I entered on the career of political writing; and, without adverting to the circumstances under

which others have entered on it, I think it will
not be believed that the pen was ever taken up
from a motive more pure and laudable.

From [that] time (the summer of 1794) to the
year 1800 my labours were without intermission.
During that space there were published from my
pen about twenty different pamphlets, the whole
number of which amounted to more than half a
million copies. During the three last years, a daily
paper, surpassing in extent of numbers, any ever
known in America, was the vehicle of my efforts;
and, [by] the year 1800, I might safely have as-
serted, that there was not in the whole country,
one single family, in which some part or the other
of my writings had not been read; and in which,
generally speaking, they had not produced some
degree of effect favourable to the interests of my
country.

The people of America, still sore from the
wounds of their war against England for liberty,
were so loud and enthusiastic in the cause of the
French, that the far greater part of the young men,
hoisted the famous tri-colour cockade; and everything seemed to indicate that the Government
would be forced into a war with England in aid of
the French. I took the English side; the force of
my writings gave them effect; that effect was prodigious; it prevented that which both Governments greatly dreaded; peace between America
and England was preserved; but the hostility excited against me produced unjust and villainous

[70]

prosecutions; and though the main part of the 1792
expense of one of the prosecutions was generously *to*
defrayed by some public-spirited men in Canada, 1795
I had to return to England in 1800 stripped of a
fortune, leaving thousands of pounds in small debts
due to me; leaving behind me my curses on the
tyrannical and corrupt Government of Pennsylvania; but leaving also my blessings on some of
the kindest friends that man ever knew.

CHAPTER VI

1796–1800

*   *   *   *   *

IN THE SPRING OF THE YEAR 1796, I TOOK
a house in Second Street, Philadelphia, for the
purpose of carrying on the book selling business,
which I looked upon as being at once a means of
getting money, and of propagating writings against
the French. I went into my house in May, but the
shop could not be gotten ready for some time; and,
from one delay and another, I was prevented from
opening till the second week in July.

Till I took this house, I had remained almost
unknown as a writer. A few persons did, indeed,
know that I was the person, who had assumed the
name of Peter Porcupine; but the fact was by no
means a matter of notoriety. The moment, however, that I had taken the lease of a large house,
the transaction became a topic of public conversation, and the eyes of the Democrats and the
French, who still lorded it over the city, and who
owed me a mutual grudge, were fixed upon me.

I thought my situation somewhat perilous. Such
truth as I had published, no man had dared to
utter, in the United States, since the rebellion. I
knew that these truths had mortally offended the
leading men amongst the Democrats, who could,

at any time, muster a mob quite sufficient to de- 1796
stroy my house, and to murder me. I had not a   *to*
friend, to whom I could look with any reasonable 1800
hope of securing efficient support; and, as to the
law, I had seen too much of republican justice, to
expect anything but persecution from that quarter.
In short, there were, in Philadelphia, about ten
thousand persons, all of whom would have re-
joiced to see me murdered; and there might, probably, be two thousand, who would have been very
sorry for it; but not above fifty of whom would
have stirred an inch to save me.

As the time approached for opening my shop,
my friends grew more anxious for my safety. It
was recommended to me, to be cautious how I
exposed, at my windows, anything that might
provoke the people; and, above all, not to put up
any aristocratical portraits, which would certainly
cause my windows to be demolished.

I saw the danger; but also saw, that I must, at
once, set all danger at defiance, or live in everlasting subjection to the prejudices and caprices of the
democratical mob. I resolved on the former; and,
as my shop was to open on a Monday morning, I
employed myself all day on Sunday, in preparing
an exhibition, that I thought would put the courage and powers of my enemies to the test. I put
up in my windows, which were very large, all the
portraits that I had in my possession of kings,
queens, princes, and nobles. I had all the English
Ministry; several of the Bishops and Judges; the

most famous Admirals; and, in short, every picture that I thought likely to excite rage in the
enemies of Great Britain. In order to make the
test as perfect as possible, I had put up some of
the worthies of the Revolution, and found out fit
companions for them. I had coupled Franklin and
Marat together; and, in another place M'Kean
and Ankerstrom.[1]

Early on the Monday morning, I took down my
shutters. Such a sight had not been seen in Philadelphia for twenty years. Never since the beginning of the rebellion, had anyone dared to hoist
at his windows the portrait of George the Third.
I had [also] put up a representation of Lord Howe's
victory[2] [from] the "European Magazine"; but,
a bookseller, with whom I was acquainted, and
who came to see how I stood it, whispered me,
while the rabble were gazing and growling at my
door, that he had two large representations of the
same action. They were about four feet long and
two wide: the things which are hawked about and
sold at farm-houses in England, and had been
crammed, more perhaps, by way of packing stuff
than otherwise, into a parcel of goods that had
been sent out from London. But the letters were
large; the mob, ten or twenty deep, could read,
and they did read aloud too, "Lord Howe's De-
cisive Victory over the French Fleet", and, therefore, though the price augmented from sixpence
to two dollars, I purchased them, and put one up
at the window. The other was sold.

At the time when I adopted my defiance, I knew not one British subject in America besides myself, who was not afraid to own his country and his King. [Yet this print] was sold to two Englishmen, who were amongst the numbers that went to America about the years 1794 and 1795, misled by the representations of Paine and others, and being, as they frankly acknowledged to me, enemies of their country when they left it. They had mixed among the crowd, had taken the part of their country, and had proposed to maintain their words with their fists. After the quarrel had, in some degree, subsided, they, partly, perhaps, by way of defiance, came into the shop to purchase each of them a picture of Lord Howe and his victory. Finding that I had but one for sale, they would have purchased that; but, as it amounted to more money than both of them were possessed of, they went, and, in their phrase, which I shall never forget, "kicked their master", that is to say got money in advance upon their labour, which was then engaged in the digging of a cellar. Having thus obtained the two dollars, each of them took an end of the print in his hand, displayed it, and thus carried it away through the mob, who, though they still cursed, could not help giving signs of admiration.

It was no sooner discovered that I was Peter Porcupine, and that I had taken [an] excellent house and shop, than the French faction began to muster their forces. Several infamous publications appeared in Bache's paper, declaring me to be a deserter, a felon, a thief who had fled from the gallows, etc. Amongst my opponents with the pen, the most persevering and bitter were the Irish emigrants, and amongst these, the most able were Mr Casey and Mr Duane, the former of whom was a bookseller in Philadelphia, and the latter the proprietor of a newspaper published in that city. These gentlemen, and the Irish emigrants generally, were distinguished amongst the most furious partisans of the French, and of course amongst the most virulent enemies of England. [But] Time, while it wears away life, softens our asperities, and, if it did not, in what a state mankind must soon be. When I was in America [in 1817,] I shook hands with Mr Casey and Mr Duane; that as our enmity rose out of error, it was put an end to by a knowledge of the truth.[3]

I cannot refrain from relating, though it be rather of a private character, a circumstance that took place in Philadelphia, because it is illustrative of my disposition. I rented my house [and shop] at more than £300 sterling a year of Mr John Oldden, of that city, who was a very rich man, a Quaker, having a wife, two sons, and a daughter. He was rather a free Quaker; liked to laugh and liked my gay and slap-dash conversation. He offered to give me the house. I refused to have it in spite of all he could say. He then wanted to give it to my wife, who also refused. Mr Oldden died suddenly in 1799, and his eldest son was surprised, that I did not come with the will and take the house, his father having told many persons that I was to have that house. I had rendered no service to Mr Oldden, and, therefore, did not think it just to take the property from his family.

From my very first outset in politics, I formed the resolution of keeping myself perfectly independent. In adherence to this resolution, I rejected, in America, many offers of great pecuniary advantage. Had I been willing to become what they call a citizen of the United States in how many ways might I have profited from it! There were no reasonable bounds, to which I might not confidently have looked forward to see my fortune extended! My perseverance in a contrary line of conduct appeared so unaccountable, upon any common principle, that the people in America, friends as well as foes, regarded me as being in the pay of the British government. I always denied the fact; but my zeal, my efforts, my sacrifices of every sort, were such that it was impossible to make men believe that I was not regularly and amply supplied with "the gold of Pitt"!

While I was making gallant and effectual stand against the French influence, our Envoy [at] Philadelphia was Sir Robert Liston, who, on the part of the Government at home, offered me, in the presence of Lord Henry Stuart, great pecuniary reward. This reward I refused. [He then] informed me, in the year 1798, I think it was, that the Ministers at home were fully sensible of the

obligations due to me from my country, and that,
if I would accept of nothing for myself, they
wished me to point out any of my relatives, in the
army or elsewhere, whom they might serve. To
which I answered, as nearly as I can recollect,
"As to my relations in the army, I can ask for
no promotion for them, because I have not an
opportunity of knowing whether such promotion
would be consistent with the good of the service;
and, with respect to my relations out of the army,
a sudden elevation might, perhaps, be very far
from contributing to their happiness, besides
which, though it would be my duty to assist them
by means of my earnings, I should not think it
just in me to be instrumental in throwing them as
a burden upon the nation". I must suppose that
[Sir Robert] was utterly astonished. The Government did nothing wrong in making the offer; for
my services to England were so great, so manifest,
that it would have been criminal not to have
made [it].

As Lord Henry Stuart was very intimate with
Lord Folkestone (now Earl of Radnor) I daresay
that the latter frequently heard my conduct described by the former; and, perhaps, to this I owe
the unbroken friendship of the Earl of Radnor for
now thirty years. The late Lord Henry Stuart told
him, that when I was at Philadelphia, [carrying]
on single-handed such a fight for my country, I
was his criterion whereby to judge men's principles; that he used to put them the question,

[78]

"How do you like Mr Cobbett's writings?" If
they applauded, he set them down as sincere
friends of England: if not, if he found them even
cold in their commendations, he set them down
as enemies.

[From the other side, too, were offers made.
The atheistical Bishop Talleyrand] assumed the
character of a gentleman, at the same time re-
moving to Philadelphia.[4] Some months after his
arrival, he left a message with a friend of his, requesting me to meet him at that friend's house.
Several days passed before the meeting took place.
I had no business to call me that way, and therefore I did not go. At last, this modern Judas and
I got seated by the same fireside. I expected that
he wanted to expostulate with me on the severe
treatment he had met with at my hands: I had
called him an apostate, a hypocrite, and every
other name of which he was deserving; I therefore
leave the reader to imagine my astonishment,
when I heard him begin with complimenting me
on my wit and learning. He praised several of my
pamphlets, the "New Year's Gift" in particular.
I did not acknowledge myself the author, of course;
but yet he would insist that I was; or, at any rate,
they reflected, he said, infinite honour on the
author. Having carried this species of flattery as
far as he judged it safe, he asked me, with a vast
deal of apparent seriousness, whether I had received my education at Oxford or at Cambridge!
Hitherto I had kept my countenance pretty well;

1796
to
1800
but this abominable stretch of hypocrisy, and the placid mien and silver accent with which it was pronounced, would have forced a laugh from a Quaker in the midst of meeting. I don't recollect what reply I made to him; but this I recollect well, I gave him to understand that I was no trout, and consequently not to be caught by tickling.

This information led him to something more solid. He began to talk about business. I taught English; and, as luck would have it, this was the very commodity that Bishop Périgord wanted. If I had taught any language, or sold sand or ashes, or pepper-pot, it would have been just the same to him. He knew the English language as well as I did; but he wanted to have dealings with me in some way or other. I therefore did not care to take him as a scholar. I told him, that, being engaged in a translation for the press, I could not possibly quit home. This difficulty the lame friend hopped over in a moment. He would very gladly come to my house. I cannot say but it would have been a great satisfaction to me to have seen the ci-devant Bishop of Autun come trudging through the dirt to receive a lesson from me; but, on the other hand, I did not want a French spy to take a survey either of my desk or my house. My price for teaching was six dollars a month; he offered me twenty; but I refused; and before I left him, I gave him clearly to understand that I was not to be purchased.

I frequently met with him in the shop of a

French bookseller, named Moreau de St Méry,[5] who had himself acted a conspicuous part in the rebellion of the famous 14th of July. One day, in a conversation respecting Buonaparte, who was just at that time beginning his robberies and murders, I observed to Talleyrand, that, seeing the state of degradation to which the French nation was sunk, I should not be at all surprised to see even this new-fledged cut-throat finish his career by wearing the crown of the Bourbons; to which Talleyrand made the remarkable reply: "Je ne sais pas, M. Cobbett, si le scélérat portera la couronne des Bourbons; mais ce que je sais, c'est que Barras l'a bien coiffé du bonnet de Moïse". In the witticism, Talleyrand evidently alluded to that appearance on the head of Moses, which painters have generally represented by horns.

I began my editorial career with the presidency of Mr Adams, and my principal object was to render his administration all the assistance in my power. I flattered myself with the hope of accompanying him through [his] voyage, and of partaking in a trifling degree, of the glory of the enterprise; but he suddenly tacked about, and I could follow him no longer. I therefore waited for the first opportunity to haul down my sails. My Gazette, instead of being a mine of gold to me, never yielded me a farthing. Gain was never a primary object with me. The other branches of my business enabled me to support the loss. It was my intention to continue it till the month of

March, 1801; but as this intention was founded entirely upon my persuasion of the public utility of the continuation, it fell, of course, the moment that persuasion was removed from my mind. [I addressed] a Farewell Number of "Porcupine's Gazette" [from New York City in January of the year 1800, and] I congratulated myself on having established a paper, carried it to a circulation unparalleled in extent, and preserved the circulation to the last number; on having, in the progress of this paper, uniformly supported with all my feeble powers, the cause of true religion, sound morality, good government, and real liberty.

When I determined to discontinue the publication of "Porcupine's Gazette", I intended to remain, for the future, if not an unconcerned, at least a silent spectator of public transactions and political points; but the unexpected and sweeping result of a lawsuit decided against me, induced me to abandon my lounging intention. The suit to which I allude, was an action of slander, commenced against me in the autumn of 1797, by Dr Benjamin Rush,[6] the noted bleeding physician of Philadelphia. It was tried on the 14th of December, [1799,] when "the upright, enlightened, and impartial republican jury" assessed, as damages, five thousand dollars; a sum surpassing the aggregate amount of all the damages assessed for all the torts of this kind, ever sued for in [the United States] from their first settlement to the time of the trial. To the five thousand dollars must be added, the costs of the suit, the loss incurred by the interruption in collecting debts in Pennsylvania, and by the sacrifice of property taken in execution, and sold by the Sheriff in public auction in Philadelphia, where a great number of books in sheets (among which was a part of a new edition of "Porcupine's Works") were sold, or rather, given away, as waste paper; so that, the total of what was wrested away from me by Rush, fell little short of eight thousand dollars.

To say that I did not feel this stroke, and very sensibly too, would be a great affectation; but, to repine at it would have been folly, and to have sunk under it cowardice. I knew an Englishman in the Royal Province of New Brunswick, who had a very valuable house, which was, I believe, at that time, nearly his all, burnt to the ground. He was out of town when the fire broke out, and happened to come home just after it had exhausted itself. He came very leisurely up to the spot, stood about five minutes looking steadily at the rubbish, and then, stripping off his coat, "Here goes", said he, "to earn another!" and immediately went to work, raking the spikes and bits of iron out of the ashes. This noble-spirited man I had the honour to call my friend; and if ever this page meet his eye, he will have the satisfaction to see, that, though it was not possible for me to follow, I, at least, remembered his example.

We came home [to England] from New York, I, my wife, and two little children, in the post-office packet, for which I paid very highly. Stopping at Halifax, I was very graciously received by the Duke of Kent, then commander-in-chief in the province of Nova Scotia. Arrived at Falmouth, I was most kindly lodged and entertained by the collector of customs. For my fame had, even then, spread very widely amongst all persons connected with the Government. Arrived in London (July, 1800) I took a hired lodging, and deliberated what I should do with my slender means, amounting to only about £500, the proceeds of the sale of goods and books at New York.

That I was most unjustly and basely treated in the American States, and by two of the Governments of that country, is a fact pretty well known to every person, who reads or hears much about America. With the exception of the Quakers of Pennsylvania, many other individuals in that State, and the people of New England, I hate the United States and all their mean and hypocritical system of rule.

I saw the defenders of America holding forth the United States as the only free and virtuous country in the world. It, therefore, became me to show, that the government of America was, in fact, one of the very worst in the world, the most profligately dishonest that I have ever seen or heard described. I say, that a judge was detected, in Philadelphia, stealing bank-notes out of the till in a shop; was afterwards driven from the bench by the shopkeeper's holding up and shaking his fist at him; and that no public proceedings, and no public expressions of indignation, were the consequence.

I lived, first and last, seven or eight years within a few hundred yards of the Court of St James. I had my ears and eyes open as well as other people, and was not much prone to give the best interpretation to acts of baseness and corruption; and I declare, that, in the whole of [those] years, I never saw and heard of so much place-hunting, profit-hunting, political intrigue, bargaining about jobs and bills; in short, no such low, filthy, odious, political corruption, as I had before my eyes, and in my ears, in one single fortnight while I was at Harrisburgh, the seat of the government of Pennsylvania. London police-runners, select vestrymen of petty parishes in England, appeared gentlemen to my recollection, during my stay at Harrisburgh.

I am, [at the end of my life,] no republican in principle, any more than I am in law and allegiance. I hold, that this, which we have [in England,] is the best sort of government in the world. I hold that a government of king, lords, and commons, the last of which chosen by all men, who are of full age, of sound mind, and untainted by indelible crime, is the best of governments. I lived eight years under the republican government of Pennsylvania; and I declare, that I believe that to have been the most corrupt and tyrannical government that the world ever knew;

[85]

added to which, were the lowness, the dirtiness of the villainy, the vulgarity, the disregard of all sense of morality and of honour, making the whole thing so disgusting, as to drive an Englishman half mad at the thought of ever seeing his country subjected to such rulers.

I must forget the votes in the legislature bought by losing a game at cards at a tavern; I must forget the great game which the Bank of Philadelphia lost, in [a] room of borrowed light in the centre of the tavern, where the card-playing was going on day and night, Sundays not excepted, during the whole of [the] session. I must forget the court-house at Harrisburgh, and the judge with a twisted silk handkerchief around his neck, and a quid of tobacco in his cheek. I must forget that dirty-faced and unshaven jury, sitting with their hats on, talking over the back of the box to the parties or their friends, and having glasses of grog handed to them to drink in the box; I must forget all these things, and a great many others, before I can begin to think that kings and lords are the worst people in the world.

The Americans, under pretences the most false, by the violent mockery of judicial proceedings, by openly avowed and boasted-of perjury, robbed me of earnings, left me to begin anew with a family dependent solely upon my exertions, and cruelly persecuted several of my friends. For the sake of these friends more than for my own sake I hate the unprincipled nation.

[Yet this applies only to officials and their political toadies: the people are good.] I lived in Philadelphia with every disposition to find fault with everything that was amiss. I never heard of any person, except in one instance, being tried for his life or her life; I never heard of a murder, a highway robbery, or of a house being broken open. I never heard of an execution of death on any person, except of three men hanged on the banks of the Delaware, for piracy and murder. These men were foreigners, and such was the horror of an execution, even in such a case, that the executioner was obliged to be disguised in such a way, that it was impossible that anyone should recognize either his person or features; being brought to the spot, in carriage, under an escort of constables, and taken away, in a similar manner, so as to make it impossible for him to become publicly known. Philadelphia, at the time I speak of, contained about 70,000 inhabitants.

[In England we had to] have laws to guard our turnip fields from robbery, and very necessary they are; for without them there is no man, in any part of the country, who could depend on having the use of his crop even of that coarse and bulky article. To steal corn out of a field, after it was cut, was punished with death by our laws; and if we had fields of Indian Corn, which is a delightful food for several weeks before it be ripe, I cannot form an idea of the means that would be necessary to preserve it from being carried away. As to

1796
to
1800

poultry, no man in England has the smallest expectation of being able ever to taste what he raises, unless he carefully locks it up in the night, and has dogs to guard the approaches to the henroost. In America, at within ten or twelve miles of Philadelphia, it is the common practice of the farmers to turn the flocks of turkeys into the woods, in the latter end of August, there to remain until towards winter, when they return half fat. A farmer in England would no more think of doing this, than he would think of depositing his purse in any of the public foot-paths across his fields. In order to preserve their fences, the farmers sometimes resorted to this expedient: they bored holes in the stoutest of their stakes, which sustained their hedges; put gunpowder in these holes; then drove in a piece of wood very firmly upon the powder; so that the stolen hedge, in place of performing its office of boiling the kettle, dashed it and all around it to pieces. This mode of preserving fences I first heard of at Alresford, a town at about twelve miles distance from Botley, [where I at one time farmed;] and although it certainly does appear at first sight, a very cruel one, what was a man to do? The thieves were so expert as to set detection at defiance.

CHAPTER VII

1800–1805

*　　*　　*　　*　　*

ARRIVED IN LONDON, ALL WHO KNEW THE history of my exploits in America, supposed as a matter of course, that showers of gold were about to fall upon me. Many persons will recollect, that, in 1803, the late Mr Windham said in the House of Commons,[1] that I, for my services in America, "merited a statue of gold". In a few days after my arrival, I was, by him, who was then Secretary of War, invited to dine at his house, with a party, of whom Pitt and Canning were two. I was, of course, very proud of this invitation: and I felt more than ever disposed to use my talents in support of the system as it was then going on; which stood in real need of support, for Buonaparte was making fearful progress; and I resolved in my mind to set up a daily paper.

While, however, I was thinking about this, Mr George Hammond, the Under Secretary of State for Foreign Affairs (Lord Grenville being the Secretary) sent for me to his office, and made me an offer of a Government paper. The Government had two, "The True Briton" and "The Sun", the former a morning and the latter an evening paper. They were their property, office, types, lease of houses, and all; and the former was offered to me as a gift, with all belonging to it. My refusal of Sir Robert Liston's offer had convinced them, that to offer money was of no use. I refused the offer, though worth several thousand pounds. From that moment, all belonging to the Government looked on me with great suspicion.

When I returned to England, after an absence from the country parts of it, of sixteen years, the trees, the hedges, even the parks and woods, seemed so small! It made me laugh to hear little gutters, that I could jump over, called Rivers! The Thames was but a "Creek"! But, when, in about a month after my arrival in London, I went to Farnham, the place of my birth, what was my surprise! Everything had become so pitifully small! I had to cross in my post-chaise, the long and dreary heath of Bagshot. Then, at the end of it, to mount a hill, called Hungry Hill; and from that hill I knew that I should look down into the beautiful and fertile vale of Farnham. My heart fluttered with impatience, mixed with a sort of fear, to see all the scenes of my childhood; for I had learnt before, the death of my father and mother. There is a hill, not far from the town, called Crooksbury Hill, which rises up out of a flat, in the form of a cone, and is planted with Scotch fir trees. Here I used to take the eggs and young ones of crows and magpies. This hill was a famous one in the neighbourhood. It served as the superlative degree of height. "As high as

Crooksbury Hill" meant, with us, the utmost de- 1800
gree of height. Therefore, the first object that my *to*
eyes sought was this hill. I would not believe my 1805
eyes! Literally speaking, I for a moment, thought
the famous hill removed, and a little heap put in
its stead; for I had seen in New Brunswick, a
single rock, or hill of solid rock, ten times as big,
and four or five times as high! The post-boy, going
downhill, and not a bad road, whisked me, in a
few minutes to the Bush Inn, from the garden of
which I could see the prodigious sandhill, where
I had begun my gardening works. What a nothing!
But now came rushing into my mind, all at once,
my pretty little garden, my little blue smock-
frock, my little nailed shoes, my pretty pigeons
that I used to feed out of my hands, the last kind
words and tears of my gentle and tenderhearted
and affectionate mother! I hastened back into
the room! If I had looked a moment longer, I
should have dropped. When I came to reflect,
what a change! I looked down at my dress. What
a change! What scenes I had gone through! How
altered my state! I had dined the day before at a
secretary of state's in company with Mr Pitt, and
had been waited upon by men in gaudy liveries!
I had had nobody to assist me in the world. No
teachers of any sort. Nobody to shelter me from
the consequences of bad, and no one to counsel
me to good, behaviour. I felt proud. The distinc-
tions of rank, birth, and wealth, all became nothing in my eyes; and from that moment (less

1800
to
1805

than a month after my arrival in England) I resolved never to bend before them.

At the time of my return, the great government
writers and political agents were[2] John Reeves,
who had been chairman of the "Loyal Associa-
tion against Republicans and Levellers"; John
Bowles; John Gifford; William Gifford; Sir Fred-
eric Eden; the Rev. Mr Ireland, now dean of
Westminster; the Rev. John Brand; the Rev.
Herbert Marsh, now Bishop of Peterborough;
Mallet du Pan; Sir Francis D'Ivernois; and Nicholas Vansittart. These were all pamphlet writers,
supporting Pitt through thick and thin. They,
looking upon me as a fellow-labourer, had all sent
their pamphlets to me at Philadelphia; and all
of them, except Marsh, Vansittart, and the two
Frenchmen, had written me laudatory letters. All
but the Parsons called themselves 'Squires in the
title-pages of their pamphlets. Look at me now:
I had been bred up with a smock-frock upon my
back; that frock I had exchanged for a "soldier's
coat"; I had been out of England almost the
whole of my time, from the age of sixteen; we used
to give, in those times, the name of 'Squire to none
but gentlemen of great landed estates, keeping
their carriages, and so forth: look at me, then, in
whose mind my boyish idea of a 'squire had been
carried about the world with me: look at me, I
say, with letters from four 'squires and from reverends on my table; and wonder not that my
head was half turned! Only think of me (who just

[92]

about twelve years before, was clumping about
with nailed shoes on my feet) [and] wonder that
I did not lose my senses! And if I had remained in
America, God knows what might have happened.

1800
to
1805

Luckily I came to England, and that steadied
my head pretty quickly. To my utter astonishment and confusion I found all my 'Squires and
Reverends and my Baronet too; all, in one way or
other dependants on the Government; and, out of
the public purse, profiting from their pamphlets.
Hey! Dear! as the Lancashire men say: I thought
it would have broken my heart!

Of all these men, Reeves and William Gifford
were the only ones of talent. The former was a
really learned lawyer, and, politics aside, as good
a man as ever lived. A clever man; a head as clear
as spring water; considerate, mild, humane; made
by nature to be an English judge. I did not break
with him on account of politics. We said nothing
about them for years. I always had the greatest
regard for him: and there he now is in the grave,
leaving, the newspapers say, two hundred thousand pounds, without hardly a soul knowing that
there ever was such a man! The fate of William
Gifford was much about the same thing. Amongst
the first things that Reeves ever said to me was:
"I tell you what, Cobbett, we have only two ways
here; we must either kiss their ——, or kick them:
and you must make your choice at once". William
Gifford had more asperity in his temper, and was
less resigned. He despised Pitt and Canning and

the whole crew; but he loved ease, was timid; he was their slave all his life, and all his life had to endure a conflict between his pecuniary interest and his conscience.

As to the rest of my 'squires and other dignified pamphleteers, they were a low, talentless, place and pension-hunting crew; and I was so disgusted with the discoveries that I had made, that I trembled at the thought of falling into the ranks with them. Love of ease was not in me; the very idea of becoming rich had not entered into my mind; and my horror at the thought of selling my talents for money, and of plundering the country with the help of the means that God had given me wherewith to assist in supporting its character, filled me with horror not to be expressed.

[For the parsons, this will show what I learnt. An] Act provided that anyone might lay an information *qui tam* against a non-resident parson; and a gentleman, whose name was Williams, who was resolved to put the law in force, laid informations against great numbers; brought them into the court of King's Bench; obtained convictions upon some, and was proceeding with the rest. Whoever has seen a shot fired into a rookery in the month of June, when the young rooks are just beginning to flutter from the nest; whoever has heard the cawing, the sort of half-squalling, and seen the fluttering and dashing about of the old ones among the boughs; whoever has witnessed this uproar amongst these feathered incumbents

of the tops of the trees, may form some faint idea
of the bustle among the black-coats and bush-
wigs, at the appearance of this bundle of *qui-tam*
actions; but no other man can have even a faint
idea of their confusion. I had a very fair opportunity of hearing the cawings of these clerical
incumbents. I well remember breakfasting with
Dr Rennel (now Dean of Winchester), he being
then Master of the Temple; and I remember that
he and his wife (daughter of Judge Blackstone)
entertained me with most strenuous efforts to excite my indignation against the men who had laid
qui-tam informations. I, who understood no more
of this matter than if I had been in China, had it
all explained to me very patiently by the Doctor,
and of course thought that the Doctor must be
right, yet, somehow or other, I perceived that the
parsons had been in fault; and my doubts were
greatly augmented by the violent railing of the
Doctor against the informer. That which took
place in the Temple, [took] place everywhere.
Jacobin, Leveller, Infidel, Atheist, Traitor, were
heard, even in the streets, poured out against this
Mr Williams. After a little while, I asked a parson
one day, why they railed so against this man; why
they had not resided; and how they came to think
of anything else than residing upon their livings;
upon which he told me that I was as bad as the
informer himself. This was a little too much, and
I, in my own mind, began to side with the informer, especially when I found that this parson

1800
to
1805
had one living in Suffolk, and one living in Surrey, and that he seldom showed his face at either of them.

It was the custom in those glorious times of Pitt and Paper, to give to the literary partisans of the Government what were called "slices" of a loan. For instance, Moses was the loan-monger; and, as the scrip, as it used to be called was always directly at a premium, a bargain was always made with the loan-monger that he should admit certain favourites of the government to have a certain portion of the scrip, at the same price that he gave for it; I was offered such portion of scrip, which, as I was told, would put a hundred pounds or two into my pocket at once. I was frightened at the idea of becoming responsible for the immense sum, upon which this would be the profit. But I soon found that the scrip was never even to be shown to me, and that I merely had to pocket the amount of the premium. I positively refused to have anything to do with the matter, for which I got heartily laughed at. But this was of great utility to me; it opened my eyes with regard to the nature of these transactions; it set me to work to understand all about the debt and the funds and the scrip and the stock and everything belonging to it. At every step I found the thing more and more black, and more and more execrable, and it soon brought my mind to a conclusion, that the system was what the accursed thing was in the camp of the Israelites,[3] and that the nation never could be

happy again until it was got rid of; in which 1800
opinion I have remained from that day to this. *to*

I set out as a sort of self-dependent politician. 1805
My opinions were my own. I dashed at all prejudices. I scorned to follow anybody in matter of
opinion. Before my time, every writer of talent
enlisted himself under the banners of one party,
or one minister, or other. I stood free from all
such connections; and, therefore, though admired
by many, I was looked upon with an evil eye by
all. All had been used to see men of no rank glad
to receive the approbation of men of rank. All
had been used to see talent crouch to power. All
were, therefore, offended at my presumption, as
they deemed it. My great success as a writer; the
great admiration which my writings frequently
excited; the effect on the public mind which they
frequently produced: these were much more than
sufficient to draw down on me the mortal hatred
of the "race that write".

[I set up a daily paper.] My undertaking was
my own; it was begun without the aid, without
the advice, and even without the knowledge of
any person, either directly or indirectly connected
with the Ministry. "The Porcupine" never was
in America, nor was it ever in England, the blind
instrument of party. In the days of youth and
ignorance, I had been led to believe that comfort,
freedom, and virtue, were exclusively the lot of
Republicans. A very short trial had convinced
me of my error. During an eight years' absence

1800
to
1805
from my country, I was not an unconcerned spectator of her perils, nor did I listen in silence to the slanders of her enemies. Once more returned, I felt an irresistible desire to communicate to my countrymen the fruit of my experience.

[It] surpassed expectations. [It] commenced at a very short notice, with 700 orders, and, in the short period of five weeks, gradually rose to upwards of 1500. "The Porcupine" could not boast of being seen in the numerous pot-houses of [London]; but had the superior advantage of being generally read by persons of property, rank, and respectability.

[At the same time] I formed a partnership [in the bookselling business] with Mr John Morgan, of Philadelphia,[4] to whom [I had] been long attached by a friendship founded in a concurrence in political principles, and on a similarity of conduct at a time when few Englishmen were to be found loyal and bold enough openly to defend the character of their King and Country. On the success of this business [I rested my] principle hope of pecuniary gain.

I had no intention to range myself in a systematic opposition to His Majesty's Ministers, or to their measures. The first object was to contribute my mite toward the support of the authority of that Sovereign, whom God had commanded me to honour and obey. The uniform intention of my writings was, and is, to counteract the effects of the enemies of monarchy in general, and of the

monarchy of England in particular, under whatever guise those enemies have appeared; to check
the spirit and oppose the progress of levelling
innovation, whether proceeding from clubs of
Jacobins, companies of traders, synagogues of
saints, or boards of government; to cherish an adherence to long-tried principles, an affection for
ancient families and ancient establishments.

[But many things led me into an opposition.]
The ancient nobility and gentry of the kingdom
had been thrown out of public employment: a
race of merchants and manufacturers, and bankers
and loan-jobbers and contractors had usurped
their place. Good honest men, plain men, men in
the middle classes of life, as Mr Wilberforce said,
may be excellent judges of public measures; but,
unfortunately, in searching after these men, we
went too far, and took them out of the lower classes
of life. Who was it that stirred up these lees? It
was Mr Pitt himself. [Another thing was the funding system. I agreed with] Lord Darnley, that,
"were all the Jew-brokers become bankrupt, and
all three-per-cent mongers no more, there would
still be a country to fight for"! Woeful experience [showed that] the funds were [not] a criterion
of the national spirit. Generally speaking, the
great evil of a national debt, of a great accumulation of personal property of any sort [is that] the
holders of such property are ever upon the rack
to increase its immediate value. Hence the sub-
serviency of statesmen to the views of money-

lenders. The funding system was eating the heart out of the nobility; stifling every high and honourable feeling. It was engaged in a desperate contest against the aristocracy and monarchy of England, and this contest must finally terminate in the destruction of one or the other.

[Mr Pitt had a] partiality for young and new men, for persons of his own creation, to the almost total exclusion of the old nobility and gentry. This upstart system was adhered to from the first moment of his administration to the last: he never voluntarily and cordially gave the hand to anything great, whether of birth, character, or talent.

[I naturally opposed the Preliminaries of the Peace of Amiens in 1801.][5] From the scenes of violence and outrage, which had taken place in some parts of the town, not far [from my shop] in Pall Mall, I had reason to expect, that, on the arrival of the Ratification of the Preliminaries, my dwelling-house there, as well as my printing-office in Southampton Street, would be attacked, because my sentiments respecting these Preliminaries were publicly known. It happened precisely as I had expected: about eight o'clock in the evening, my dwelling-house was attacked by an innumerable mob, all my windows were broken, and when this was done, the villains were preparing to break into my shop. The attack continued at intervals, till past one o'clock. During the whole of this time, not a constable nor peace officer of any description made his appearance;

nor was the smallest interruption given to the proceedings of this ignorant and brutal mob, who were thus celebrating the Peace. "The Porcupine" office experienced a similar fate.

[With the signing of the Peace in a few months' time, this scene was repeated.] In the same degree that I perceived the illumination on this [occasion] was to be compulsory, I became resolved not to submit to the degradation, and, therefore, it was with great mortification, that, on the evening before the Proclamation, I saw my wife actually confined in that situation, which, above all others, requires comfort and tranquillity. I wrote immediately to Lord Pelham, informed him of this untoward circumstance, but, at the same time, expressed my resolution not to illuminate my house. His Lordship assured me that he had given orders to protect from insolence, my family, and my premises.

I began to grow apprehensive of the consequences of resistance. To hazard the life of her, who had been my companion and support through all the storms I had endured; to make this sacrifice was no longer to be thought of, and I had made up my mind to yield, when she bravely determined to be removed to the house of a friend, rather than her husband should submit to the mandates of a base and hireling mob. A private individual may, with propriety, yield to the torrent, and subject himself to the imputation of openly approving what he secretly condemns. But

1800
to
1805
the man who aspires to the honours of attracting the attention, and influencing the opinions of others, must submit his conduct to the guidance of a different principle. His ease and comfort [must] never be consulted at the expense of his consistency; he must never be seduced by persuasion, allured by promises, nor intimidated by threats, to swerve, in the smallest degree, from the straight line of duty.

[My wife's] removal had not taken place many hours before I had reason to congratulate myself upon it. A numerous and boisterous rabble, coming from Cockspur Street, began to assault the house, at about half past nine o'clock. The Bow Street Magistrate with his men, used their utmost exertions to prevent violence, but in vain. The attack continued, with more or less fury, for about an hour and a half, during which time a party of horse-guards were called in to the aid of the civil power. Great part of the windows were broken; the sash frames of the ground floor almost entirely demolished; the panels of the window shutters were dashed in; the door nearly forced open; and much other damage done to several parts of the house.

[With such troubles, and since] I knew nothing of business which demanded thousands in place of a few hundreds [of pounds], my daily paper was soon gone,[6] and with it more than all that I possessed in the money way. I lost about £450, which was enough, in all conscience, to reward me for all my exertions, dangers, and losses in America. The light was extinguished completely. One half of the [public] papers were devoted to France, and the other half to the Ministry. I had done all I could do without exposing my family to beggary.

I had not the means, fairly my own, of establishing a [new work]. The risk of a beginning was more than I dared to encounter; was more than I should have been justified in encountering. If I had not been aided by a private subscription, set on foot by Mr Windham and the good Dr Lawrence, gentlemen conspicuous in what was then called the New Opposition,[7] [the now] famous " Register " never could have been begun. I should explicitly state in what light I viewed the proposed enterprise. I had sunk about £450 in " The Porcupine ". The remainder of my capital was joined to that of my partner, Mr Morgan, who, soon after our partnership was formed, had returned to the United States of America, with many of the towns of which we carried on a sort of mercantile trade of considerable magnitude, and not contemptible in point of profit. From that trade I could not withdraw any considerable sum. [Nor could] I think of setting on foot any sort of subscription, or collection, of which my emolument should be regarded as the object. I disclaimed all desire to derive pecuniary advantage from the proposed undertaking, and all idea of personal obligation towards anyone who [might have thought] proper to contribute toward it. I

was willing; even anxiously desirous, to conduct
the publication; but, that desire, great as it was,
would not suffer me to do, or to accept of, anything, that should, in the smallest degree, work
a forfeiture of that independence, to preserve
which, I had all my life time, practised, and I still
do practise, industry and economy to their utmost
extent. Thus the foundation of "The Register"
was laid; being, I trust it will be thought, a foundation as fair and as honourable as any of which
the mind of man can possibly form an idea. It
was building upon a rock; and the house has
stood, accordingly, in spite of the winds and the
floods. [In a year,] there were sold weekly, of this
work, upon an average, in the United Kingdom
alone, more than two thousand numbers, an instance of success unparalleled in the history of
periodical literature.

Indulging, as I [did,] and as I yet do, the hope
of being, for a few years, at least, now and then
remembered as one of those, whom the spirit-
stirring circumstances of those awful times drew
forth from their native obscurity, I never ceased
anxiously to desire, that the events, amidst which
I had lived, and in which I had taken so deep an
interest, might be handed down to posterity un-
disfigured by falsehood. Actuated by this desire,
I bent my mind on securing a faithful record of
these events. [I published "The Political Register", "The Parliamentary Debates", "The
Spirit of the Public Journals ", "The State Trials ",

"The Parliamentary History"]; and it appeared to me, that in possession of [these] works, the politician and the historian [would] possess every help afforded to them by the press relative to the feelings, opinions, and the facts of the times. If popular delusion and popular baseness, fed by the corruptions of the commercial system, should contrive to triumph till the very names of liberty and honour shall be expunged from the English language, and till every man be brought to lend his hand to the muzzling of his neighbour, I shall still have the satisfaction to reflect, that, on my part, no effort has been wanting to prevent this consummation of national infamy.

[My opinions were strengthened by my experience of the changes undergoing in the nation.] I liked not the never-ending recurrence to Acts of Parliament. Something must be left and something ought to be left, to the sense and reason and morality and religion of the people. There were a set of "well-meaning" men in the country, who would have passed laws for the regulating and restraining of every feeling of the human breast, and every motion of the human frame: they would have bound us down, hair by hair, as the Lilliputians did Gulliver. Instead of retrenching the enormous sinecures and pensions; instead of endeavouring to lessen taxes, which were the cause, and the sole cause, of the fearful and deplorable pauperism, instead of measures of this sort, [they] proposed schools and badges for the poor. [They

The Progress of a Plough-boy

were hostile] to rural and athletic sports;[8] to those sports which string the nerves and strengthen the frame, which excite an emulation in deeds of hardihood and valour, and which imperceptibly instil honour, generosity, and a love of glory. Men thus formed are unfit for the puritanical school; therefore it was, that the sect were incessantly labouring to eradicate, fibre by fibre, the last poor remains of English manners. Their pretexts were plausible: gentleness and humanity were the cant of the day. Instead of preserving those assemblages and those sports, in which the nobleman mixed with his peasants, which made the poor man proud of his inferiority, and created in his breast a personal affection for his lord, too many of the rulers of this land were hunting the common people from every scene of diversion, and driving them to a Club or a Conventicle, at the former of which they sucked in the delicious rudiments of earthly equality, at the latter, the no less delicious doctrine, that there was no lawful king but King Jesus.

[William Wilberforce,] with talents, which in spite of twenty years cultivation, still remained far beneath mediocrity; with an abundant stock of that presumption of which a conceit of extraordinary purity was at once the cause and the effect: all at once started forth, a puritan in religion and in law, a reformer of the church and the parliament. [Yet,] the full force of [his] philanthropy [never moved] in behalf of the more than

a million paupers in existence in England. Yes, in
England! English men and women and children!
One eighth of our whole population! But they
were not slaves. Say, rather, they were not black;
a thing which they might, seeing the preference
which was given to that colour, have well regarded
as extremely unfortunate. The politics of the whole
sect of the Methodists were very bad. Never was
anything done by them, which bespoke an attachment to public liberty. "Their kingdom", they
told us, "was not of this world"; but they did,
nevertheless, not neglect the good things of it;
and, some of them were to be found amongst the
rankest jobbers in the Country. Indeed, it was
well known, that that set of politicians, ironically
called the Saints, were the main prop of the Pitt
System; it was well known, that under the garb of
sanctity, they aided and abetted in all the worst
things that were done. The political history of the
Saints, would exhibit a series of the most infamous
intrigues and most rapacious plunder, that, perhaps, ever was heard of in the world. They were
never found wanting at any dirty job; and invariably lent their aid in those acts, which were
the most inimical to the liberty of England.

[On the other hand was the Pitt System of
government, with all its debasing effects.] The
tendency of [his] funding and taxing system was
to draw the produce of labour into unnatural
channels, into the hands of upstart cormorants,
and to deal it back again in driblets, under the

1800
to
1805

name of relief, or of charity, just to support the life of those from whose pores it had been drained. "Well", some overgorged upstart [would] say, "and what matter is it, so they are supported, whence the support comes?" The matter was this, that the labourers were humbled, debased, and enslaved. And thus was the nation debased; thus, without any direct abolition of the liberties of the common people, those liberties were being destroyed.

When you had restrained your surprise, and could hardly restrain your indignation, at seeing a broker, a contractor, a placeman, or speculator of any description, start all at once from the dunghill to a coach and four, you were told that his rise was a proof of his merit. For my part, I generally drew an exactly opposite conclusion.

[In consequence of these opinions publicly expressed, the Ministers] attempted to establish no less than six periodical papers for the express and openly avowed purpose of destroying "The Register", all of which papers, in due succession, perished, not from want of funds but for want of readers. To obtain success for these publications, no expense, no device was spared; advertisements and handbills, announcing a determination to "detect and expose Cobbett" were published in numbers far exceeding those of the several works to which they related. The wretches published a thing which they pretended was a true account of [the] Court-Martial, in which I was concerned, at

the time of my leaving the army. They sent 1800
hundreds and thousands of copies into Hamp- *to*
shire, [where my farm was.] All the gentlemen 1805
received them for nothing. The post-office at
Winchester charged only a penny for their trans-
mission, for instance. The robbers, as they came
down from London in their carriages, brought
with them whole bales, which they tossed out to
all whom they met or overtook on the road. A
landau full of he and she peculators passed through
Alton, tossing out these pamphlets as they went.
The thing was put into all the Inns, and other
public places, particularly at Winchester, where
it would certainly have been put into the churches,
had they been places of public resort.

[In 1806, I announced my intention to stand
for the borough of Honiton. My expressed prin-
ciples] were the necessity for a strong front against
bribery; never to touch the public money either
by [my] own hands, or by those of relatives. All
professions, short of this, I accounted as nothing.

Before I set off from London, having fixed
upon the hour of my departure on Friday morning the 6th [of June], I met Mr Johnstone (Lord
Cochrane's uncle), and asked him if he had any
news of his nephew, of whose recent gallant
conduct the newspapers had just informed us.
Mr Johnstone said, that he was then going to the
Admiralty, in order to get him leave of absence to
come part of the way [from Plymouth] to London
to meet him upon some business; whereupon I

observed, that as I was going to Honiton, he might
as well go with me. Mr Johnstone accepted of my
offer, and we set off accordingly at three o'clock
on Friday. We arrived at Honiton on Saturday,
and, on the same day, Mr Johnstone received a
letter from Lord Cochrane informing him that his
Lordship could not leave Plymouth just then.
But, on Sunday, while we were at dinner, there
came an express from Lord Cochrane, bearing a
letter for me, informing me, that his Lordship,
having read my address to the people of Honiton
in the London newspapers, and having perceived
that I had resolved to stand myself merely because I could find no other independent man, he
had determined to accept of my general invitation, and that he was actually on his way (dating
his letter from Exeter) to put his purpose in execution. In an hour afterward, having stopped at
Exeter to provide lawyers, his Lordship arrived.
I declined proceeding to the poll.

Now, as to the state of this borough, who shall
describe it? Who shall describe the gulph wherein
have been swallowed the fortunes of so many
ancient and respectable families? There was, the
electors would tell you, no bribery. They took a
certain sum of money each, according to their
consequence; "but this", they said, "came in the
shape of a reward after the election, and, therefore, the oath might be safely taken". Considered
as a question of morality, how contemptible this
subterfuge was need hardly be noticed; but, to say

the truth, they did not deceive themselves, and I must do them the justice to say, that they were not very anxious to deceive anybody else. They told you, flatly and plainly, that the money which they obtained for their votes, was absolutely necessary to enable them to live; that, without it, they could not pay their rents; and that, from election to election, poor men ran up scores at the shops, and were trusted by the shopkeepers, expressly upon the credit of the ensuing election; and that, thus, the whole of the inhabitants of the borough, the whole of the persons who returned two of the members to every parliament, were bound together in an indissoluble chain of venality.

The poorest of the people made a sort of pun upon my name as descriptive of my non-bribing principles, and moulded their sentiments into a cry of: "Bread and Cheese, and no empty Cupboard"; and some of them in a very serious and mild manner, remonstrated with me upon my endeavour to deprive them of the profits of their vote, or, in their own phrase, "to take the bread out of poor people's mouths".

In quitting this scene, looking back from one of the many hills that surrounded the fertile and beautiful valley in which Honiton lay, with its houses spreading down the side of an inferior eminence crowned by its ancient and venerable church; in surveying the fields, the crops, the cattle, all the blessings that nature could bestow, all the sources of plenty and all the means of com-

fort and happiness, it was impossible to divest
myself of a feeling of horror at reflecting upon the
deeds which the sun witnessed upon this one of
his most favoured spots.

The more I reflected upon what I had seen with
my own eyes, the more firm my conviction became, that [such] was the cause of our calamities
and our dangers, and that it was not, as was vainly
imagined, to be removed by laws [then] in existence. The greater fault was in those who exposed
the poor and miserable to the temptation of selling
their votes; [and for these something more radical
was needed.]

CHAPTER VIII

1805–1810

*　　*　　*　　*　　*

[I MUST NOW TELL OF MY OTHER ACTIVI-
ties; for, I was a countryman and a father before
I was a writer on political subjects.] The first
thing that I did, when [my] fourth child had come,
was to get into the country, and so far as to render
a going backward and forward to London, at short
intervals, quite out of the question. [While in
Hampshire, in 1804, I saw the village of Botley,
and determined on living there.] Botley was the
most delightful village in the world. It had everything in a village, that I loved; and none of the
things that I hated. It was in a valley, the soil
was rich, thick, set with woods; the farms were
small, the cottages neat; it had neither workhouse, nor barber, nor attorney, nor justice of the
peace. There was no justice within six miles, and
the barber came three miles once a week to shave
and cut hair! Would I were poetical, I would
write a poem in praise of Botley. [Within a year,
I had purchased land and a house there, and removed my family from London.]

Born and bred up in the sweet air myself, I was
resolved that [my children] should be bred up in
it too. Enjoying rural scenes and sports, as I had

1805
to
1810

done, when a boy, as much as anyone that ever was born, I was resolved that they should have the same enjoyments tendered to them. When I was a little boy, I was, in the barley-sowing season, going along by the side of a field, near Waverley Abbey; the primroses and bluebells new spangling the banks on both sides of me; a thousand linnets singing in a spreading oak over my head; while the jingle of the traces and the whistling of the plough-boys saluted my ears from over the hedge; and, as it were to snatch me from the enchantment, the hounds, at that instant, having started a hare in the hanger on the other side of the field, came scampering over it in full cry, taking me after them many a mile. I was not more than eight years old; but this particular scene presented itself to my mind every year from that day. I always enjoyed it over again; and I was resolved to give, if possible, the same enjoyments to my children.

I did not lead an idle life; I had to work constantly for the means of my living; my occupation required unremitted attention; I always saw the possibility, and even the probability, of being totally ruined by the hand of power; but happen what would, I was resolved, as long as I could cause them to do it, my children should lead happy lives; and happy lives they did lead, if ever children did in this whole world.

My intention was to make the boys fit to fight their way through life, for, who [could have been]

so weak as to imagine, that they would ever see 1805
many days of tranquillity! To write English; to *to*
speak French; to read a little Latin, perhaps; to 1810
ride, to play at single-stick, and, above all, to
work at husbandry. It was my intention to teach
them, in all by precept and in the most instances
by example. I had seen too many proofs of the
insufficiency of riches in the obtaining of happiness
and too many instances of the misery to which a
dependence on patronage led. [I had no wish] to
stifle genius; but if it were not of a stamp to rise
of itself, there was no raising it.*

* Cobbett left no detailed description of Botley, but
Miss Mitford's is very good, and gives exactly the picture
wanted.

"He had at that time a large house at Botley, with a
lawn and gardens sweeping down to the Bursledon River
...His...house, large, high, massive, red, and square,
and perched on a considerable eminence, always struck
me as not being unlike its proprietor.... There was a large
fluctuating series of guests for the hour or guests for the
day, of almost all ranks and descriptions, from the Earl
and his Countess to the farmer and his dame. The house
had room for all, and the hearts of the owners would have
had room for three times the number.

"I never saw hospitality more genuine, more simple, or
more thoroughly successful in the great end of hospitality,
the putting everybody completely at ease. There was not
the slightest attempt at finery, or display, or gentility.
They called it a farm-house, and everything was in
accordance with the largest idea of a great English
yeoman of the old time. Everything was excellent—
everything abundant—all served with the greatest nicety
by trim waiting damsels; and everything went on with
such quiet regularity that of the large circle of guests not

1805
to
1810

My two eldest sons, when about eight years old, were, for the sake of their health, placed, for a short time, at a clergyman's at Micheldever, and my daughter, a little older, at a school a few miles from Botley, to avoid taking them to London in the winter. But, with these exceptions, never had they, while children, teacher of any description. What need had we of schools? What need of scolding and force, to induce children to read, write, and love books? We did not want to "kill time"; we were always busy, wet weather or dry weather, winter or summer. There was no force, in any case; no command; none of these was ever wanted. To teach the children the habit of early rising was the great object; and everyone knows how young people cling to their beds. This was a capital matter; because here were industry and health one could find himself in the way. I need not say a word more in praise of the good wife...to whom this admirable order was mainly due.

"...fields lay along the Bursledon River, and might have been shown to a foreigner as a specimen of the richest and lovliest English scenery....Few persons excelled him in the management of vegetable, fruit, and flowers....His wall-fruit was...splendid, and much as flowers have been studied since that day, I never saw a more glowing or more fragrant autumn garden than that at Botley, with its pyramids of hollyhocks, and its masses of china-asters, of cloves, of mignonette, and of variegated geranium. The chances of life soon parted us, as, without grave faults on either side, people do lose sight of one another; but I shall always look back with pleasure and regret to that visit."

Recollections of a Literary Life, Chap. XVII.

both at stake. The child that was downstairs first, 1805
was called the lark for that day, and, further, sat *to*
at my right hand at dinner. They soon discovered, 1810
that to rise early, they must go to bed early; and
thus was this most important object secured,
with regard to girls as well as boys. Nothing is
more inconvenient, more disgusting, than to have
to do with girls, or young women, who lounge in
bed: "A little more sleep, a little more slumber,
a little more folding of the hands to sleep". Solo-
mon knew them well: he had, I daresay, seen the
breakfast cooling, carriages and horses and servants waiting, the sun coming burning on, the day
wasting, the night growing dark too early, ap-
pointments broken, and objects of journeys defeated; and all from the lolloping in bed of persons
who ought to have risen with the sun.

Health, the greatest of all things, was provided
for. Next, my being always at home was secured
as far as possible; always with them to set an
example of early rising, sobriety, and application
to something or other. Children will have some
out-of-doors pursuits; and it was my duty to lead
them to choose such as combined future utility
with present innocence. Each his flower-bed,
little garden, plantation of trees; rabbits, dogs,
asses, horses, pheasants and hares; hoes, spades,
whips, guns; always some object of lively interest, and as much earnestness and bustle as if
our living had solely depended on them.

In the meanwhile the book-learning crept in of

1805
to
1810

its own accord. Children naturally want to be like their parents, and to do what they do; and as I was always writing or reading, mine naturally desired to do something in the same way. Fond of book-learning, and knowing well its powers, I naturally wished them to possess it too; but never did I impose it upon anyone of them.

I accomplished my purpose indirectly. Health was secured by the deeply interesting and never-ending sports of the field and pleasures of the garden. Luckily these things were treated of in books and pictures of endless variety; so that, on wet days, in long evenings, these came into play. A large strong table in the middle of the room, their mother sitting at her work, used to be surrounded with them, the baby, if big enough, set up in a high chair. Here were inkstands, pens, pencils, india-rubber, and paper, all in abundance, and everyone scrabbled about as he or she pleased. There were prints of animals of all sorts; books treating of them; others treating of gardening, of flowers, of husbandry, of hunting, coursing, shooting, fishing, planting, and, in short, of everything with regard to which we had something to do. One would be trying to imitate a bit of my writing, another drawing the pictures of some of our horses and dogs, a third poking over Bewick's "Quadrupeds", and picking out what he said about them; but our book of never-failing resource was the French "Maison Rustique", which, it is said, was the book that first tempted Dusquesnois, the famous physician, in the reign of Louis XIV, to 1805 learn to read. And there was I, in my leisure *to* moments, to join this inquisitive group, to read 1810 the French, and tell them what it meaned in English. When my business kept me away from the scrabbling-table, a petition often came, that I would go and talk with the group, and the bearer generally was the youngest, being the most likely to succeed.

To do the things I did, you must love your home yourself; to rear up children in this manner, you must live with them; you must make them, too, feel by your conduct, that you prefer this to any other mode of passing your time. My occupation, to be sure, was chiefly carried on at home. Many a score of papers have I written amidst the noise of children, and in my whole life never bade them be still. When they grew up to be big enough to gallop about the house, I have written the whole day amidst noise that would have made some authors half mad. That which you are pleased with, however noisy, does not disturb you. I found time to talk with them, to walk, to ride about, with them; and when forced to go from home, always took one or more with me.

I remember that, one year, I raised a prodigious crop of fine melons, under handglasses; and I learned how to do it from a gardening-book; or, at least, that book was necessary to remind me of the details. Having passed part of an evening in talking to the boys about getting this crop,

1805
to
1810

"Come", said I, "now, let us read the book". Then the book came forth, and to work we went, following very strictly the precepts of the book. I read the thing but once, but the eldest boy read it, perhaps twenty times, over; and explained all about the matter to the others. [There] was a motive! Then he had to tell the garden labourer what to do to the melons. Now, I will engage, that more was really learned by this single lesson, than would have been learned by spending at this son's age, a year at school and he happy, and delighted all the while.

They began writing by taking words out of printed books; finding out which letter was which, by asking me, or those who knew the letters one from another; and by imitating bits of my writing, it is surprising how soon they began to write a hand like mine, very small, very faint-stroked, and nearly as plain as print. The first use that anyone of them made of the pen, was to write to me, though in the same house with them. They began doing this in mere scratches, before they knew how to make any one letter; and as I was always folding up letters and directing them, so were they; and they were sure to receive a prompt answer, with most encouraging compliments.

All the meddlings and teazings of friends, and, what was more serious, the pressing prayers of their anxious mother, about sending them to school, I withstood without the slightest effect on

my resolution. "Bless me, so tall, and not learned
anything yet!", [a meddling woman friend would
say of one of my sons]. "Oh, yes, he has", I used
to say, "he has learned to ride, and hunt, and
shoot, and fish, and look after cattle and sheep,
and to work in the garden, and to feed his dogs,
and to go from village to village in the dark." This
was the way I used to manage with troublesome
customers of this sort. And how glad the children
used to be when they got clear of such criticising
people!

1805
to
1810

The great business of life, in the country, ap-
pertains, in some way or other, to the game. If it
were not for the game, a country life would be
like an everlasting honeymoon, which would, in
about half a century, put an end to the human
race. In towns, or large villages, people make a
shift to find the means of rubbing the rust off from
each other by a vast variety of sources of contest.
A couple of wives meeting in the street, and giving
each other a wry look, or a look not quite civil
enough, will, if the parties be hard pushed for a
ground of contention, do pretty well. But in the
country, there is, alas, no such resource. [There]
are no walls for people to take of each other.
[There] is more room of every sort, elbow, leg,
horse, or carriage, for them all. Even at Church
(most of the people being in meeting-houses) the
pews are surprisingly too large. Where all circumstances seem calculated to cause never-ceasing
concord with its accompanying dullness, there

would be no relief at all, were it not for the game.
This, happily, supplies the place of all other sources
of alternate dispute and reconciliation; it keeps
all in life and motion, from the lord down to the
hedger. The wives and daughters hear so much of
it, that they inevitably get engaged in the dis-
putes; and thus all are kept in a state of vivid
animation.

I always encouraged my sons to pursue these
sports. I remembered, too, that I myself had had
a sportsman-education. I many and many a day
followed the hounds, and returned home at dark-
night, with my legs full of thorns and my belly
empty to go supperless to bed, and to congratulate
myself if I escaped a flogging. All the lectures, all
the threats, vanished from my mind in a moment
upon hearing the first cry of the hounds. I remembered all this, and resolved to leave the same
course freely open to my sons. They, until the ages
of 14 or 15, spent their time, by day, chiefly
amongst horses and dogs, and in the fields and
farmyard; and their candle-light chiefly in reading
books about hunting and shooting, and about dogs
and horses.

I always admired the sentiment of Rousseau:
"The boy dies, perhaps, at the age of ten or
twelve. Of what use, then, all the restraints, all
the privations, all the pain, that you have inflicted upon him? He falls, and leaves your mind
to brood over the possibility of your having
abridged a life so dear to you". I do not recall

the very words; but the passage made a deep impression upon my mind, just at the time when I
was about to become a father; and I was resolved
never to bring upon myself remorse from such a
cause. I was resolved to forgo·all the means of
making money, all the means of living in anything
like fashion, all the means of obtaining fame or
distinction, to give up everything, to become a
common labourer rather than make my children
lead a life of restraint and rebuke: I could not be
sure that my children would love me as they loved
their own lives; but I was, at any rate, resolved to
deserve such love at their hands.

[I learnt much of the state of the country
through going into Hampshire.] It was when the
madness for enclosure raged most furiously. I
[used to go] around a little common, called Horton
Heath on a Sunday. I found the husbands at
home. The Common contained about 150 acres;
and I found round the skirts of it, and near to the
skirts, about 30 cottages and gardens, the latter
chiefly encroachments on the common, which
was waste (as it was called) in a manor of which
the Bishop was the lord. I took down the names
of all the cottagers, the number and ages of their
children, and number of their cows, heifers, calves,
ewes, pigs, geese, ducks, fowls, and stalls of bees;
the extent of their little bits of ground, the worth
of what was growing, the number of apple trees,
of the black-cherry trees, called by them "mer-
ries", which was a great article in that part of

1805
to
1810

Hampshire. I have lost my paper, and, therefore, I cannot speak positively as to any one point; but, I remember one hundred and twenty five, or thirty five stalls of bees, worth at that time ten shillings a stall, at least. Cows there were about fifteen, besides heifers and calves; about sixty pigs great and small; and not less than five hundred head of poultry! The cattle and sheep of the neighbouring farmers grazed the common all the while besides. The bees alone were worth more annually than the common, if it had been enclosed, would have let for deducting the expense of fences. The farmers used the Common for their purposes; and my calculation was, that the cottagers produced from their little bits, in food, for themselves, and in things to be sold at market, more than any neighbouring farm of 200 acres! The cottagers consisted, fathers, mothers, and children, grandfathers, grandmothers, and grandchildren, of more than two hundred persons!

[I learnt to hate] a system that could lead English gentlemen to disregard matters like these! That could induce them to tear up "wastes" and sweep away occupiers like those I have described! Wastes indeed! Give a dog an ill name. Was Horton Heath a waste? Was it a "waste" when a hundred, perhaps, of healthy boys and girls were playing there of a Sunday, instead of creeping about covered with filth in the alleys of a town?

[I always was a good] master and employer. I never higgled as to prices in any case whatsoever;

I never attempted to cheapen anything; never **1805** wasted any of the precious moments of life in this *to* sort of lying and cheating. Accordingly I have **1810** been, and am, better served than anybody else. Those who have been long employed by me, not only like my employment, but they like me personally better than they like any other man in the world; and this, not from any cant about humanity; but on account of the frankness and sincerity which they always experienced from me, that freedom in conversation, that unrestrained familiarity, and that absence of anything like superciliousness or austerity, which have always marked my character, and, in all which, to the surprise of most observers, I indulged with my children as well as with all others under me, without at all lessening my authority.

I made it a rule that I [would] have the labour of no man who received parish relief. I gave my men constant pay, all seasons and all weathers, and though I had no rule about sickness, I never had, among my constant labourers, a sick man, whom I did not pay all the same as if he were well. I do not pretend, that it was from a regard for my labourers that I gave such great wages; for, I was convinced, that it was to my interest to do it. One of my labourers was worth two or three half-famished creatures. But, my great motive was, the lessening of the number of paupers; to raise part, at least, of the labouring people from that state of slavery, commonly called pauperism.

1805
to
1810
[Farming showed me much of these things.] That one half, or more, of the labourers of a country should have been paupers, was really something too disgraceful to think of. A constant state of pauperism would debase the best nature that man ever possessed. A labourer in this state was always studying deceit; he was afraid of nothing so much as of appearing prosperous, healthy, or happy; he contracted a plaintive language and manner. His children were studiously clad in rags and covered with filth; his wife was always "poorly". A family, thus reared, not only was likely to be, but was sure to be, a nest of thieves and imposters. The way in which we proceeded [in Hampshire,] is really worth being [mentioned]. As an instance: we had two families, one of which contained nine children and the other seven, the whole of whom, drawn up in rank entire, and set off to the best advantage, that is to say, half hung over with rags, the rest of the body being naked, were arrayed against us, [the farmers,] before a bench of magistrates. We were satisfied, that owing to particular circumstances they had quite a sufficient income; but, as we could not prove it upon oath, the magistrates were about to order them relief, when I offered to pay them weekly all that they said they earned, and, besides that, as much as they received from the parish, rather than suffer them to continue paupers. They declined my offer, got no relief, and not only did without relief, but gradually

assumed a more decent appearance; and, for this obvious reason, that they had no longer an interest in being thought miserable. [This was better than] the comforting system; the cow system; the child-bed-linen system; and the industry system; all which, like the schools of Mrs Hannah More, did more harm than good.

A lad, about 16 or 17 years of age, named Jesse Burgess, was my servant in husbandry, [in the year 1809]. In the latter end of February, I found fault with him for coming into breakfast before he had cleaned out his stable; and, [again in] March, I found fault with him, and that, too, in very sharp language, for lying in bed after I myself was up, that is to say, after 5 o'clock. The next morning the boy got up very early and set off from his service. There was, in the case of a servant running away and setting me at defiance, a duty which I owed to the community, and especially to my neighbours, occupying lands, who would have experienced great injury from such an example, if this boy had been suffered to get off with impunity. The mother of the boy had come, a few days before his running away, and had got his wages up to the 1st of March. It was, therefore, clear, that the intention was to get the boy away for the spring and summer, after having placed him in good keep during that part of the year when there was little to do. This was a very common trick through the country; my neighbours, the farmers, were plagued half out of their

1805
to
1810
lives with these desertions, which always took place, just when the sun began to shine on both sides of the hedge; that is to say, when those who had been warmed and fed all the winter, were called upon to make some remuneration by their labour. Nothing was so common as the sending people to prison for this offence.

I got a warrant from Southampton, and delivered it to Mr Astlett, the constable of Botley, in order that he might take up the boy. Mr Astlett took him at his father's house, and brought him to Botley, to a public-house called the Dolphin, whither, by the indulgence of the constable, he was accompanied by his mother and his elder brother, William. In the morning, Mr Astlett, who was a blacksmith, had occasion to go to his own house, and, while he was away, he left his prisoner in the hands of the tythingman, whose name was Dubber. While the boy was in the custody of Dubber, the mother came with a pretended message from me, desiring that the boy might be permitted to come to my house. He thereupon let the boy go, and the mother and the two sons went off together. [The boy] ran away somewhere, and the mother and her elder son made the best of their way towards their home.

Mr Astlett, finding what had taken place, set out, ordering Dubber to go with him, in pursuit of them. The boy was not to be found; but, they took the brother and the old woman, for having aided in the escape, and brought them to Botley.

They were suffered to depart, [on the advice of 1805
the magistrate at Southampton], having been in *to*
duress for not more than nine hours, having 1810
suffered no assault, and having sustained no other
injury than the loss of a day's work.

Upon principle, when the boy had escaped, I
spared no pains or expense to recover him. In
about a fortnight, Mr Astlett and Dubber found
him at his father's house. Things took a turn, that
Mr Astlett came to Botley for assistance, while
Dubber was left in the garden to see that the boy
did not escape. A new character came upon the
scene—one Stone, bailiff to Mr Goodlad (whose
house stood at a little distance) came to Dubber,
and told him to go away, for that he had no
business there. Suffice it to say, that the boy was
taken to Winchester, and was, after a full ex-
amination, and a remarkably patient hearing of
all he had to say, committed to prison. The example was of general utility.

I was very much surprised when the constable
told me, that the Burgesses boasted of having the
support of Mr Goodlad. I accordingly wrote to
him, stating to him the whole of the circumstances, and expressing a hope, that he, as a
magistrate, would give the constable countenance
and support. To my utter astonishment, the
answer I received was, as nearly as I can recollect,
this:—that the whole of the fault of resistance lay
with the constable of Botley, whose ignorance of
his duty had induced him to execute a warrant

out of his own hundred. The answer further informed me, that the old woman and her son William had been at the bench at Droxford, where they had been told, that, if their story was true, they might bring an action for false imprisonment. It appeared that the Magistrates at this bench, sitting in their capacity as magistrates, not only told the old woman and her son, that they had a ground for action, but advised them to go to the Attorney for the purpose of commencing the action.

The Attorney was soon in motion. Botley, Droxford, Hill-Pound, Southampton, and the borders of the Forest, heard the sound of his horse's feet, and were struck with the eager countenance of the rider. I was sued for £333. 6*s.* 8*d.* and the jury said, that, at most, I ought to pay the odd £3. 6*s.* 8*d.*

[Another thing followed. I was] informed, that, the very day after the trial, the walls of London were covered over with large bills about the "Oppressions of Cobbett"; and, "Cobbett the Oppressor of the Poor", etc. These posting bills cost, perhaps, fifty pounds a day! Notwithstanding the great events that were passing upon the continent of Europe, there was, in England, no subject whatever, which excited so much public interest as the character and conduct of William Cobbett.

[The conclusion of this incident will show that I had raised up the government and its supporters

against me. I had come over to the cause of Parliamentary Reform.] A remark or two seems
necessary here, [to show] the insinuation, and,
indeed, open accusation, brought against all those,
who stood prominently forward in the cause of
Reform: it was this, that they wished for confusion; for the annihilation of property; and for
uproar and bloodshed. This has always been the
charge against all those, who have had the courage
to take the lead in endeavouring to root out corruption. From the nature of things it is a charge
that must be preferred against such men; because
the corrupt will naturally seek to disarm those
who attack them, and, it being impossible to say
that corruption is right, there is no mode of at-
tacking its assailants, other than that of representing them as wishing for confusion and uproar,
by which representations, the uninformed are
misled and the timid frightened. By this mode,
the nation was long deceived and alarmed. Posterity will, I hope, hardly believe; I hope that our
children will hardly credit the true history of the
delusions and alarms [from the years 1792 to
1809]. The disgraceful days of alarm had passed
by then; and, I thought, it would be difficult for
the friends of corruption to cause their return;
but, still they harped upon the dangers of change,
though they could not deny that change would be
for the better; still they accused us of a wish to
introduce confusion and uproar and bloodshed.

The greatest compliment that could be paid to

any writer, to answer his arguments by an attack upon his person, [or, to appeal] to his opinions formerly expressed, especially under a total change of circumstances, was made most liberal use of against me.[1] Just as if opinions formed and expressed, when I was not much more than half as old, and when I had, in fact, no experience at all, could invalidate, or have any weight, against the arguments that I [later had] to offer. Upon my return from America I received marks of approbation from all the men then in power. When Mr Canning looked back to the time, when I dined at his house at Putney, and when he paid me so many just compliments for my exertions in my country's cause, I can hardly think, that he did not view with some degree of shame [such] attempts on the part of persons, who were publicly said to have written under his particular patronage.

[On the occasion of King George's Jubilee in October, 1809], the Jubilee Crew exhibited at Charing Cross, a placard respecting me, with the following words:

MAY GOD
disperse
The Votaries of
COBBETT
As the Clouds
of this Day.

The effect of this placard is worthy being re-

corded. Some persons among the many thousands, who composed the continually shifting
crowd of gazers at the placard, asked a very
worthy friend of [mine], what the thing meant,
and who "Cobbett" was; to which he answered,
that Mr Cobbett was a gentleman, who wished
to see sinecure places and unmerited pensions
abolished, who wanted all peculators and public
robbers to be punished, and by such means to
lessen the taxes and give people encouragement
to fight for their country. This ran, of course,
from one to another; and, it was no wonder, that,
on the fourth night after it was put up, the stupid
wretch who had ordered it to be hoisted, found
somebody to beat into his addled brains the
prudent measure of taking it down.

The best of it was, that, while these senseless
creatures were plotting and conspiring against
me, I was leading a life the most pleasing and un-
disturbed that could be conceived; I was walking
over a very beautiful farm and pleasure grounds.
And, at the very moment when the placard was
hoisted, I was in a farm-yard in Berkshire, taking
and noting down the dimensions of a sheep-crib.

CHAPTER IX

1810–1812

*   *   *   *   *

IN 1809, SOME YOUNG MEN AT ELY, IN WHAT
was called the "local militia", had refused to
march without the "marching guinea", which the
Act of Parliament awarded them. This was called
Mutiny; and a body of Hanoverian horse were
brought from Bury St Edmunds, to compel these
young Englishmen to submit to be flogged! They
were flogged, while surrounded by these Hano-
verians; and the transaction was recorded in "The
Courier" ministerial paper. I, in my "Register",
expressed my indignation at this, and to express
it too strongly was not in the power of man. The
Attorney-General, Gibbs, was set upon me; he
harassed me for nearly a year, then brought me
to trial. [This] took place on the 15th of June,
1810, when I was found guilty [of treasonous
libel] by a Special Jury. On the 20th, I was compelled to give bail for my appearance in court to
receive judgement, and, as I came from Botley (to
which place I had returned on the evening of the
15th) a Tip-Staff went down in order to seize me
personally, and to bring me up to London to give
bail.

I went home to pass the remaining short space of

personal freedom with my family. I had just begun 1810
farming projects, and also planting trees, with the *to*
hope of seeing them grow up as my children 1812
grew. I had a daughter fifteen years of age, whose
birthday was just then approaching, and, destined
to be one of the happiest and one of the most unhappy of my life, on that day my dreadful sentence
was passed. One son eleven years old, another
nine years old, another six years old, another
daughter five years old, and another child nearly
at hand. It was at this crisis, no matter by what
feelings actuated, I wrote to my Attorney, Mr
White, to make the proposition, "if I were not
brought to justice, I never would publish another
'Register' or any other thing". But, fits of fear
and despair [were] never of long duration in my
family. The letter was hardly got to the Post
Office at Southampton before the courage of my
wife and eldest daughter returned. Indignation
and resentment took place of grief and alarm; and
they cheerfully consented to my stopping the
letter. Mr Peter Finnerty was at my house at the
time; a post-chaise was got; and he came off to
London during the night, and prevented Mr White
from acting on the letter.

I was brought up to receive judgement on the
5th of July, when, after the Attorney-General had
made the speech, I was sent to the King's Bench
Prison, and ordered to be brought up again on the
9th of July. On this day I was, by Ellenborough,
Grose, LeBlanc and Bailey, sentenced to be im-

1810
to
1812

prisoned two years in Newgate amongst felons, to pay a fine to the King of a thousand pounds, and to be held in heavy bail for seven years after the expiration of the imprisonment! And, what was never heard of before, my printer, my publisher, and a bookseller, were all prosecuted and put in prison. Everyone regarded it as a sentence of death, and it was intended to be a sentence of death. I lived in the country, seventy miles from London; I had a farm on my hands; I had a family of small children, amongst whom I constantly lived; I had a most anxious and devoted wife, who was, too, in that state which rendered the separation more painful tenfold.

During the time that I was absent from home for the purpose of giving bail, a man, dressed like a gentleman, went upon my land in the neighbourhood of Botley, got into conversation with my servants, asked them how much property I had, where it lay, of whom I had purchased it, what I had given for it, and a great many other questions of the same sort. When he went away from one of them, he told him: "You'll not have Cobbett here again for one while"; or words to that effect. I leave [my readers] to form their opinions as to the object of this visit. Another person, of a similar description, went to another man who worked for me, asked him what sort of man I was, what he had heard me say about the King or the Government, and told him that some people thought me a very great enemy of the

government. He heard nothing but good of me
as a neighbour and a master; and, as to politics,
not a soul that he talked to knew what he meant,
never having in their lives heard me utter a word
upon any subject of the sort.

I was followed to prison by an excellent friend,
Mr Peter Walker, Major Cartwright, and Mr
Asbury Dickins, an American, whom I had known
in Philadelphia. [The first had] found me in
King's Bench Prison, previous to my being taken
up for judgement [the second time]. It had been
expected [then], that, in order to disable me from
writing for the press, I [was to] be sent to some
distant jail. In this expectation [he] had proposed,
that a certain number of friends should agree to
succeed each other in living, at their own expense,
in whatever town that jail should be, in order to
afford me society and assistance; and, he proposed
to fill this part [himself] for the first four months.

I was hardly arrived at Newgate when the brave
old Major Cartwright came. "And", exclaimed
he, "is this the place they have sent you to! I am
seventy years old, but— —I shall yet live to see
— —!" [Mr Walker was] the next to arrive, and
when, by dint of money, I had obtained the favour
to be put into a room by myself, [he] hurried
home and brought me bedstead, chairs, tables,
bedding, and everything; and, I think I see [him]
now, stripped in [his] shirt, putting the bedstead
together and making up my bed.

My wife arrived in about half an hour; but

1810
to
1812

before that time I had bought myself out of the company of felons. By great favour I finally obtained leave to occupy two rooms in the jailer's house, paying for them twelve guineas a week, and it required eight more to fee the various persons, and to get leave to walk an hour in the leads of the prison in the morning: so that here were £2080 during the two years besides the £1000 to the good old King. These direct losses were, however, trifling compared with the indirect. I was engaged in the publication of two works, called "The State Trials" and "The Parliamentary History". There had been a great outlay for these works; several thousands of pounds were due to the paper-maker and the printer. These works were, as far as regarded me, ruined. I had bought land in 1806 and 1809. This land, about 500 acres, was in hand. I had made plantations, and had made preparations for others. I had then a trifling mortgage to pay off, but quite within reach of my earnings; and, in short, if it had not been for this savage sentence, I should, by the year 1814, have had my estate cleared. [Almost] exactly ten years [after landing] in England, having lost a fortune in America, solely for the sake of England, I was sent to prison in that same England! It was quite impossible for me to banish reflections of this sort from my mind.

Many gentlemen, by letter as well as verbally, proposed to me the putting forward a subscription, for the purpose of indemnifying me and my

family against the heavy expense and loss, which
had been incurred in consequence of the prosecution. I was, however, happy to say, that I had
been not only able to withstand all pressure; but,
that, without any extraordinary aid, from any
quarter, I felt confident of my ability to proceed,
and, with the blessing of continued health, make
a suitable provision for all my children. My
health, thank God, was as good as ever it was.
But, I had no security for either health or life;
any more than other men; and, if I had attempted
an insurance upon my life, Newgate would have
told pretty strongly against me. It was, therefore,
impossible for me not to feel an anxious desire to
see my family, at least, guarded against certain
expense and loss.

Everyone will easily imagine, that every debt
that I owed,[1] of every description, came pouring
in for payment. The whole nation was cowed down
at the time, and under the sway of Perceval,
Gibbs, and Ellenborough, and with several parts
of the country actually under the command of
Hanoverian generals; the people seemed like
chickens, creeping and piping to find a hiding
place, while the kite was hovering in the air. The
sons and daughters of corruption openly chuckled
at what they thought my extinguishment. Almost
everyone stood aloof, except my creditors (never
the last to visit you in such a season), who pressed
on amain; so that I really forgot that I was in
prison, so great and so numerous were the tor-

1810
to
1812

ments arising. I was looked upon as a man given over by the doctors; and everyone to whom I owed a shilling, brought me sighs of sorrow indeed; but, along with these, brought me his bill. Why, the truth is, that had it not been for one thing, I should not have been able to bear up under this accumulation of evil; and, that one thing was that, I had a friend, to whom, on the third day after I entered the accursed jail, I wrote, requesting him, in case of my death, to send for, and take care of my wife and children, and from whom I received an answer, containing, amongst others, these words: "Give thyself no trouble about Nancy and the children. If thee should die, which I hope thee will not for years to come, thy dear family shall find a home under my roof, and shall be to me and all of us as our own kindred". At [70] years of age, I feel the tears of gratitude on my cheeks as I transcribe his words. It was James Paull,[2] a Quaker farmer, of Lower Dublin Township, in the state of Pennsylvania; a native American; a man, on whom I had never conferred a favour to the amount of the value of a pin.

My children [were] at Botley. The tears of the postman, a rough and hardy fellow, who had lost an arm in the military service, prepared my daughter for the news. The three boys were in the garden hoeing some peas. My daughter called the eldest to tell him what had been done. He returned to the others, and they hearing their sister cry,

asked him what was the matter. He could make 1810
them no answer, but, pulling his hat over his eyes, *to*
took up the hoe in a sort of wild manner and 1812
began to chop about, cutting up the peas and all
that came his way. The second took hold of him,
and seeing his face bathed with tears, got, at last,
an account of what had been done to a father,
who had never given either of them a harsh word
since they were born. By that very night's post
I got a letter from my eldest son, and he concluded his in these words: "I would rather be now
in the place of my dear Papa, than in that of
those who have sent him to prison". I wrote them
back for answer, that I was very well; that imprisonment would not hurt my health; and concluded by saying, "be you good children, and we
shall all have ample revenge"

In a few days after this, five big brutal farmers,
trotting along towards Fareham Market, on a
road by the side of which my carpenter was
erecting a sort of picket fence, called out to him,
"where be the iron bars?" and then set up a loud
laugh. Need I say, that it gave me pleasure to
know, that every one of these unfeeling monsters
was reduced to insolvency [in 1822], brought into
that state, too, by [the] very paper-money system,
for endeavouring to check which in time was my
real offence.

The sentence, though it proved not to be one of
death, was, in effect, one of ruin, as far as then
possessed property went. But this really appeared

as nothing compared with the circumstance that I would have a child born in a felon's jail, or be absent from the scene at the time of birth. My wife, who had come to see me for the last time previous to her lying-in, perceiving my deep dejection at the approach of her departure for Botley, resolved not to go, and actually went and took a lodging as near to Newgate as she could find one, in order that the communication between us might be as speedy as possible, and in order that I might see the doctor, and receive assurances from him relative to her state. The nearest lodging that she could find was in Skinner Street, at the corner of a street leading to Smithfield. So that there she was, amidst the incessant rattle of coaches, dogs, and bawling men, instead of being in a quiet and commodious country house, with neighbours and servants and everything necessary about her. Yet, so great is the power of the mind in such cases, she, though the circumstances proved uncommonly perilous, and were attended with the loss of the child, bore her sufferings with the greatest composure, because at any minute she could send a message to, and hear from me. If she had gone to Botley, leaving me in that state of anxiety in which she saw me, I am satisfied that she would have died; and that event taking place at such a distance from me, how was I to contemplate her corpse, surrounded by her distracted children, and to have escaped death or madness myself? If such was not the effect of this merciless act of the Government towards me, that amiable **1810** body may be well assured that I [took] and re- *to* corded the will for the deed, and that as such it **1812** will live in my memory as long as that memory shall last.

When the Government crammed me into a jail amongst felons it added to the difficulties of my task of teaching [my children;] for now I was snatched away from the only scene in which it could, as I thought, properly be executed. But even these difficulties were got over. The blow was, to be sure, a terrible one; and, O God! how it was felt by [those] poor children! [The] account [of their feelings,] when it reached me, filled me with deeper resentment, than any other circumstance. And, oh! how I despise the wretches who talk of my vindictiveness; of my exultation at the confusion of those who inflicted those sufferings! How I despise the base creatures, the crawling slaves, the callous and cowardly hypo- crites, who affected to be "shocked" (tender souls!) at my expressions of joy, at the death of Gibbs, Ellenborough, Perceval, Liverpool, Can- ning, and the rest of the tribe that I have already seen out, and at the fatal workings of [their] system.

[This was the way we worked at education.] I had a farm in hand. It was necessary that I should be constantly informed of what was doing. I gave all the orders, whether as to purchases, sales, ploughing, sowing, breeding; in short, with

regard to everything, and the things were endless
in number and variety, and always full of interest.
My eldest son and daughter could now write well
and fast. One or the other of them was always at
Botley; and I had with me one or two, besides
either this brother or sister; the mother coming up
to town about once in two or three months, leaving the house and children in the care of her sister.
We had a hamper, with a lock and two keys, which
came up once a week, or oftener, bringing me fruit
and all sorts of country fare, for the carriage of
which, cost free, I was indebted to as good a man
as ever God created, the late Mr George Rogers, of
Southampton.

This hamper, which was always, at both ends
of the line, looked for with the most lively feelings,
became our school. It brought me a journal of
labours, proceedings, and occurrences, written on
paper of shape and size uniform, and so contrived,
as to margins, as to admit of binding.[3] The journal
used, when my son was the writer, to be interspersed with drawings of our dogs, colts, or anything that he wanted me to have a correct idea of.
The hamper brought me plants, bulbs, and the
like, that I might see the size of them; and always
everyone sent his or her most beautiful flowers;
the earliest violets, and primroses, and cowslips,
and bluebells; the earliest twigs of trees; and, in
short, everything that they thought calculated to
delight me. The moment the hamper arrived, I,
casting aside everything else, set to work to answer

every question, to give new directions, and to add 1810
anything likely to give pleasure at Botley. Every *to*
hamper brought one "letter", as they called it, 1812
if not more, from every child; and to every letter
I wrote an answer, sealed up, and sent to the
party, being sure that that was the way to produce
other and better letters; for though they could not
read what I wrote, and though their own consisted at first of mere scratches, and afterwards,
for a while, of a few words written down for them
to imitate, I always thanked them for their "pretty
letter", and never expressed any wish to see them
write better; but took care to write in a very neat
and plain manner myself, and to do up my letter
in a very neat manner.

Thus, while the ferocious tigers thought I was
doomed to incessant mortification, and to rage
that must extinguish my mental powers, I found
in my children, and in their spotless and courageous
and most affectionate mother, delights to which
the callous hearts of those tigers were strangers.
"Heaven first taught letters for some wretches'
aid." How often did this line of Pope occur to me
when I opened the little spuddling "letters" from
Botley! This correspondence occupied a good part
of my time: I had all the children with me turn
and turn about; and, in order to give the boys
exercise, and to give the two eldest an opportunity of beginning to learn French, I used, for a
part of the two years, to send them a few hours in
the day to an Abbé, who lived in Castle Street,

1810
to
1812

Holborn. All this was a great relaxation to my mind; and, when I had to return to my literary labours, I returned fresh and cheerful, full of vigour, and full of hope, of finally seeing my unjust foes at my feet.

The paying of the work-people, the keeping of the accounts, the referring to books, the writing and reading of letters; this everlasting mixture of amusement with book-learning, made me, almost to my own suprise, find, at the end of two years, that I had a parcel of scholars growing up about me; and, long before the end of the time, I had dictated many "Registers" to my two eldest children. Then there was copying-out of books, which taught spelling correctly. The calculations about the farming affairs forced arithmetic on us: the use, the necessity of the thing led to the study. By and by, we had to look into the laws, to know what to do about the high-ways, about the game, about the poor, and all rural and parochial affairs.

I was, indeed, by the fangs of the Government, defeated in my fondly cherished projects of making my sons farmers on their own land, and keeping them from all temptation to seek vicious and enervating enjoyments; but these fangs were not able to prevent me from laying in for their lives a store of useful information, habits of industry, care, sobriety, and a taste for innocent, healthful, and manly pleasures; the fangs had me and them penniless; but they were not able to take from us our health or our mental possessions; and these

were ready for application as circumstances might
ordain.

Judges Grose and Ellenborough and Bailey and
LeBlanc did, indeed, sentence me to be im-
prisoned for two years, but they did not sentence
me to be blindfolded and have my hands tied all
the time. They did, indeed further adjudge that a
thousand pounds should be taken from me and
paid to the King, but they did not condemn me to
be bereft of my reason, they passed no sentence of
imprisonment upon my thoughts. [While] I was in
this jail, I was never ill for a single moment; I
never had even a headache, and I felt myself as
strong as at any period of my life.

[Shortly] after I had been got safe in Newgate,
an American friend of mine, who had the clearest
and soundest head of almost any man I ever knew
in my life, came to see me. Being seated, one of
us on each side of a little bit of table he said,
looking up into my face, with his arms folded
upon the edge of the table, "Well! they have
got you, at last. And now what will you do?"
After a moment or two I answered, "What do you
think I ought to do?" He then gave me his
opinion, and entered pretty much into a plan of
proceedings. I heard him out, and then, I spoke
to him in much about these words: "No, Dickins,
that will never do. This nation is drunk, it is as
mad as a March hare, and mad it will be till this
beastly frolic [the war] is over. The only mode
of proceeding to get satisfaction requires great

[147]

1810
to
1812

patience". I then described to him the outline of what I intended to do with regard to the paper-system; and, after passing a very pleasant afternoon, during which we selected and rejected several titles, we at last fixed upon that of "Paper Against Gold", which I began to write and to publish in a few weeks afterward.

I had long had it in contemplation to make the Paper Money system familiar to the understandings of the nation at large; but, until I was put into jail, I wanted the time to do the thing to my wish. Nothing [could] make me quit it, till it was made so plain, that children at school, and even, Doctors at the University, nay, that the Pitt Statesmen themselves, [could] understand it as well as they understood how to calculate the amount of their salaries. The Government gave me the leisure, and I in return, gave the world the true history of its Funding System.

For seven years previous to 1810, I had contended, and, indeed, I had been repeatedly proving, that the paper-money was depreciated, and that it must in the end, produce a convulsion in the country, unless prevented by a diminution in the Debt, and a return to payments in gold, always considering the latter as impossible without the former. On account of these opinions, I had to undergo the almost incessant abuse of the base press of London; and, indeed, of the whole country; and, which was a more serious matter, I had to undergo the consequences of the wrath of the people in power, including that of the far greater part of the members of the two Houses of Parliament. Really, from the acrimony and rage, to which, upon this subject, my opponents gave way, a stranger to the controversy would, were he first to dip into their writings, were he to hear them reviling me, certainly have concluded, that I myself owed the whole of the [national] debt.

I remember the time, when there was scarcely ever seen a bank-note among Tradesmen and Farmers; and, when the Farmers in my country hardly ever saw a bank-note except when they sold their hops at Wey-hill Fair. People, in those days, used to carry little bags to keep their money in, instead of the paste-board or leather cases that they now carry. If you looked back, and took a little time to think, you could trace the gradual increase of paper-money, and the like decrease of gold and silver money. At first there were no bank-notes under 20 pounds; next they came to 15 pounds; next to 10 pounds: at the beginning of the last war, they came down to 5 pounds; and, before the end of it they came down to 3 and to 1 pounds. How long it was before they came down to parts of a pound, it would, perhaps be difficult to say; but in Kent, at least, there were country notes in circulation to an amount as low as that of seven shillings.

I long saw, that the Bank could never pay again in Gold and Silver, and, at the same time, pay the full interest of the debt. For several years, I en-

1810
to
1812

deavoured to persuade the Government to lower the interest. In 1806, I published an argument to prove, that it was just, as well as necessary, to make this reduction. Many and many a time did I endeavour to convince Mr Windham, that, unless this measure was adopted in time, a complete convulsion must finally be the consequence. I never could get him to pay attention to me. Indeed, I was a great fool for my pains in this private way. I ought to have put my opinions boldly forth to the world, and have left talking alone.

Just about the time that there needed something to take to school the young men who succeeded those that had been taught by Mr Paine, "The Register" made its appearance; and, in a short time it entered upon that series of teachings, the fair fruits of which [did not become] visible [for twenty years]. The great subject of "The Register" always was, the Paper Money. I knew nothing of this matter in the year 1802, any more, and perhaps not quite so much as Mr Canning or the Old Doctor, [Lord Sidmouth, knew] of it [in] 1822. I did not know what had made the Bank of England. I did not know what the slang terms of Consols meant. I did not know what Dividend, Omnium Scrip, or any of the rest of it, imported. Finding it necessary to understand something of the matter, and about taxation, and other things relating thereto; I read, by the advice of that excellent man, Dr Lawrence, the work of that old Scotch tax-gatherer, Adam Smith. I could make

neither top nor tail of the thing. After a great
hunting about in search of books to give me information, I set to work to read the Act of Parliament by which the Bank of England was created,
and all the Acts about loans, and funds, and divi-
dends and payings-off and sinking-funds; and
disgusting as this would have been to almost any
other man upon the face of the earth, to me it was
pleasant; for I soon got something of an insight;
and I soon began to perceive that the fate of the
Kingdom must finally turn upon what should be
done with regard to the accursed thing called the
National Debt. I saw the purpose for which it
had been founded; I saw how completely it had
answered that purpose; I saw how it had been the
instrument of putting unbounded power into the
hands of the Government; I saw how it had drawn
the wealth of the country into masses, how it had
destroyed the lower and middle classes of farmers,
how it had added to the list of paupers, how it had
beggared and degraded the country.

I took up a little essay by Paine.[4] Here I saw to
the bottom at once. Paine not only told me what
would come to pass, but showed me, gave me con-
vincing reasons, why it must come to pass, and he
convinced me also, that it was my duty to endeavour to open the eyes of my countrymen to the
truths which I myself had learnt from him; because his reasoning taught me, that, the longer
these truths remained hidden from their view, the
more fatal must be the consequences. How happy

1810
to
1812

would it have been for this nation, if the opinions of Mr Paine had produced, at the time, their wished-for effect! In my opinion, [his] little work, in the space of twenty-five pages, conveyed more useful knowledge upon this subject, and discovered infinitely greater depths of thought and general powers of mind, than were to be found in all the pamphlets of the three-score and two financiers, who favoured the world with their opinions upon the state of our money system. I saw, but not without the assistance of Mr Paine, how the Bank came to be restrained in 1797. I soon arrived at a conclusion of this truth; that, the Nation must destroy that monster the Debt: or that the monster must destroy this form of government.

This was in the year 1804. From this time, a new era commenced in the political education of the people of England. I attacked a thing which Mr Paine had but lightly touched on, for, before his "Decline and Fall" came out, his writings had been suppressed by brute force; and, when that came out, he had, unfortunately rendered himself unpopular amongst the very best part of the people, by his gratuitous and rude assault on the Christian religion. My manner of attack on the accursed system of funding had its charms in its boldness and originality. My style was such as to please all those who read with a desire of acquiring knowledge. I always reasoned, and yet in a sort of way, that seldom created weariness in the reader.

Now, out of this arose that new sort of educa- 1810
tion, that new turn in the minds of men, of which *to*
I have before spoken. During all this time, the 1812
people were reading; and especially the labouring
classes. So that England presented to the world
this singular spectacle. The Government, the
Parliament, the rich, the pretended learned, ignorant of the causes, which were shaking society
to its base, while a considerable part of the middle
class and a large part of the very poorest class of
all, understood these causes perfectly well.

At last, however, [in the year 1810], a portion of
the Parliament came to make the assertion, that a
depreciation in the value of paper-money had
actually taken place; and, finally a Committee of
the people who had got into the Commons House,
was appointed to inquire into the matter. This
Committee, which might have been called the
Paper-Committee, was called the Bullion-Com-
mittee, had for its Chairman one Horner, a
Scotch lawyer. After immense volumes of "evidence" [it] reported to the House, that bank-
notes were depreciated, and that, in order to
prevent future fatal consequences, a law ought to
be passed to compel the Bank to pay in gold at the
end of two years from that time. The Ministry
contended, that bank-notes were not depreciated,
and that the notes could, at any time, be paid
in gold, but that during the war, the proposed
measure was inexpedient.

I contended that both sides were totally ignorant in the subject; and that the bank-notes, without a great reduction in the interest of the debt, and of all other out-goings, never could be paid in gold, without plunging the country into ruin. To prove this opinion to be correct, and to show that I understood more of the matter than both sides of the House put together, I wrote and published "Paper Against Gold", with an avowed intention, too, of having it to produce, when time should have verified its doctrines, and when the sufferings of the nation should have disposed it to listen to truth and reason.

[An example of the nation's fate was very soon given by] the scenes at Salisbury, on account of the failure of the Banks of that City. Poor people were without victuals or drink for some time, and many persons, in a respectable way of life, were for many days together, obliged to sit down to dine upon little more than bread, no meat being to be purchased [with paper money]. Many persons, who had gathered together a few pounds, the fruit of long labour and anxious care, of frugality, and of forbearance from enjoyment; many of these very best of people, saw their little all vanish in a moment, and themselves reduced to the same state with the improvident, the careless, the lazy, the spendthrift, the drunkard, and the glutton. Here Pitt, if he had still been alive, [would] have seen a specimen of the fruits of his system!

[My work on Paper Money, I believe to be the

best of my life, but] I was [only] regarded as a 1810
very clever man,[5] with rather a twist in the head; *to*
and being of an odd taste, having selected the 1812
subject of the Debt and Paper Money as my
particular hobby. [I continued], however, to ride
this hobby without anyone to trot along side of
me for fourteen years.

[In addition to this labour], during my imprisonment, I wrote and published 364 Essays
and Letters upon political subjects; during the
same time, I was visited by persons from 197
cities and towns, many of them as a sort of
deputies from Societies and Clubs; and, at the
expiration of my imprisonment, on the 9th of
July, 1812, a great dinner was given in London
for the sake of receiving me, at which dinner upwards of 600 persons were present, and at which
Sir Francis Burdett presided. Dinners and other
parties were held on the same occasion in many
other places in England. On my way home [to
Botley], I was received at Alton, the first town in
Hampshire, with the ringing of the church bells.
A respectable company met me and gave me
dinner at Winchester. I was drawn for more than
the distance of a mile into Botley by the people;
upon my arrival in the village, I found all the
people assembled to receive me. I concluded the
day by explaining to them the cause of my imprisonment.*

* Anne Cobbett, who accompanied her father on his

The Progress of a Plough-boy

return from prison, wrote of the journey to her uncle, Lieut. Frederick Reid.

" ...We got to Bagshot about ten o'clock on Friday evening, where we slept, and the next morning left it about six o'clock, and breakfasted at Alton, the bells rung a merry peal as we entered the town and continued to ring about an hour. We proceeded from Alton to Alresford, and from thence to Winchester, where we arrived about one. About five minutes after we got there, Mama came in a post-chaise with all the children. After staying there a little while, Mama returned home with her three daughters, leaving the three boys to come home with Papa after the dinner. Parson Baker refused the keys of the church, so that the people could not ring the bells which they wished very much to do. However, they sufficiently testified their respect to Papa, and their pleasure at his return, without the assistance of the church. For a party of young men...accompanied by a band of music which they had hired themselves for the purpose met him about a mile out of Botley...where they insisted upon taking the horses out of the carriage, which they did, and with colours flying, and the band of music marching before them, they brought him into Botley.... Mama had ordered four hogsheads of ale one at each of the public-houses, in the morning, but she had no idea of what was to be done. Papa arrived here about eight o'clock, and after we had drank tea about nine, the band came and stationed themselves on the lawn where they continued playing for some time, after which we called them into the hall, and gave the young men and young women of the village a dance. Mr Walker and your humble servant opening the ball. They danced till Sunday morning and then dispersed."

The Cobbett Papers. Letter dated from Botley House, 13 July, 1812.

CHAPTER X

1812–1817

*   *   *   *   *

WHEN I LEFT PRISON, IN 1812, I THOUGHT
it prudent to quit so large a house as my own [at
Botley] was, and to lessen all my expenses. I,
therefore, took [the] place [of a] Mr Kempt, which
had a neat little gentleman's house on it, and the
best gardens in the country, having nearly three
quarters of a mile of high walls, for fruit trees. I
laid out more than £150 in purchasing and planting the walls and gardens with all the finest sort
of peaches, nectarines, apricots, plums, cherries,
pears, and apples. The vines against the walls,
which bore nothing scarcely before I went to the
place, I made, by my management, [in time] bear
half a ton of grapes. There were three vines in a
grape-house, which bore the first summer only
five or six bunches of grapes. I cut out two of
them, leaving one, and, [four years later], that
one bore me more than 300 pounds of grapes. I
trusted nobody to prune this vine but myself.
My excellent friend, Mr Brown, of Peckham
Lodge, measured one single grape from this vine,
which was three inches and three quarters in cir-
cumference. I mention these things to show what
pains I took with these gardens, where I grew as

[157]

great a weight of melons as was grown in any 20 gentlemen's gardens round the country; where I had very large watermelons, which I never saw in England except in my gardens. In short, I never saw myself down in any spot in my whole life, without causing fruits and flowers and trees (if there was time) and all the beauties of vegetation to rise up around me.

My imprisonment gave me, as to money matters, a blow not easily recovered. The Peace came, too, in about twenty months afterward, which was greatly injurious to me as a farmer, and at the same time as a writer; for, in its fit of drunken joy, the nation in general laughed at me.

The intelligence of this grand event reached me in the following manner. I had been out very early in the morning, and, in returning home to breakfast, I met a populous gang of gypsies. At the first view of them, I thought of nothing but the robberies which they constantly committed upon us, and I began to plan my measures of defence. But, upon a nearer approach to them, I perceived the whole caravan decorated with laurel. The blackguard ruffians of men had laurel boughs in their hats; the nasty ferocious-looking women, with pipes in their jaws, and straddling along like German trulls, had laurel leaves pinned against their sides. The poor asses, that went bending along beneath their burdens laid on them by their merciless masters, and that were quivering their skins to get the swarms of flies from

those parts of their bodies which the wretched
drivers had beaten raw, had their bridles and
halters and pads stuck over with laurel. Somewhat
staggered by this symbol of victory, I hesitated
what to do, passed the gang in silence, until I met
an extraordinarily ill-looking fellow, who, with
two half-starved dogs, performed the office of
rear-guard. I asked him the meaning of the
laurel boughs, and he informed me, that they were
hoisted on account of the "glorious victory obtained by the Duke of Wellington over Boney";
that they were furnished them by a good gentleman, whose house they had passed the day before,
between Andover and Botley, and who had given
them several pots of ale, wherein to drink the
Duke's health. "And to be sure", added he, "it
is glorious news, and we may now hope to see the
gallon loaf at a 'grate' [a groat] again, as 'twas
in my old father's time." I left this political
economist, this "loyal man and friend of social
order", to overtake his companions, I went home-
ward with a mind far from being as completely
made up as that of the Gipsey and his black-
coated and white-wigged benefactor.

[But], which was the heaviest blow of all, I,
under such heavy bonds [to keep the peace], did
not dare to be the proprietor of "The Register";
it was transferred to another, in order to screen
me. That other, of course, had the greater share of
the profits. By the beginning of the year 1816, my
pecuniary affairs became so desperate as to make

me determine on selling my land and everything else, and on beginning the world afresh. [I did not, however, become poor at once; and I saw the nation grow poor along with me.]

When I looked back [ten years or so] and considered how the country then stood, what a contrast presented itself to my mind! The preliminaries of peace had just then been concluded; the price of provisions had just then been lowered; the people were on tiptoe for commerce and manufactures; every print-shop window presented something demonstrative of friendship with Buonaparte. What was the picture [that followed]? A war with that same Buonaparte, [which] led to the overthrow of every state formerly in alliance with us, [which] put into the hands of that same Buonaparte the whole of Italy from the confines of France down to the shores of Calabria, [which] raised a new kingdom in the heart of Germany.

It added five hundred millions to the National Debt of England. It banished gold from circulation. It ruined commerce and manufactures in England; [in which] respect, it produced a new order of things both in Europe and America, both of which could then dispense with English goods. What inroads were made upon English liberty during this period, I need not attempt to describe; and, as to the weight of taxes, who needs to be told of that?

[If you asked] any man, be he of what party he

might, what he thought of the state of things, you found, that he expected, that a great change of some sort or other, would take place ere long. He could not tell what it would be; he could not even guess; he was full of fears, and that was all. The very hirelings of the press, whose trade it was to buoy up the spirits of the people, had no longer any plausible grounds of hope to hold out.

At any rate, the people could not blame the "Jacobins and Levellers". They had been against the war; they had been for letting the French Republicans alone. They had no hand in any of the measures that were pursued, and were liable to no responsibility and no blame. [Yet] they were an object of incessant abuse. The next ten years showed whether they merited this.

It is the common practice of men to judge from experience; but, it really seemed, that governments acted upon no such principle; that they were wholly deaf to the voice of experience; that they either did not see, or they heeded not, the consequences of their measures. Were this not the case, how could it possibly be, that no change took place in the measures of any of the old governments that we saw annihilated [during these years]? In no instance did we see them attempt to make any change; nay, they [seemed to grow] more and more attached to their several systems in proportion as the evil consequences of them became manifest to all the world. It could only be accounted for in this way: that the persons in the enjoyment of power and of the emoluments belonging to power thought, that they would lose both by a reformation as effectually as by a destruction of the government; and, therefore, that, as they could lose no more by the latter than by the former, they, in every case, endeavoured to uphold corruptions and abuses to the last possible moment.

We here see, also, the cause of that persecution of opinions, which invariably increased as the old governments felt their dangers increase. The persecution was the effect of fear; and, it is well known, that cruelty is never so great as when it has such a foundation. When men have expressed their surprise at seeing these old governments grow more and more tyrannical and cruel in proportion as their situation became perilous, they have not duly considered the motive of these governments; if they had, they would have felt no surprise.

[In these ten years] the reputation of party was wholly destroyed. The people became weary of the thing. They saw that no change of men did them any good; they saw that the difficulties of the country and their own burdens still went on increasing; hope was, at last, dead within them. This was an awful state for a country to be in. Was there one man, who sincerely believed, that we could, without some great change of system, extricate ourselves from this state? There were men, and some of them very well-meaning men,

who still railed against Jacobins and Levellers. 1812
The railing against them might, at one time, have *to*
proceeded from alarm; but, it was now the effect of 1817
a sort of senseless resentment that knew not what
to fall upon. If there had been any great body of
the nobility and gentry, standing forward for a
reform of the system, the spirit of the country
would have been very different from what it was;
but, we saw no such body. The gentlemen of
England seemed to have given up the country to
the Minister of the day. Each seemed to care for
nobody but himself; and to think himself pretty
well off, if he had weight enough left to secure him
the permission to have a sufficiency to live upon.
The barriers erected by the pride and circumstance of family worth and by the circles of
hospitality, were all swept away. There was no
longer any intermediate link. The natural magis-
tracy, as Hume calls it, was extinguished. All
authority proceeded immediately from the government. There was not a village in England where
the Surveyor of Taxes was not a more powerful
man than the Lord of the Manor. The principle of
obedience was that of fear and not of love.

What must have been the feelings of an English
gentleman, if there was one with any feeling left,
who had first mounted his hunter fifty years ago,
and who now saw his son a subscriber to a county
pack; and, in public places, instead of a bold
assertor of his country's rights, an humble and
awkward imitator of the special pleaders of the

1812
to
1817
day, anxious only not to be thought the friend of those few, who still were not ashamed to contend for the liberties of England. The lot of such a father was not to be envied even by the hoary beggar that swept the crossing of the streets. Both were but one remove from a return to the earth whence they had sprung; but the latter, if not quite unconscious of the fallen state of his country, had, at least, the consolation of knowing that he had never, by act of omission, contributed toward the cause by which it was produced.

[By 1816], whole parishes were left destitute of the means of feeding the poor. It has been thought to be an exaggeration to say this, but, from what passed under my own eyes, I have not the smallest doubt of the fact. The misery of the country seemed to have travelled in all directions towards [Botley]. From the North, from the East, from the West, it crept on to what the country people call, the "zunny zide 'o Lunnon". At last, it reached us there, upon the verge of the channel, where less misery has always existed, I believe, than in any other part of the kingdom. The paupers swarmed about our fields and hedges. Or, rather, the labouring people were almost all become paupers. The notions about daily and weekly and yearly wages seemed to be all disappearing from men's minds. Nothing struck me so forcibly as to find that this was the case in the adjoining parish of Titchfield. A parish rich in its soil, in its woods, in its waters, in its inhabitants, consisting

of many gentlemen of fortune, and of numerous 1812
opulent and most excellent farmers, and of a neat *to*
little town, not surpassed in point of appearance 1817
by any in England. And yet, in this parish,
decent, honest, able, and well-behaved labourers,
and those in great numbers, too, were compelled
to become paupers. So that really, one-half of the
people were, at this time, living upon the means
possessed by the other half. I am here, not stating
what I have been told, what I have heard; but
what I have seen, and what I daily saw with my
own eyes.

Just after Easter Tuesday, [in 1816,] the
officers of the several Parishes [near me,] held a
meeting, at which, by way of lottery, they distributed amongst the most able parishioners, young
paupers to be kept by the said parishioners and
brought up by them in their own houses, or, at
any rate, maintained by them, clothed, fed,
lodged, and doctored, at their own particular
expense, until they grew up to be men, or women.
I had drawn for me in this lottery, a girl about 10
or 12 years of age. If I had had all my share of
paupers quartered upon me as this girl was, I
should have had about twenty-eight of all ages.
In my own house we were twelve altogether. So
that I had more than one pauper to every other
human being moving within the sphere of my
support.

It is from facts like these that we are enabled to
judge of the real state of the nation. The coaches

The Progress of a Plough-boy

and chariots and landaus that rattled through the squares and streets of London; the forests of masts that rose in the seaports; the loads of pearls and diamonds that shone at the court; even the beautiful mansions and pleasure grounds that were seen all around the metropolis; these: no one, no, nor all of these put together, were proof of the prosperity of a nation: all these could exist, and the nation [yet] be plunged into the deepest of misery and degradation.

[By the enclosing of land] numerous families of the children of labourers were crammed into the stinking suburbs of towns, amidst filth of all sorts, and congregated together in the practice of every species of idleness and vice. In the stinking houses of towns, the labourer's children could not have health. If they had not health they were miserable in themselves and a burden to the parish. [The potato became] a favourite because it was the suitable companion of misery and filth. It could be seized hold of before it was half ripe, it could be raked out of the ground with the paws, and without the help of any utensils, except, perhaps, a stick to rake it from the fire, could be conveyed into the stomach in the space of an hour. We had but one step further to go, and that was, to eat it raw, side by side with our bristly fellow-creatures, who, by the by, reject it as long as they can get at any species of grain or at any other vegetable. I can remember when the first acre of potatoes was planted in a field, in the

[166]

neighbourhood of the place where I was born; and I very well remember, that even the poorest of the people would not eat them. They called them hog-potatoes.

Before the year had expired, "agricultural distress" began to make the nation listen to the call for parliamentary reform; and the latter part of 1816, saw the kingdom agitated from one end to the other.[1] Now was the time for me to lay on. Sometime in the month of September, I was conversing on this subject with a neighbour, and we both agreed, that, if the people could but be enabled to see the matter in its true light, there would be an end to all such acts of violence, [as food-riots,] at once, and, of course, to the ignominious deaths of fathers and sons, and the miseries of wives, children, and parents, produced in the end by these acts of violence. My neighbour was of opinion, that it was in my power to effect this desirable purpose, by writing an Essay upon the subject. But, though I had a strong desire to do it, I was aware, that the high price of "The Register", though it had not prevented it from being more read than any other publication, still, it prevented it from being so generally read as would be necessary to put the people right upon this important subject. Hence came the observation from one of us, I forget which, that if, for this one time, for this particular purpose, the price could be, by some means or other, reduced to twopence, then the desired effect would be produced

[167]

1812
to
1817

at once. I said, before we parted, that this should
be done.

But, as it was impossible for me to prove to the
people what was *not* the cause of their misery,
without proving to them what was the cause of
their misery; as the remedy, at last, came to a
Reform of Parliament; and, as I feared, that the
best time was not come for urging on this grand
question, I delayed, from time to time, the ful-
filment of my promise to my neighbour, who, on
his part, never saw me without pressing me hard
upon the subject; and, on the 2nd of November, I
wrote an "Address to the Journeymen and
Labourers", on the aforementioned subject.[2]

As the topics had long been passing through
my mind, they came very naturally and easily
into their place upon paper; and, as I most
sincerely felt the truth and justice of all that I
wrote, I wrote with as much force both of language
and argument as I had at my command. The
arrangements had been made the week before for
the manner and price of publication; and I felt
quite confident not only of a great sale, but of a
very great effect. [I changed] the price of "The
Register" from 1*s.* to 2*d.*, publishing it without a
stamp, and keeping myself sheltered from the law
by not being the legal proprietor.

After the manuscript had gone off, my fears of
premature effect returned; and, after two days
resolving and re-resolving and misgiving, I sent
off my son John by the night coach to prevent the

Cheap Edition being published for a short time at any rate. But, instead of informing me that he had obeyed my orders, he informed me that six thousand of the Cheap Edition had been sold before his arrival. It was too late to balance. I had put myself before the wind, which I well knew would prove too strong to suffer me to stop, or to slacken my pace. It was impossible now, in this new scene, to remain at Botley. I went off to London in a few days, and remained there until my final departure for Liverpool; and, of the eventful days of my wonderful life, these were certainly the most eventful.

The effects of No. 18, [the first cheap "Register]", were prodigious.[3] It occupied the conversation of three-fourths of all the acting men in the kingdom. The whole town was in a buz. The labouring classes of people seemed as if they had never heard a word on politics before. The effect on their minds was like what might be expected to be produced on the eyes of one bred up in the dark, and brought out, all of a sudden, into broad daylight. In town and country, there were, in two months, more than two hundred thousand of this one Number printed and sold; and this, too, in spite of all the means which the Government, the Church, the Military, the Naval Half-Pay, and all the innumerable swarms of Tax-Gatherers and Tax-Eaters, were able to do to check the circulation. The "Paper Against Gold", was selling in weekly numbers at the rate of twenty to thirty thousand a week. In short, clear of all expenses, there was a profit of £200 a week; so that, if I had been let alone, if no law had been passed to stop and ruin me, my estate would have been clear at the end of two years, and I should have been as rich as I ever wanted to be.

Amongst the striking and instantaneous effects of this Cheap Register was the unlocking of the jaws of the London Press with regard to me and my writings. For nearly five years I had been unable to extort a word from this Press. Upon the appearance, however, of No. 18, away went all the *chuchutments*, and all the pretendings of ignorance; and the corrupt part of the press, instead of its apparently sworn silence, treated the public with volleys of lies and execrations against me that never had a parallel in the world. It seemed as if the curses of these hirelings had, for years past, been kept without sound, like those of Mandeville's sailors, which having been uttered during a terrible hard frost, filled the air with their cracklings when the thaw came.

Early in December, Mr Becket, the Under Secretary of State to Lord Sidmouth, said, in answer to a proposition for silencing me in some very atrocious manner, "No: he must be written down". Accordingly, up sprang little pamphlets at Norwich, at Romsey, at Oxford, and at many other places, while in London, there were several, one of which could not cost less than two thousand guineas in advertising and in large and expensive

[170]

placards, which were pulled down, or effaced, the 1812
hour they were put up, and which were replaced *to*
the next hour, as one wave succeeds another in the 1817
sea. At last, after all the other efforts of this kind,
came "Anti-Cobbett", written "by a Society of
Gentlemen", amongst whom, I was told, were
Canning, Mr Gifford, and Southey. Not content
with advertisements in three hundred newspapers;
not content with endless reams of placards; the
managers of this concern actually sent out two
hundred thousand circular letters, addressed to
persons by name, urging them to circulate this
work amongst all their tradesmen, farmers, work
people, and to give it their strong recommendation; and this they were told was absolutely
necessary to prevent bloody revolution.

By the beginning of January, [1817,] or thereabouts, the Government had discovered that it was
quite useless to carry on any longer this contest
with the pen. But, though open force appears
now to have been resolved on, it was very hard to
make out any pretext for employing such force.
Sidmouth and Castlereagh were authorized to shut
up in prison every one "suspected of treasonable
practices"; and, when Sidmouth brought in the
bill, he distinctly stated, as a reason for it, that
the publications then going on were such that the
law-officers of the crown *could find nothing in them
to prosecute with any chance of success*!!! Lord
Holland asked Sidmouth, why, if there were such
seditious works going forth from the press, he did

1812
to
1817

not cause them to be prosecuted; to which the latter answered, that he had laid them all before the law-officers, and that they could find nothing to prosecute, such was the art and malignity of the writers! Therefore, the Power of Imprisonment Bill was passed![4] a law to enable some of *themselves* to shut me up in prison *at their pleasure*; to keep me in a dungeon as long as they pleased; and this too without even telling me what I was accused of; and all this they did, as expressly stated by Sidmouth, because I had committed no offence against the laws; because the law-officers could find nothing to prosecute in my publications.

One of my sons brought me, from the House of Lords, an account of this speech of Sidmouth. "Oh! then", said I, "we must strike our tent and be off." If I had had a mind to touch the public money, I might have remained in safety, and with ten thousand pounds in my pocket; or, at least, such an offer was made me, by a gentleman in whose word and authority I firmly believed. The sole condition was *future silence*.

I gave no answer, but, with my two eldest sons, resolved upon flight, it being manifest that silence, or a dungeon, must attend my staying. I sent for my wife to come up from Botley, and told her what I had resolved on. She did not utter a single plaintive accent; a few big tears rolled down her face; she resumed her smiles in an instant, and, having come up in the night, she

prepared for returning (seventy miles) to her 1812
children the next night, which she did.

Nothing could have induced me to quit [my] 1817
country, while there remained the smallest chance
of my being able, by remaining, to continue to aid
her cause. The laws which had just been passed,
forbade [me] to entertain the idea, that it would
be possible to write on political subjects according
to the dictates of truth and reason, without drawing down upon [my] head certain and swift
destruction. If I removed to a country where I
could write with perfect freedom, it was not only
possible, but very probable, that I should, sooner
or later, be able to render that cause important
and lasting service.

Upon this conclusion it was, that I made my
determination: for though life would have been
scarcely worth preserving, with the consciousness
that I walked about my fields, or slept in my bed,
merely at the mercy of a Secretary of State;
though, under such circumstances, neither the
song of the birds in spring, nor the well-thatched
homestead in winter, could make me forget that I
and my family were slaves, still there was something so powerful in the thought of country, and
neighbourhood, and home, and friends, there was
something so strong in the numerous and united
ties with which these and endless other objects
fastened the mind to a long-inhabited spot, that
to tear oneself away nearly approached to the
separating of the soul from the body.

[173]

1812
to
1817

A few years [before], being at Barnett Fair, I saw a battle going on, arising out of some sudden quarrel, between a Butcher and the servant of a West-country grazier. The Butcher, though vastly superior in point of size, finding that he was getting the worst of it, recoiled a step or two, and drew out his knife. Upon the sight of this weapon, the Grazier turned about and ran off till he came up to a Scotchman who was guarding his herd, and out of whose hand the former snatched a good ash stick about four feet long. Having thus got what he called a long arm, he returned to the combat, and, in a very short time, he gave the Butcher a blow upon the wrist which brought his knife to the ground. The Grazier then fell to work with his stick in such a style as I never before witnessed. The Butcher fell down and rolled and kicked; but, he seemed only to change his position in order to insure to every part of his carcase a due share of the penalty of his baseness. After the Grazier had, apparently, tired himself, he was coming away, when, happening to cast his eye upon the knife, he ran back and renewed the basting, exclaiming every now and then, as he caught his breath: "dra thy knife wo't!" till at last the Butcher was so bruised, that he was actually unable to stand, or even to get up; and yet, such amongst English-men was the abhorrence of foul fighting, that not a soul attempted to interfere, and nobody seemed to pity a man thus unmercifully beaten. It was my intention to imitate the conduct of this

Grazier; to resort to a long arm, [by going to America,] and to combat Corruption while I kept myself out of the reach of her knife. Nobody called the Grazier a coward, because he did not stay to oppose his fists to a pointed and cutting instrument.

I and my two sons, William and John, set off from London early in the morning of Saturday, the 22nd of March [1817]. We reached Litchfield that night, and Liverpool the next night about ten o'clock. Of the whole country, through which we passed (and all of which was very fine) we were more delighted with the ten miles from Dunchurch to Coventry, in Warwickshire. The road very wide and smooth; rows of fine trees on the sides of it; beautiful white-thorn hedges and rows of ash and elm dividing the fields; the fields so neatly kept; the soil so rich; the herds and flocks of fine fat cattle and sheep on every side; the beautiful homesteads and numerous stacks of wheat! Every object seemed to say: here are resources! here is wealth! Here are all the means of national power, and of individual plenty and happiness! And, yet, at the end of those ten beautiful miles, we entered that city of Coventry, which, out of twenty thousand inhabitants contained at that very moment, upwards of eight thousand miserable paupers.

As we passed onwards through Staffordshire and Cheshire all the same signs of wealth and of the sources of power, on the surface of the earth struck us by day; and, by night, those more sub-

lime signs, which issued from the furnaces on the
hills. The causeways for foot-passengers, paved,
in some instances, for tens of miles, together; the
beautiful rows of trees shading these causeways;
the canals winding about through the valleys,
conveying coal, lime, stone, merchandise of all
sorts; the immense and lofty woods of the hills;
every object seemed to pronounce an eulogium
on the industry, skill, and perseverance of the
people. And, why, then, were those people in a
state of such misery and degradation?

On Wednesday evening, the 27th of March, we
embarked on board the ship "Importer", D.
Ogden master, bound to New York. When we
went on board it was nearly dark. The boat was
so full that some of the passengers were obliged to
quit it and go to another boat. Amongst these
was a youngish man, who, in a voice half nasal
and half squeal, cried out, "but where is my
Portfolio! I cannot go and leave my Portfolio!
I shall be ruined if my Portfolio gets wet!" The
Captain, who was going with us, pledged his life
for the safety of everything. One of my sons, who
said in my ear, "who can that be?" was answered
by me, "Oh, he is only an Envoy-Extraordinary
from some Dry Good Store, be assured", which
afterward proved to be the case to the very letter.

The next day, when we came to muster, we
found our cabin companions to be, a Mr Astor,[5]
son of a respectable merchant of New York, who
had been some years in Europe, who had travelled

over the greater part of it, and who was perfectly
civil and polite. Two young men, who belonged to
Manchester establishments at Manchester, who
were going out with goods, and who, from the very
little that I heard them say, seemed to think that
sinecures were no bad things, because, as one of
them explained the matter, every man would get
one if he could. The fourth was the Captain's
brother, a tailor of New York, who reviled Paine's
memory without being able to tell why, and who
approved of the employment of spies, asserting,
that spies were constantly employed by the
Corporation of New York. The fifth was a very
pretty woman from Manchester, with two small
children, going out to her husband, who, if it was
impossible for her wholly to avoid giving us
annoyance, conducted herself with the most exemplary patience, never uttering one word of
complaint or of apprehension, during a most disagreeable and perilous voyage. The Captain's
brother, the aristocratical tailor, died at the end
of about three weeks of a lingering disease, the
effects of which, while he was alive (confined in so
small a place as we were), formed a subject, not
only of most horrible disgust, but of some apprehension on account of possible infection. The sixth
and last of our inmates was the Envoy-Extraordinary, who called himself a Federalist, as did
also the Captain call himself, and certainly, with
the exception of Mr Astor, we could not well have
fallen into more disagreeable company.

1812
to
1817

The few times that I have ever travelled in a stage coach, I have held my tongue, and, in order to keep all quite quiet, I have generally taken a French book to read. However, as my sons spoke French as well as myself, we could talk and laugh about all sorts of things quite at our ease, and without interfering with the people. We had also some books, and sometimes we would write a little. Nevertheless, talk amongst us all would sometimes arise; and, as it was one of the features in the Envoy's character to affect an understanding in matters that he knew nothing of, he one day told us, that Dr Mitchell of New York, was writing a very interesting work on "The Theology of Fishes". I ought to have let it pass; but the Envoy was a great stickler for religion as he called it, and I could not help exclaiming, "I wonder what religion they are of!" A laugh ensued, and the Envoy curled up his sharp nose a quarter of an inch beyond its usual point of altitude.

One Sunday morning, the weather being fine, the Envoy had dressed himself out in all his Bond Street gear, not by any means forgetting his high-heeled boots, and perceiving, without doubt, the obduracy of our feelings, which remained wholly unmoved towards admiration by all these attempts, seemed to have resolved, as a last shift, to try the virtues of his portfolio upon us. Out, therefore, it came, and with a thundering slap upon the table, at which we sat attentively reading, having been, for a short time, delivered from the company of the sick tailor. Down came the portfolio, and I could have cursed the impertinent fop most heartily for the interruption; but, I had scarcely had time to look up, when a part of the contents of this important depository was laid before me for my inspection.

I, at first, looked at it merely because I could no longer read; but, my eye was soon attracted more closely; not by the snips of cloth, but by an engraving at the top of the card. This card had been made for the purpose of being exhibited in the Store, or Shop, in Connecticut; at the head of it was an engraving as follows. In the middle was a shield, on the right hand America represented by a fair Virgin, surrounded with the emblems of wisdom, science, agriculture and commerce, on the left an old lion with a figure seated on him in the shape of a woman with a spear in her hand and some bales of goods behind her. To the American flag the post of honour was given, and, at the top, the British crown was represented as stricken down by the beak of the American Eagle, which was waving its wings over it in triumph. Could you, taking the motive into view, imagine anything more base than this, on the part of the English manufacturer? Another ruffian, a crockery-ware man, had furnished mugs with engravings on them representing an old crazy lion, all skin and bones, with an American standing with his foot on his neck.

Every morning of my passage I was up, shaved

1812
to
1817

and dressed, before any other person was stirring. Then I called up my sons. Our place was swept out, or washed out, aired and beds made by ourselves before breakfast. While others were lolling in their berths, we were out on deck. During the time of sea-sickness, which I had none of, I took care of my sons, attended them on deck, brought them down, waited on them like a nurse, gave no trouble to anybody; and when that was over, our room was, at all times, night as well as day, fair weather or foul, as clear from all annoyances as one of our fields at Botley. We were stinted to one tumbler of fresh water a day, to wash in. We never complained of this, and we kept ourselves perfectly clean. The consequence was, we landed at New York as fresh as we were when we went on board the ship. We arrived on the 5th of May. In all respects that can be named our passage was disagreeable; and, upon one occasion, very perilous from lightning, which struck the ship twice, shivered two of the masts, killed a man, struck several people slightly, between two of whom I was sitting without at all feeling the blow.

CHAPTER XI

1817–1819

*   *   *   *   *

WE [WENT TO] AN INN, 13 MILES FROM
New York, in [Long Island]. It was on the main
road to [the] city. We lodged and boarded in this
Inn, had each a bedroom and a good bed, had a
room to sit in to ourselves, ate by ourselves; and
it really was eating. We had smoaked fish, chops,
butter and eggs, for breakfast, with bread,
crackers, sweet cakes; and, when I say, that we
had such and such things, I do not mean that we
had them for show, or just enough to smell to;
but in loads. Not an egg, but a dish full of eggs.
Not a snip of meat or of fish; but a plate full.
Lump sugar for our tea and coffee; not broke into
little bits the size of a hazel-nut; but in good
thumping pieces. For dinner we had the finest of
fish, bass, mackerel, lobsters; of meat, lamb, veal,
ham, etc. Asparagus in plenty, apple pies (though
in the middle of May). And for all this an excellent
cider to drink, with the kindest and most obliging
treatment, on the part of the Landlord and Landlady and their sons and daughters, we paid no
more than twenty-two shillings and sixpence a
week.

But, there were two things which no money

1817
to
1819

could purchase anywhere. The first was, no grumbling on the part of the Landlady, except on account of our eating and drinking too little; and the other was, that Mr Wiggins had no fastening but a bit of a chip run in over the latch of the door to a house which was full of valuable things of all sorts. All this was the effect of good government, of just and mild government, which took so little from the people in taxes, that they had the means of happiness fully left in their hands.

We [soon, however, took] a place, pleasant and agreeable, a beautiful place, called Hyde Park; a fine park, orchards, gardens, and fields and woods. It was at North Hempstead in Long Island. A fine house too, but out of repair. Everybody was kind and obliging. If this untaxed, beautiful, fertile, and salubrious island had been inhabited by Englishmen, it would very far have surpassed the Garden of Eden; for here the trees produced golden fruit, and we were forbidden to eat none of them. I had good servants in my man Churcher and his Wife, and I heard their Hampshire tongues so often, that I almost conceited myself at home; only the fine sun, the fine roads, the fine fruits and the happy labourers told me that I was not. Tranquillity I enjoyed unalloyed by one single bitter reflection as to any one act of my whole life. Simply to preserve life and health was all that reason, or common sense, permitted me to go to the expense of.

At the place where I lived, which was in

Queen's County, and very nearly in the middle of the island, crosswise, we had no water, except in a well seventy feet deep, and from the clouds; yet, we never experienced a want of water. A large rain-water cistern to take the run from the house, and a duck-pond to take that from the barn, afforded an ample supply. The rains came about once in fifteen days; they came in abundance for about twenty-four hours; and then all was fair and all was dry again immediately. [The summers] were very, very hot. The thermometer 85 degrees in the shade; but a breeze. I worked in the land morning and evening, and wrote in the day in a north room. The dress became very convenient, or, rather, a very little inconvenient affair. Shoes, trousers, shirt, and hat. No plague of dressing and undressing! I never slept better in all my life. No covering. A sheet under me, and a straw bed. My window looked to the East. The moment Aurora appeared, I was in the Orchard. It was impossible for any human being to lead a pleasanter life than this. How I pitied those, who were compelled to endure the stench of cities! The dews were equal to showers; I frequently, in the morning, washed hands and face, feet and legs, in the dew on the high grass.

[In the winter], the frost made us jump and skip about like larks. Very seasonable for a sluggish fellow. [To prepare] for the winter, [I] patched up a boarded building, which had formerly been a coach-house; but, which was not so necessary to me, in that capacity, as in that of a fowl-house. The neighbours told me, that the poultry would roost out on the trees all the winter; and, indeed, they must, if they had no house, which was almost universally the case. However, I meant to give them a choice. I lined the said coach-house with corn-stalks and leaves of trees, and tacked up cedar boughs to hold the lining to the boards, and laid a bed of leaves a foot thick all over the floor. I secured all against dogs, and made ladders for the fowls to go in at holes six feet from the ground. I made pig-styes, lined round with cedar-boughs and well covered. Also a sheep-yard, for a score of ewes to have lambs in the spring, surrounded with a hedge of cedar-boughs and well covered, and with a shed for the ewes to lie under, if they liked. The oxen and cows were tied up in a stall. The dogs had a place well covered, and lined with corn-stalks and leaves. And I could without anxiety, sit by the fire, or lie in bed, and hear the North Wester whistle.

Let not my countrymen, who may happen to read this suppose, that these, or any other, pursuits, withdrew my attention from, or slackened my zeal in that cause, which was common to us all. That cause claimed, and had, my first attention and best exertion; that was the business of my life, these other pursuits were my recreation. King Alfred allowed eight hours for recreation, in the twenty-four, eight for sleep, and eight for business. I did not take my allowance of the two former.

[Early in 1818, I made] a journey into Pennsylvania, [which] had, for its principal object, an appeal to the justice of the Legislature of that state for redress for great loss and injury sustained by me, nearly twenty years [before], in consequence of the tyranny of one M'Kean, who was then Chief Justice of that State.[1] The appeal was not successful; but, my journey was productive of much and various observation, and, of useful knowledge.

[I went] over a space of more than two hundred miles, passing through the city of New York; through a list of towns in the State of New Jersey; then crossing the Delaware [River] into Pennsylvania; stopping some days to see my old friends at Bustleton and Philadelphia. The question eagerly put to me by everyone in Philadelphia was, "Don't you think the city greatly improved?" They seemed to me to confound augmentation with improvement. It always had been a fine city, since I first knew it; and it was very greatly augmented. It had, I believe, nearly doubled its extent and number of houses since the year 1799. But, after having been, for so long a time, familiar with London, every other place appeared little. After having lived within a few hundred yards of Westminster Hall, and the Abbey Church and the Bridge, and looked from my own windows into St James's Park, all other buildings and spots appeared mean and insignificant. I went to see the house I had formerly occupied. How small! It is always thus: the words *large* and *small* are carried about with us in our minds, and we forget real *dimensions*. All nations like to boast of their populousness. It is the same with cities and towns. The great subject of rivalship between those two fine cities, New York and Philadelphia, was that of the number of their inhabitants. Nothing tickles the vanity of the mass of a community more than the idea of an increasing population. The greater part of mankind like to make part of a crowd. Divide a crowd at any time: send one part to the right and the other to the left: let there be a great many more in one parcel than in the other, and the beggar man who is in the big parcel, will, for the moment, think himself better than the 'squire that is in the other parcel.

Leaving Philadelphia, [I passed] through a most beautiful country, studded with neat towns and villages, and with farm-houses, barns, and homesteads, such as I never before saw, and of which, without actually seeing them, I could have formed no idea; over all this space, amongst all these various scenes, I never saw a beggar, nor did I see, or hear of, a single person in distress. The skirts of the towns were not, as in England, rendered loathsome and dismal by miserable habitations. [However], the dwellings and gardens and little out-houses of labourers, which form so striking a feature of beauty in England, and especially in Kent, Sussex, Surrey, and Hampshire, and which constitute a sort of fairy-land, were what I, for my part, most felt the want of seeing. Instead of the neat and warm little cottage, the yard, cow-stable, pig-sty, hen-house, all in miniature, and the garden, nicely laid out and the paths bordered with flowers, while the cottage door is crowned with a garland of roses and honey-suckle; instead of these, we here saw the labourer content with a shell of boards, while all around him was as barren as the sea-beach; though the natural earth would have sent melons, the finest in the world, creeping around his door, and though there was no English shrub, or flower, which would not grow and flourish. This want of atten-tion in such cases was hereditary from the first settlers. They found land so plenty, that they treated small spots with contempt. Besides, the example of neatness was wanting. There were no gentlemen's gardens, kept as clean as drawing rooms, with grass as even as a carpet. From endeavouring to imitate perfection, men arrive at mediocrity; and, those who have never seen, or heard of perfection, in these matters, would naturally be slovens. Yet, notwithstanding these blots, as I deemed them, the face of the country was very fine.

[On my way I saw a great many Pennsylvania wagons.][2] Perhaps nothing of the kind was ever seen in the world so worthy of admiration as every-thing belonging to these Pennsylvania wagons. They have a tilt over them, neatly put upon hoops

1817
to
1819

of hickory wood, as slender as whale-bone would be, and as tough, if not tougher. A manger for horses is hung at the tail of the wagon. The wagon carries the provender for man and horse. A Pennsylvania wagon is loaded with barrels full of fine flour, at three or four hundred miles westward of Philadelphia. It carries from three to four ton weight. It comes over rocks and along roads upon which an Englishman would not believe it possible for an empty wagon to go. It has two horses abreast next the wagon, with a pole between them; two horses abreast before them; and one horse in front. The left-hand pole horse has a saddle upon him. This horse, the driver occasionally rides; and, with the enormous load, you see it rattling down hills and over rocks at a full trot.

In summer time, the man, wrapped in his blanket, sleeps in the wagon. In winter time, wrapped in his blanket, he sleeps upon the floor of the tavern where he halts, with his feet to the fire and his head upon a log of wood. And, as to the horses, never do they, in these their journeys, see the inside of a stable or feel covering of any sort. Five hundred of these wagons, and five times five hundred horses may be seen in the high street of Philadelphia at one and the same moment. The men are taking out their flour or taking in loads to carry back; and you see the horses feeding at the tail of the wagon, or lying about in the dirt, in the snow, or the dust.

[But yet], in everything where horses are the chief instruments (and horses are second only to men) the English so far surpass all the rest of the world, that there is no room for comparison. The man who has a mind to know something of England in this respect, should walk from the Tower of London to Charing Cross a little after daybreak in the morning, while the streets are clear of people. He would then see the teams of immense horses, drawing up from the bank of the Thames, coals, timber, stone, and other heavy materials. One morning I counted in various places, more than a hundred of these teams, worth each of them, harness, wagon, load and all, little less than a thousand pounds. The horses, upon an average, weigh more than a ton. But, next after a fox-hunt, the finest sight in England is a stage-coach just ready to start. A great sheep or cattle fair is a beautiful sight; but, in the stage-coach you see more of what man is capable of performing. The vehicle itself, the harness, all so complete and so neatly arranged; so strong and clean and good. The beautiful horses impatient to be off. The inside full, and the outside covered in every part, with men, women, children, boxes, bags, bundles. The coach-man, taking his reins in one hand and his whip in the other, gives a signal with his foot, and away go, at the rate of seven miles an hour, the population and the property of a hamlet. The horses are now all sweat and foam, the reek from their bodies ascending like a cloud.

[189]

The whole equipage is covered, perhaps, with dust or dirt. But still, on it comes as steady as the hand of a clock. As a proof of the perfection, to which this mode of travelling has been brought, there is one coach which goes between Exeter and London, the proprietors of which agree to forfeit eightpence for every minute that the coach is behind its time at any of its stages; and this coach, I believe, travels eight miles an hour, and that, too, upon very hilly, and, at some seasons, very deep roads.

[I reached] Harrisburgh, which lay about a hundred miles from Philadelphia. It had been laid out about thirty years [before], and contained a population nearly equal to that of Winchester. It was close on the left bank of the river Susquehanna, which had not frozen over, but had large quantities of ice floating on its waters. I tired to death of the tavern at Harrisburgh, though a very good one. I was weary of the ever-lasting loads of meat. Weary of being idle. How few such days had I spent in my whole life.

My business not coming on, I went to a country tavern, to get a room to myself, in which to read my English papers, and [to] sit down to writing. McAllister's tavern was situated at the foot of the first ridge of mountains; or rather, upon a little nook of land, where the river had found a way through a break in the chain of mountains. I had great enjoyment here. My mind was again in England. Mrs McAllister just suited me. [She

did] not pester me with questions, did not cram 1817
me with meat, let me eat and drink what I liked, *to*
and when I liked, and gave mugs of nice milk. The 1819
spot was the most delightful that my eyes ever
beheld. It was at once the most rich and the most
romantic. From one side of my room I looked out
into a farm-yard, full of fodder, and of cattle,
sheep, hogs, and multitudes of poultry, while, at
a few paces beyond the yard, ran the river Susquehanna, which was wider than the Thames, and
had innumerable islands lying in it, a quarter of
an acre to five or six acres in extent. From the
other side of my room I looked into an Orchard of
Apples and Peaches of forty acres, lying in a
narrow valley, which ran up between two mountains, about a quarter of a mile high, formed
precisely like the ridge of a house, the gable ends
being towards the river. These mountains were
covered with woods. [One] night it rained: it
froze before morning, and the frost caught the
drops hanging upon the trees; so that the sun,
shining as bright as in England in the month of
May, exhibited these icicles in countless millions
of sparkling diamonds.

[I] quitted Harrisburgh, very much displeased
[at the failure of my petition]. Lancaster, [on the
road to Philadelphia], was a pretty place. No fine
buildings, but no mean ones. The people of this
town seemed to have had the prayer of Hagar
granted them: "Give me, O Lord, neither poverty
nor riches". This was a fine part of America. Big

barns, and modest dwelling-houses. Barns of stone, a hundred feet long and forty wide, with two floors, and raised roads to go into them, so that the wagons went into the first floor upstairs. Below were stables, stalls, pens, and all sorts of conveniences. These were very fine buildings. And, then, all about them looked so comfortable, and gave such manifest proofs of ease, plenty, and happiness!

It was a curious thing to observe the farm-houses in this country. They consisted, almost without exception, of a considerably large and a very neat house, with sash windows, and of a small house, which seemed to have been tacked on to the large one; and, the proportion they bore to each other, in point of dimensions, was, as nearly as possible, the proportion of size between a Cow and her Calf, the latter a month old. But, as to the cause, the process was the opposite of this instance of the works of nature, for, it was the large house which grew out of the small one. The father, or grandfather, while he was toiling for his children, lived in the small house, constructed chiefly by himself, and consisting of rude materials. The means, accumulated in the small house, enabled a son to rear a large one; and though, when pride entered the door, the small house was sometimes demolished, few sons in America had the folly or want of feeling to commit such acts of filial ingratitude, and of real self-debasement. For, what inheritance so valuable and so honourable could a son enjoy as the proofs of his father's industry and virtue? The progress of wealth and ease and enjoyment, evinced by this regular increase of the size of the farmer's dwelling, was a spectacle, at once pleasing, in a very high degree in itself, and, in the same degree, it spoke the praise of the system of government, under which it had taken place.

[When] I arrived at Philadelphia, they were roasting an ox on the Delaware. The fooleries of England [were being] copied here, and every-where, with wonderful avidity. [Soon, however, there was a] complete thaw. I hated this weather; hot upon my back, and melting ice under my feet. The people (those who had been lazy) were chopping away with axes the ice, which had grown out of the snows and rains, before their doors, during the winter. The hogs (best of scavengers) were very busy in the streets seeking out the bones and bits of meat, which had been flung out and frozen down amidst water and snow, during the two foregoing months. At New York (and, I think, at Philadelphia also) they had corporation laws to prevent hogs from being in the streets. For what reason, I knew not, except putrid meat was pleasant to the smell of the inhabitants. But, Corporations are seldom the wisest of law-makers. It was argued, that, if there were no hogs in the streets, the people would not throw out their orts of flesh and vegetables. Indeed! What would they have done with those orts, then? Made

1817
to
1819

their hired servants eat them? The very proposition would have left them to cook and wash for themselves.

[In returning to New York, I went] in what is called a Jersey-wagon, through such mud as I never saw before. Up to the stock of the wheel; and yet a pair of very little horses dragged us through it. The best horses and driver, and the worst roads I ever set my eyes upon. New Jersey was a sad spectacle, after leaving the brightest of all the bright parts of Pennsylvania. My driver, who was a tavern-keeper, would have been a very pleasant companion, if he had not drunk so much spirits on the road. This is the great misfortune of America! As we were going up a hill very slowly, I could perceive him looking very hard at my cheek for some time. At last, he said: "I am wondering, Sir, to see you look so fresh and so young, considering what you've gone through in the world", though I could not imagine how he had learnt who I was. "I'll tell you", said I, "how I contrived the thing. I rise early, go to bed early, eat sparingly, never drink anything stronger than small-beer, shave once a day, and wash my hands and face clean three times a day, at the very least." He said, that was too much to think of doing.

I got, [at length,] to Elizabeth Town Point through beds of mud, twenty minutes too late for the steam-boat. [The next day,] I went to New York by the steam-boat; over to [Long Island] by

another, took a little light wagon, that whisked
me home over roads as dry and smooth as gravel
walks in an English bishop's garden in the month
of July. [It was] a great contrast with the
bottomless muds of New Jersey!

There were two things, which were almost
wholly wanting in America: the singing birds and
the flowers. There were many birds in summer,
and some of very beautiful plumage. There were
some wild flowers, and some English flowers in the
best gardens. But, generally speaking, they were
birds without song, and flowers without smell. The
linnet (more than a thousand of which I have
heard warbling upon one scrubbed oak on the
sandhills of Surrey), the skylark, the goldfinch,
the woodlark, the nightingale, the bullfinch, the
blackbird, the thrush, and all the rest of the
singing tribe were wanting in these beautiful
woods and orchards of garlands. When these
latter had dropped their bloom, all was gone in
the flowery way. No shepherd's rose, no honey-
suckle, none of that endless variety of beauties
that decorate the hedges and the meadows in
England. No daisies, no primroses, no cowslips,
no bluebells, no daffodils, which, as if it were not
enough for them to charm the sight and the smell,
must have names, too, to delight the ear. All
these were wanting in America. [There were,]
indeed, birds, which bore the name of robin,
blackbird, thrush, and goldfinch; but, alas! the
thing at Westminster has, in like manner, the

name of parliament, and speaks the voice of the people whom it pretends to represent, in much about the same degree that the blackbird [in America] spoke the voice of its namesake in England.

I met with an accident from fire [in the summer of 1819]. The house, in which I lived, was burnt down. I should have gone to New York, and remained there till the time of my departure for England; but, when I considered the interruptions which such a removal would occasion, and when I thought of the injury that these and the air of a city might be to my literary labours; I resolved on making a sort of thatched tent, in which I might enjoy tranquillity and in which I might labour without intermission. From this tent, made of poles, thatch, and English newspapers, I had the honour to address [many "Registers"]. Happiness never depends upon mere place. It depends little more on food or raiment. My diet all came from my own fields, and my cow was my vintner and brewer. I was asleep on my straw by nine o'clock, and I was in my orchard before four o'clock. Books and documents were rescued from the flames in Long Island, in consequence only of the extraordinary fidelity, zeal, and courage of my housekeeper, to whom, in my absence, my books and papers had been entrusted. She rushed into the room, which was in flames, and when no man was bold enough to enter it, and dragged out the trunk to the door at the manifest risk of her life.

I had given her particular charge about the trunk, 1817
and in her confusion she had forgotten it until it *to*
was nearly too late. Oh! let us not talk, then, 1819
about being sick of the world, because we now
and then meet with ingratitude and perfidy.
[They] would not weigh a feather in the scale
against Mrs Churcher.

That melancholy, mean fellow, Doctor Johnson,
observes, that when a man plants a tree, he
begins to think of dying. If this were the fact, is
that to prevent the planting of trees? I have been
planting of trees in every spot that I have ever
occupied, all my life time; and, [in America,] I
collected seeds of trees to carry home, and to sow
in England. I expected to sit under the shade of
the trees which [those] seeds would produce; and,
if I only saw them six inches high, had I not the
enjoyment of so much of them? [The same,] in
seeking justice on our oppressors: if we die before
we have obtained that justice, we enjoy, in the
meanwhile, the blows we inflict on them. We
enjoy their fears, their embarrassments, their
disgrace, their infamy. If I wrote grammars, if I
wrote on agriculture; if I sowed, planted, or dealt
in seeds; whatever I did had first in view the
destruction of infamous tyrants.

I resolved, while in [America], to write an
account of the Life, Labours, and death of that
famous Englishman, Thomas Paine;[3] and, perhaps, to collect and republish the whole of his
writings complete in a cheap form, and with some

[197]

1817
to
1819
explanatory notes to the "Rights of Man" particularly. I had within my reach all the means of correct information. There was only Long Island Sound and a few miles of land between me and the spot where he died. Justice in his memory, justice to the cause of freedom, justice to the country that gave him birth, justice to his friends on both sides the Atlantic, demanded at my hands an earnest endeavour to perform this task in a manner worthy of the subject. [For in spite of my early hatred], old age having laid his hand upon this truly great man, this truly philosophical politician, at his expiring flambeau I lighted my taper.

I published my intention of writing an account of [his] life. Soon after this, a Quaker at New York, named Charles Collins, made many applications for an interview with me, which at last, he obtained. I found that his object was to persuade me that Paine had recanted. I laughed at him, and sent him away. But, he returned again and again to the charge. He wanted me to promise him that I would say "that it was said" that Paine recanted. "No", said I, "but, I will say, that you say it, and that you tell a lie unless you prove the truth of what you say; and if you do that, I shall gladly insert the fact." This posed "friend Charley", whom I suspected to be a most consummate hypocrite. He had a sodden face, a simper, and manoeuvred his features, precisely like the most perfidious wretch. He was the reverse of my honest, open, and sincere Quaker friends, the Paulls of Pennsylvania. Friend Charley plied me with remembrances and reasonings; but, I always answered him, "Give me proof; or I denounce you as a liar". Thus put to his trumps, Friend Charley resorted to the aid of a person of his own stamp; and, at last, brought me a paper, very cautiously and craftily drawn up, [containing] only the initials of the names. I made him, at last, put down the full name and the address of the informer, "Mary Hinsdale, No. 10 Albany Street, New York".

The informer was a Quaker woman, who, at the time of Mr Paine's last illness, was a servant in the family of Mr Willett Hicks, an eminent merchant, a Quaker, and even, I believe, a Quaker preacher. Mr Hicks, a kind and liberal rich man, visited Mr Paine in his illness, and, from his house, which was near that of Mr Paine, little nice things (as is the practice in America) were sometimes sent to him; of which this servant, friend Mary, was the bearer, and this was the way, in which the lying cant got into the room of Mr Paine.

To "Friend Mary" I went, with friend Charley's paper in my pocket. I found her in a lodging in a back room up one flight of stairs. I knew that I had no common cunning to set my wits against. I began with all the art that I was master of. I had got a prodigiously broad-brimmed hat on. I patted a little child that she had sitting beside her; I called her *friend* and played all the awkward tricks of an undisciplined wheedler. But, I was compelled to come quickly to business. She asked, "What's thy name, friend"? and, the moment I said *William Cobbett*, up went her mouth as tight as a purse! Sack-making appeared to be her occupation; and that I might not extract through her eyes that which she was resolved I should not get out of her mouth, she went and took up a sack, and began to sew: and not another look or glance could I get from her.

However, I took out my paper, read it, and stopping at several points, asked her if it was true. She shuffled; she evaded, she equivocated, she warded off; she affected not to understand the paper, not to remember. The result was: that it was so long ago, that she could not speak positively: and that she had never given "friend Charley" authority to say anything about the matter in her name. "Oh! no! Friend, I tell thee, that I have no recollection of any person or anything that I saw at Thomas Paine's house."

I had now nothing to do but bring Friend Charley's nose to the grindstone. But, Charley, who was a grocer, living in Cherry Street, though so pious a man, and, doubtless, in great haste to get to everlasting bliss, had moved out of the city for fear of the [Yellow] Fever. And thus he escaped me, who sailed from New York in four days afterward. [My business with Paine, for other reasons, was never completed.]

After twenty-one days sailing over a sea almost

as smooth as the beautiful Long Island Lake, I arrived at Liverpool, on a Sunday evening, [in November 1819]. We were not permitted to land until Monday about two o'clock. There had been a great multitude assembled on the wharf the whole of the day; and, when I landed, I was received with cheers and with shakings of the hand, which made me feel that I was once again in England. I soon learned that the whole county of Lancashire was in a stir to give me a hearty welcome. The news of my arrival, upon reaching Bolton, was announced by a man, who went round the town with a bell. He stopped at different parts of the town, and, after ringing his bell, said: "Our countryman, William Cobbett, is arrived at Liverpool in good health." This man, for this act, was taken before a Magistrate.

On Sunday, the 28th of November, I, accompanied by [my sons] William and John, left Liverpool, on my road to Manchester, which I had been invited to visit, and where I had been invited to partake of a dinner on the Monday. We proceeded on our way to an Inn at a little hamlet called Irlam, which was within ten miles of Manchester. There we slept, and, the next morning prepared to get into our coach and to go to receive the welcome intended for us. A deputation had arrived to accompany us on the way, when, not to my surprise at all, arrived a messenger on horseback with a notification from the Boroughreeves and Constables of Manchester and Salford,

1817
to
1819

interdicting any further advance toward the Town! It would have been really criminal in me to proceed, for the purpose of receiving marks of approbation, and without any other purpose, when there manifestly would have been danger to the lives of some persons or other if the military had been brought out to obstruct my entrance into Manchester.[4]

We went back to Warrington and took the road to London; not, however, before I took an opportunity to make a short address to about two hundred persons who had assembled round the Inn, some of whom had come on foot all the way from Manchester. I shall never forget the looks of these men, and, indeed, of these women, for there were some of both sexes. My hand yet reminds me of the hard squeezes I had from them; and, [it is well known,] how great a favourite of mine a hard squeeze of the hand is.

We arrived at Coventry late on the evening of the 30th. When I came down into a front room of the house to breakfast, [the next day,] I found a great number of persons assembled in the street opposite the house; and finding that they were there for the purpose of seeing me, I informed them that I should set off in precisely an hour. When we started a great number followed us to a distance of about a mile out of the city, where there was an open space on the side of the road, surrounded by some high banks. Having drawn the chaise up in a suitable position, and having

placed myself upon the outside of the chaise on
the foot-board, I found myself surrounded by
several thousands of persons of both sexes, the
females forming a very beautiful battalion, many
of them with children in their arms, in one part
of the circle, not mixed among the men, while
other persons were running towards us not only
along the track of the chaise from the city, but in
all directions over the fields and meadows. This
was not a meeting. There had been nothing done
to call it together. It was spontaneous, it was
collected of itself, by the mere sound of my name.
Never did I behold any spectacle in my whole life
that gave me so much pleasure as this.

[My son] William and I [went] down from
London [to Botley in December]. The people of
the village, notwithstanding the threats of the
Parson, came to meet us upon the hill on the
Winchester road. They took out the horses and
drew us into the village, whence, after I had
shortly addressed them, they took us to [my]
house. The farm was in very neat order, the turnpike perfectly good, the trees monstrously grown;
the American trees of finer growth than any that
I ever saw in America of the same age.

CHAPTER XII

1820–1825

* * * * *

[AFTER MY RETURN, THOUGH] MY HEART
was always at home, [I had to] have my mind and
hand [in London]. We started a daily paper.[1] It
was a trying time and fortitude was required.
[My] boys were wonders of activity and sense and
spirit. [And then, the opportunity coming, I
resolved to stand for Parliament again.]

I set off for Coventry with [my eldest daughter],
on the 28th of February. We went all the night
(the coldest of the winter) in a post-chaise; breakfasted at Daventry, and then proceeded on towards Dunchurch, which is eleven miles from
Coventry. Here we were met by messengers who
brought accounts that I should certainly be murdered, if I attempted to enter the city. A band of
rich ruffians had leagued together against me.
They had got together a parcel of men, whom they
made partly drunk, and whom they gave orders
to go out, meet me at a bridge about a mile from
the city, and if I refused to return to London, to
fling me over the bridge.

While we were deliberating on what course to
pursue, a gentleman arrived with intelligence,
that the enemy had drawn up, rank and file, in

the city; that they were marching off with fourteen banners waving over their heads, and with
drums and music in their front; and that they had
not reached the outside of the city, when our
friends sallied forth upon them, took away their
banners, staved in their drums, dispersed them
in all directions, and set off to meet me.

At about four miles from Coventry, we met
with small advanced parties of young men, with
leaves of laurel in their hats and boughs in their
hands. The groups grew more frequent and larger
as we approached the city. The curiosity to see
me was so strongly expressed, that I was obliged
to get out of the chaise and stand upon the foot-
board with my hat off. I was drawn through all
the principal streets [for] two hours, in [the] frosty
evening, part after sunset, [and] the loss of my
voice, [from the chill,] was nearly as complete as
if I had been dumb from my birth.

[My] friends, satisfied with the victory of the
day, had retired to their houses, when the savages
sallied forth, dashed in the windows of the house
of Mr Serjeant, at which I was, and made many
brutal attacks upon individuals, whom they took
unawares in the street or at public-houses. Even
at this early period they cut several persons with
knives. On Monday, the sixth of March, Moore
and Ellice [my opponents] arrived, and as a
signal of their arrival, their hired savages again
dashed in the windows of Mr Serjeant. Upon this
occasion, [they] made an attempt to enter the

house; but, they, after getting into the passage, were beaten back into the street.

On Wednesday morning, the election began; and the poll closed in the afternoon, leaving me at the head of it! On Thursday, the savages came well fed and well supplied, all the day long, with gin and brandy, brought out to them in glass bottles, and handed about from one to another. I, that day, saw about twenty of my voters actually torn away from the polling-place, and ripped up behind, and stripped of their coats. During the afternoon, several fresh bands of savages [arrived] from the country; so that, by the hours of closing the poll, an immense multitude of these wretches roaring like wolves, and foaming with rage and drink, were collected round the Booth.

[As] I went out of the Booth, I had to pass through bands of savages; and I was scarcely among them, when they began an endeavour to *press me down.* I got many blows in the sides, and, if I had been either a short or a weak man, I would have been pressed under foot, and inevitably killed. However, the crowd took a sway toward a row of houses, standing on a pavement above the level of the area of the open street. With a good deal of difficulty I reached the pavement keeping my feet. I had to fight with my right hand. I had to strike back-handed. One of the sharp corners of [my] snuff-box, which stuck out beyond the bottom of my little finger, did good service. It cut noses and eyes at a famous rate, and assisted mainly in securing my safe arrival, on the raised pavement. Just at this time, one of the savages exclaimed: "damn him, I'll rip him up". He was running his hand into his breeches pocket, apparently to take out his knife, but I drew up my right leg, armed with a new and sharp gallashe over my boot, [and] dealt [the] ripping savage so delightful a blow, just between his two eyes, that he fell back upon his followers. For this I should certainly have been killed in a few moments, had not Mr Frank Serjeant made shift to get along, by the side of the houses, to the spot where I was. [Getting] to me, he turned round, saying, *follow me, Sir*, and, beating back three or four so as to make them press upon others behind them, the whole body turned about, while he with thumps on some, with kicks bestowed on others, set the body on a sway toward the house, at which we arrived safely.

[The next day], we were informed that the bands had been greatly augmented from the country; that they were now divided in regular bodies, fed and drenched at different houses, regularly paid, and ready to be brought out in succession, in order to relieve each other. When the poll opened, we had between three and four hundred men, all ready to poll; all was quiet. The Booth had no railway, or any other protection for the voters. The ground, too, was sloping, and the slope ran longways of the Booth. So that, though

[207]

1820
to
1825

my men might be ready to poll, it was by no means difficult to force them away.

The Ruffians came, not less than five hundred in number, in regular order, about eight or ten deep, with drums and banners at their head. They made their approach by the higher part of the ground, [and] began the attack upon my voters. All attempts to resist were in vain. And, in five minutes, three hundred of my voters were as completely driven away as if an army had made an attack upon them. After this, not a man dared to show his face to vote for me.

The way I managed [these] brutes was well calculated to sting them and their employers to madness. My way was to stand and look upon the yelling beasts with a most good-humoured smile, turning my head now and then, as it were to take different views. Now and then, I would put my mouth close to the ear of some friend, and then point to some beast, giving him at the same time a laughing look, such as we bestow on a dog that is chained up and barking at us. I never had so good an opportunity to philosophize before. The scene was far more horrible than anything of which any man not actually present, could have formed an idea. The bottles of gin and brandy continually passed from mouth to mouth; and, from the mass of heads which were closely jammed together, there arose a reek, or steam, just like the reek that rises, in a morning, from a heating dung hill. What was still more shocking and disgusting

than all the rest, was the sight of the wives and 1820
daughters of the Rich Ruffians, who were seated *to*
on the balconies and at the windows, looking 1825
directly down upon this scene, and discovering
every symptom of satisfaction and delight, at
hearing what would have made a bevy of common
prostitutes hang their heads with shame. I remember seeing crowds of prostitutes on the Point
at Portsmouth; and, I once saw three hundred on
board of a Seventy-Four at Spithead; but I never
before saw anything in the shape of woman, that
would have remained and listened to what appeared to give delight to [those] wives and
daughters.

The [savages finally] conceived the idea of
driving me out of the city. [They] made a regular
attack upon Mr Serjeant's house. They first dashed
in the upper-room windows; next they pulled
down the shutters of the ground-floor room. They
then broke into the house passage by forcing the
door; and while the main body were entering in
front, others were (as we could see from the window of our room) scaling a wall to get into the
house in the rear. I, who was very ill with a cold,
was sitting in my bedroom with my [daughter]
Nancy. Some gentlemen came running up for our
poker and tongs. One or two took station at the
top of the stairs; while I fixed the bedstead in a
way to let the door open no wider than to admit
one man only at a time, and stood with a sword.
I had pulled off my coat, and was prepared to give

1820
to
1825

with a clear conscience, as hearty a thrust as was ever given by man.

However, their cowardize soon put an end to the siege. They entered the passage, stabbed one man twice in his arm and did some other mischief: retreated hastily into the street. The thing went off without bodily hurt to any but our friends! And the natural consequence was, that the poor men who wished to vote for me dared no longer even talk of it! We got some firearms, and were quite secure in the house; but, as to the election, there remained nothing belonging to it worthy of the name. [I stood at the bottom of the poll.]*

[In this same year, money troubles came upon me again. I owed money to Sir Francis Burdett and others, and I had written the former] a letter from America, containing an assertion, that a man against whom ruinous laws had been singly pointed, was, by the law of nations, exonerated from obligations by which men, not so singled

* Letter from J. M. Cobbett to his brother James, at New York; dated London: 12 April 1820.

"Papa has failed in his election, and he has been so ill-used by several persons, to whom he owed money, that he will shortly be compelled to surrender himself, and to yield up all the property he has, though he could so easily clear off all the claims upon him, and though he is so anxious to do it to the last farthing. But, the spiteful villains, urged on no doubt by the Government, will not give him any time at all, and, therefore, he must take the usual protection of the law, and be either a bankrupt or an insolvent; and we all insist that he ought to do it...." See *Cobbett Papers*.

[210]

out, were bound; but, at the same time, saying, that I would not avail myself of that principle.[2] [Though,] for seven long years, I had been his sole prop, the ungrateful fellow, keeping the letter out of sight, published an answer to it, misrepresenting its meaning. A good large volume would not have contained the facts that I had collected for him; the notes that I had made for his speeches; the various things that I had written to uphold him. Two particularly I must mention. His sensible speech on the currency, recorded in "Paper Against Gold", I wrote out for him, and then published it and praised it as his. In 1812, he moved the answer to the King's Speech, or, rather, the Regent's. I wrote the answer and the speech; and the former was copied by his own daughter, that my hand might not appear. Nay, these were published in a pamphlet, by subscription, and I was myself the greatest subscriber! Shame, indeed, would it be to relate this; but, what has he left undone that he thought had a tendency to destroy my character!

I had sent a copy of the same letter [from America] to my friend Mr Timothy Brown. He did [not] cavil at it; but, though then bandaged up for the gout, took me to his house [and] brought on my bankruptcy in the most friendly manner. [And] Mr Tipper, a paper-maker, to whom I owed £3000, and with whom I was but slenderly acquainted, signed my certificate at the first possible moment; and he, or Mr Brown, I forget which, actually gave me a pound note and a few shillings, that I might, for form's sake, have something to surrender to the commissioners. [These] commissioners, seeing a great crowd in Guildhall staring at me, behaved towards me in a manner that showed the best of feelings; put no questions to me, dismissed me in a minute, and very kindly shook me by the hand when I went away. Everyone, even the bitterest political enemy; everyone felt, but Burdett. The old Lord Chancellor [Eldon], though he had advocated the bills that had ruined me, signed my certificate out of rule: "It is too late", said the officer: "his Lordship will not sign any more until such a day". I wrote my name upon a bit of paper, and begged him just to show it to the Chancellor. When he came out, he smiled with surprise, and said, "His Lordship will sign it". Every soul but that of Burdett was softened.

In January 1821, my family, after having for years been scattered about like a covey of part-ridges that had been sprung and shot at, got once more together in a hired lodging at Brompton. I was without one single article of furniture of my own; and, when we were all got together in that lodging, all that we could muster out of all our pockets, were three shillings and a few halfpence! No man to let me have paper to print the next Register upon, without having the money first; no man to print that Register, unless he had the money down before he began to print, or unless he had guarantee for that money from somebody besides me! A friend lent me twenty pounds to purchase the paper with, and the printing was done by some arrangement which I have now forgotten.

This was a season to try what a man and his family were made of. Here, indeed, was fortitude required, not only on my part, but on the part of every one of my family old enough to think. Mrs Williams of Brompton [could tell] whether she ever lodged a more happy or cheerful family. Our delight and our mutual caresses, and our tears of joy, experienced no abatement at our actually finding ourselves with only three shillings in the whole world.

Since that day, what, Good God!, have been my labours! A "Register" every week; nearly 500 "Registers", more than enough to occupy the whole time of any other man; my French Grammar, Woodlands, Gardening Book, Cottage Economy, Sermons, Protestant Reformation, Corn-Book, Advice to Young Men, and Guide to Emigrants, besides all my labours and cares about everything that I could possibly think of, leading to the good of my country.

My endeavours to stop the evil [facing my country] in time [had now] cost me the earnings of twenty long years! I did not sink, no, nor bend, beneath the heavy and reiterated blows of the accursed system, [but] dealt back blow for blow; and, blessed be God, I now saw it reel! It was

1820
to
1825

staggering about like a sheep with water in the head: turning its pate up on one side: seeming to listen, but had no hearing: seeming to look, but had no sight: one day it capered and danced: the next it moped and seemed ready to die.

Approbation [was again] bestowed on my "Trash",[3] which had, for so many years, been a mark for the finger of scorn to be pointed at by ignorant and arrogant and selfish power. [That] "Trash" was now triumphant; its triumph [people] met to celebrate. Proofs of its triumph I myself witnessed [at Norwich at a public dinner given to me]. In walking through St Andrew's hall [there], my mind was not so much engaged on the grandeur of the place, or on the gratifying reception I met with. The melancholy reflection engaged my mind, that, of the two thousand farmers then in my view, there were probably three-fourths who came with aching hearts. What a thing to contemplate! A set of men, occupiers of the land; producers of all that we ate, drank, wore, and of all that formed the buildings that sheltered us; a set of men industrious and careful by habit; cool, thoughtful, and sensitive from the instructions of nature; engaged in pursuits in their nature as stable as the very earth they tilled: to see a set of men like this plunged into anxiety, embarrassments, jeopardy, would have been more than sufficient to sink my heart within me, had I not been upheld by the reflection, that I had done all in my power to prevent calamities, and

that I still had in reserve that which, with the 1820
assistance of the sufferers themselves, would re- *to*
store them and the nation to happiness. 1825

[In April I went, with my family, to a convenient house at Kensington.] I was here most
delightfully situated. We kept five fine cows. We
had a pigeon-house to hold a hundred pair; and
[my youngest son] Dick was the grand pigeon-
master. Pigs in stye, and a most abundant and
fruitful garden. [My] publications, particularly
the "Sermons", were more famous than ever;
[there were] no villains to cheat us any more.

[I began, too, to ride about the country, and
when] I had put an end to my ride of August,
September, and October 1826, I had travelled
[hundreds of miles]. I had been in cities, market
towns, and villages. During the whole of [these
rides] I was rarely abed after daylight; I drank
neither wine nor spirits. As to drink, the less the
better; and mine was milk and water, or, not-sour
small beer, if I could get the latter. I liked the
milk and water best; for, if I drank much milk, it
loaded and stupefied and made me fat. I ate no
vegetables, and only a very moderate quantity of
meat. Many days I had no breakfast and no
dinner. I sometimes took, from a friend's house,
a little bit of meat between two bits of bread,
which I ate as I rode along. Whoever tries it will
find, that the less they eat and drink, when travelling, the better they will be. But, whatever I
saved from this fasting work, I thought I had a

1820
to
1825

clear right to give away; and, accordingly, I
generally put the amount, in copper, into my
waistcoat pocket, and disposed of it during the
day. I knew well, that I was better for not stuffing
and blowing myself out, and with the savings I
now and then gave a whole family a good meal
with the cost of a breakfast, or a dinner, that
would have done me mischief.

During [these rides] I was several times wet to
the skin. At some times of my life, after having
indulged for a long while in coddling myself up in
the house, these soakings would have frightened
me half out of my senses; but I [learnt to] care
very little about them, and, it was very seldom
that rain, come when it would, prevented me from
performing the day's journey that I had laid out
beforehand. Now, this was the advantage of
going about on horseback. On foot, the fatigue
was too great and you went too slowly. In any
sort of carriage you could not get into the real
country places. To travel in stage-coaches was to
be hurried along by force, in a box, with an air-
hole in it, and constantly exposed to broken
limbs, the danger being much greater than that
of shipboard, and the noise much more disagreeable, while the company was frequently not a
great deal more to one's liking.

Could you have seen and heard what I saw and
heard during [my] Rural [Rides], you would [not
have said] that the House "worked well". [There]
were two hundred thousand men, who by the Acts

of this same House, saw wives and children doomed to beggary, and to beggary too never thought of, never regarded as more likely than a blowing up of the earth or a falling of the sun. It was reserved for this "working well" House to make the firesides of the farmers scenes of gloom. These facts were notorious: the House had made all the loans which constituted the Debt: the House had put a stop to gold payments in 1819; the House had unanimously passed Peel's Bill [in 1819].[4] Here were all the causes of the ruin, the misery, the anguish, the despair.

[In 1822] I went to Beauworth to inquire after the family of a worthy old farmer, whom I had known there some years [before]. A bridle road over some fields and through a coppice took me to Kilmston, formerly a large village, but now mouldered into two farms, and a few miserable tumble-down houses for the labourers. Here was a house, that had been the residence of the landlord of the place, but was now occupied by one of the farmers. Kilmston had belonged to a Mr Ridge who had been a famous fox-hunter, and who was accused of having spent his fortune in that way. He had a right to spend his income, as his father's had done before him. It was the Pitt-system, and not the fox-hunting, that took away the principal.

[On the same journey I] crossed the River Wey. Here I found a parcel of labourers at parish-work. Amongst them was an old playmate of mine. The account they gave me of their situation was very

[217]

1820
to
1825

dismal. The harvest was over early. The hop-picking was over; and they were employed by the parish; that was to say, not absolutely digging holes one day and filling them up the next, but at the expense of half-ruined farmers and tradesmen and landlords, to break stones into very small pieces to make nice smooth roads lest the jolting, in going along them, should create bile in the stomachs of tax-eaters. [This] was a state of things where all was out of order; where self-preservation, that great law of nature, seemed to be set at defiance; for here were farmers unable to pay men to work for them, and yet compelled to pay them for working in doing that which was really of no use to any human being. There lay the hop-poles unstripped. You saw a hundred things in the neighbouring fields that wanted doing. The fences were not nearly what they ought to have been. The very meadows, to my right and left in crossing [the] little valley, would have occupied these men advantageously until the setting in of the frost; and here were they, not, as I said before, actually digging holes one day and filling them up the next; but, to all intents and purposes, as uselessly employed.

I am sure I saw produce enough in [some] farm-yards, to feed the whole of the population of [some] parishes. But the infernal system caused it all to be carried away. Not a bit of good beef, or mutton, or veal, and scarcely a bit of bacon was left for those who raised all this food. The

labourers looked as if they were half-starved. 1820
Good God! what a life to live! What a life to see *to*
people live; to see this sight in our own country, 1825
and to have had the base vanity to boast of that
country, and to talk of our "constitution" and
our "liberties". The fact was, that, where honest
and laborious men could be compelled to starve
quietly, with old wheat ricks and fat cattle under
their eyes, it was a mockery to talk of their
"liberty" of any sort; for, the sum total of their
state was this, they had "liberty" to choose between death by starvation (quick or slow) and
death by the halter! I really was ashamed to ride
a fat horse, to have a full belly, and to have a clean
shirt on my back, while I looked at these wretched
countrymen of mine.

However, even this was necessary, as long as
[the] bank-note system continued; and all com-
plaints about severity of laws, levelled at the poor,
were useless and foolish. What, short of such laws,
could prevent starving men from coming to take
away the dinners of those who had plenty? "Education"! Despicable cant and nonsense! What
education, what moral precepts, could quiet the
cravings and ragings of hunger?

[Look,] for a minute, to the little village of
Stoke-Charity, near to Winchester, that grand
scene of ancient learning, piety, and munificence.
The parish formerly contained ten farms, and it
contained but two [in 1824]. There used to be ten
well-fed families in this parish, at any rate; and

1820
to
1825

[in 1824] all were half starved except the curate
and two families. The blame was not the landlord's; it was nobody's; it was due to the infernal
funding and taxing system, which of necessity
drove property into large masses in order to save
itself; which crushed little proprietors down into
labourers; and which pressed them down in that
state and made them paupers, their share of food
and raiment being taken away to support debt
and dead-weight and army and all the rest of the
enormous expenses, which were required to sustain [the] intolerable system. Those, therefore,
were fools or hypocrites, who affected to wish to
better the lot of the poor labourers, while they, at
the same time, either actively or passively, upheld
the system which was the manifest cause of [all].
The coaxing work of schools could only add to
what was quite enough without them.

I have never been able clearly to comprehend
what the beastly Scotch *feelosofers* meant by their
"national wealth"; but, as far as I could understand them, this was their meaning: that national
wealth meant, that which was left of the products
of the country over and above what was consumed,
or used, by those whose labour had caused the
products to be. This being the notion, it followed,
of course, that the fewer poor devils you could
screw the products out of, the richer the nation
was. What, then, was to be done with this over-
produce? Was it to go to pensioners, placemen,
gendarmerie, and, in short, to whole millions, who

did no work at all? By national prosperity, [such] 1820
writers meant something very different indeed *to*
from that which I, who had no desire to live upon 1825
taxes, should have called national prosperity.
They looked upon it as being demonstrated in the
increase of the number of chariots and fine-dressed
people in and about the purlieus of the court. This
was a demonstration of the increase of the taxes,
and nothing more. National prosperity shows itself in very different ways: in the plentiful meal,
the comfortable dwelling, the decent furniture
and dress, the healthy and happy countenances,
and the good morals of the labouring classes of
the people. National wealth means, the Common-
wealth, or Commonweal; and these mean, the
general good, or happiness of the people, and the
safety and honour of the state; and, these were
not to be secured by robbing those who laboured,
in order to support a large part of the community
in idleness.

[One had only] to look at the face of the country,
including [the] Wen [of London], to behold the
effects of taking property from one man and
giving it to another. The monstrous streets and
squares, and circuits, and crescents; the pulling
down of streets and building up new ones; the
making of bridges and tunnels, till the Thames
itself trembled at the danger of being marched
and undermined: the everlasting ripping-up of
pavements and the tumblings up of the earth to
form drains and sewers, till all beneath us was like a

1820
to
1825

honeycomb.* [One had only] to look at the thousands employed in cracking the stones upon the
highways, while the docks and thistles and couch-
grass were choking the land on the other side of
the hedges; to see England, land of plenty and
never-ending stores, without an old wheat rick,
and with not more than a stock of two-thirds the
former cattle upon the farms: to see the troops of
half-starved creatures flocking from the fields,
and, in their smock-frocks and nailed shoes, beg-
ging their way up to [the cities], in order to get a
chance snap at the crumbs and the orts rejected by
idleness and luxury—of all the destructive things
that could fall upon a nation; of all the horrid
curses that could afflict it, none was equal to that
of robbing productive labour of its reward, of
taking from the industrious and giving to the idle.

* My Lord Holland disfigured and half spoiled his
beautiful park and farm at Kensington, during the
building madness of "matchless prosperity" of 1824 and
1825. When, in the former of those years, I saw "Addison
Road" come and cut his beautiful farm across, and when
I saw "Cato Cottage" and "Homer Villa" start up on the
side of that road, I said, My Lord will pay pretty dearly
for his taste for the "classics". These "classics" are,
sometimes, not very safe guides even in matters of a
merely literary nature. So long, however, as you confine
your enthusiasm to paper and print, you merely expose
yourself to ridicule; but when your taste pushes you on to
the levelling of banks, the tearing up of trees, the felling of
oaks fifty years old, and, above all the rest, to dabbling in
brick and mortar, the classics become most perilous and
pernicious companions!

To have plenty of everything that made life 1820
easy and pleasant was formerly one of the great *to*
characteristics of the English people. Good eating, 1825
good drinking, good clothing, good lodging; without these people do not really live: it is staying
upon the earth. Good government is known from
bad government by this infallible test: that, under
the former the labouring people are well fed and
well clothed, and under the latter, they are badly
fed and badly clothed.

It was deeply interesting to observe how the
taste of this country appeared to have changed.
The fashion became to cry up spare diet, and to
preach content with hunger. One of the Tracts
put forth by canting hypocrites who pretended to
exclusive grace, was entitled "The Life of Peter
Kennedy, who lived on, and saved money out of
eighteen pence a week". And this to his praise,
mind! I never considered empty bellies and
ragged backs as marks of the grace of God. [Never]
did we, until these days, hear of millions of
"Tracts, Moral and Religious" for the purpose of
keeping the poor from cutting the throats of the
rich. The parson's sermon, once a week or a fortnight, used to be quite sufficient for the religion
and morals of a village. Now we had a busy creature or two in every village, dancing about with
"Tracts" for the benefit of the souls of the labourers and their families. The gist of the whole
of the "Tracts" was to inculcate content in a
state of misery! To teach people to starve without

making a noise! What did all this show? Why, a consciousness on the part of the rich, that the poor had not fair play; and that the former wished to obtain security against the latter by coaxing.

A parson said to me, once, by letter: "Your religion, Mr Cobbett, seems to me to be altogether political". "Very much so indeed", answered I, "and well it may, since I have been furnished with a creed which makes part of an Act of Parliament." And, the fact is, I am no Doctor of Divinity, and like a religion, any religion, that tends to make men innocent and benevolent and happy, by taking the best possible means of furnishing them with plenty to eat and drink and wear.

Once, coming through the village of Benenden, I heard a man talking very loudly about houses! houses! houses! It was a Methodist parson, in a house, close by the roadside. I pulled up, and stood still, in the middle of the road, but looking, in silent soberness, into the window (which was open) of the room in which the preacher was at work. I believe my stopping rather disconcerted him; for he got into shocking repetition. "Do you KNOW", said he, laying great stress on the word KNOW: "do you KNOW, that you have ready for you houses, houses I say; I say do you KNOW; do you KNOW that you have houses in the heavens not made with hands?" And, on he went to say, that, if Jesus had told them so, they would be saved, and that if he had not, and did not, they would be damned. Some girls whom I saw in the room, plump and rosy as could be, did not seem at all daunted by these menaces; and indeed, they appeared to me to be thinking much more about getting houses in this world first: houses with pig-styes and little snug gardens attached to them, together with all other domestic and conjugal circumstances. The truth is, these fellows had no power over the minds of any but the miserable.

A full belly to the labourer was, in my opinion, the foundation of public morals and the only source of real public peace. It was with this opinion in my mind, that I wrote and published my little work, called "Cottage Economy".[5] It was written at North Lodge, a farm-house in Sussex, whither I had gone to reside for some time, for the purpose of teaching [my] youngest son how to go about in the fields and the woods and the lanes; teaching him to ride upon a pony, and to begin to be hardy and strong. I do not deny that Mrs Brazier, the farmer's wife, helped me a great deal; for she, though then nearly eighty years of age, had brought up forty children and grand-children, and had it said of her, that she had done more work herself than any woman in Sussex; and that there was not a working-man or woman in the parish who had not, first or last, either resided or been fed under her roof; and though she could neither write nor read, understood well the making of bread, the brewing of beer, the keeping of cows, the rearing of pigs, and was able to teach me practically, all that I myself did not know

1820
to
1825

touching the subjects upon which I was writing. To her, who is now dead, I thus record my acknowledgements.

[With this book] I did more good than Bailey, [who once judged me,] ever did in the whole course of his life, notwithstanding his pious Commentary on the Book of Common Prayer. I will allow nothing to be good, with regard to the labouring classes, unless it make an addition to their victuals, drink, or clothing. As to their minds, that was much too sublime a matter for me to think about. I knew that they were in rags, and that they had not a belly-full; and I knew that the way to make them good, to make them honest, to make them dutiful, to make them kind to one another, was to enable them to live well; and I also knew that none of these things would ever be accomplished by Methodist sermons, and by stupid, at once stupid and malignant things, and roguish things, called Religious Tracts.

[I must add that I brought back from my rides] the most pleasing impressions. It is not for [me] to descend to particulars in characterizing personal friends; and, therefore, I will content myself with saying, that the treatment I met with was much more than sufficient to compensate me, personally, for all the atrocious calamities, which, for twenty years, I had had to endure.

CHAPTER XIII

1825–1830

*   *   *   *   *

ALL OUR PROPERTIES, ALL OUR LAWS, ALL
our manners, all our minds changed. This, which
I noticed, took place within forty, and, most of it,
within ten years. The small gentry, to about the
third rank upwards (considering there to be five
ranks from the smallest gentry up to the greatest
nobility), all went, nearly to a man, and the small
farmers along with them. The Barings alone,[1] I
should think, swallowed up thirty or forty of these
small gentry without perceiving it. They, indeed,
swallowed up the biggest race of all; but, innumerable small fry slipped down unperceived,
like caplins down the throats of sharks while these
latter feel only the cod-fish. It frequently happened, too, that a big gentleman or nobleman,
whose estate had been big enough to resist for a
long while, and who had swilled-up many caplin-
gentry, went down the throat of the loan-dealer
with all the caplins in his belly.

Thus the rivulet went on, shifting property
from hand to hand. My Lord, De Bombastville
(the Norman, who came in with the Conqueror),
had, for instance, mortgaged his estate to Moses
Oraculo, the Jew, who had come in with the Dutch

[227]   15-2

1825
to
1830

and the Devil. The estate, when mortgaged in 1812, had been worth two hundred thousand pounds, and Moses lent a hundred thousand upon it. Peel's Bill passed in the memorable year 1819, and in 1821, the estate was the Jew's. The three great estates near the place where I was born were the Bishop of Winchester's Castle; Moor Park, occupied by the descendants of Sir William Temple; and Waverley Abbey, which belonged to Sir Robert Rich. [During my Rides I found] Moor Park in the hands of Mr Timson, and Waverley Abbey in those of Mr Tomson, the one a dealer in spirits and the other a dealer in wine. The Bishop was standing his ground. And, really, it was a consolation to me to find something [the same].

[You added, too], the work of sublimating farmers out of their senses, [that had been] promoted by the Nobility and Gentlemen of great estates, who, by means of agricultural societies, cattle shows, and the like, had given every encouragement to this class of men to become conceited and presumptuous. The King, too, had had to have a farm. It was "Farmer George"! Between the commercial people on the one side and the farmers on the other, the far greater part of the country gentlemen in England were fairly squeezed out of existence.

Now, this process produced no diminution of consumption, no falling off of revenue. What the Norman had before, the Jew had now. The rents, which the Norman had spent, were now spent by

the Jew, who lived in a square of London where
the Norman had lived before. The land was just
what it was before. It yielded the same produce.
[And then the farmers themselves, under the
effects of Peel's Bill, began to sink.] I had an
opportunity of hearing something about this. I
asked the farmers of my old neighbourhood, one
by one, of the condition of the country; and the
answers I received only tended to confirm me in
the opinion, that the whole race would be destroyed; and that a new race would come, and
enter upon farms without capital and without
stock; be a sort of bailiff to the landlord for a
while, and then, if the funding system went on,
bailiffs to the Government as trustee for the
fundholder.

The big [men], to save themselves from being
"swallowed up quick" (as we used to say, in our
church prayers against Buonaparte), made use of
their voices to get, through place, pension, or
sinecure, something back from the taxes. Others
of them fell in love with the daughters and widows
of paper-money people, big brewers, and the like;
and sometimes their daughters fell in love with
the paper-money people's sons, or the fathers of
those sons; and, whether they were Jews or not,
seemed to be little matter with this all-subduing
passion of love. But, the small gentry had no resource. While the war lasted, "glorious war",
there had been a resource; but now, alas! not only
was there no war, but there was no hope of war.

1825
to
1830

There was no place for them in the army, church, navy, customs, excise, pension-list, or anywhere else. All these were now wanted by "their betters". A stock-jobber's family would not look at such pennyless things. So that while they had been the active, the zealous, the efficient instruments, in compelling the working classes to submit to half-starvation, they had, at any rate, been brought to the most abject ruin themselves. I should not have minded this sweeping away of the little old aristocracy, if a worse had not come in its place, which invariably looked upon every labourer as a thief.

[Once], at Up-Street, [near Canterbury], I was struck with the words written upon a board which was fastened upon a pole, which pole was standing in a garden near a neat little box of a house. The words were these: "Paradise Place. Spring guns and steel traps are set here". A pretty idea it gave of Paradise to know that spring guns and steel traps were set in it! This was doubtless some stock-jobber's place; for, in the first place, the name was likely to have been selected by one of that crew; and, in the next place, whenever any of them went to the country, they looked upon it that they were to begin a sort of warfare against everything around them.

Some were ready to cry, and I knew one that did actually cry to a farmer (his tenant) in 1822. The tenant had told him, that "Mr Cobbett had been right about this matter [of the funds]"

"What!" exclaimed he, "I hope you do not read 1825
Cobbett! He will ruin you, and he would ruin us *to*
all. He would introduce anarchy, confusion, and 1830
the destruction of property!" Oh, no Jolterhead!
There was no destruction of property. Matter,
the philosophers say, is indestructible. It was
[only] all easily transferable, as [became] well
known to the base jolterheads.

[In these days, too], Wens devoured market
towns and villages; and shops devoured markets
and fairs; and this, too, to the infinite injury of
the most numerous classes of the people. All was
looked for at shops: all was to be had by traffick-
ing: scarcely anyone thought of providing for his
own wants out of his own land and out of his own
domestic means. To buy the thing, ready made,
was the taste of the day: thousands, who were
housekeepers, bought their dinners ready cooked:
nothing was so common as to rent breasts for
children to suck: a man actually advertised, in the
London papers, to supply childless husbands with
heirs! In this case, the articles were, of course, to
be ready made.

Shopkeeping, merely as shopkeeping, is injurious to any community. The shop must be paid
for; the shopkeeper must be kept; and the one
must be paid for and the other must be kept by
the consumer of the produce. When fairs were
very frequent, shops were not needed. A manufacturer of shoes, of stockings, of hats, of almost
anything that man wanted, could manufacture at

1825
to
1830

home in an obscure hamlet, with cheap house-rent, good air, and plenty of room. He needed pay no heavy rent for shop: and no disadvantages from confined situation: and, then, by attending three or four or five or six fairs in a year, he sold the work of his hands, unloaded with a heavy expense attending the keeping of a shop. Could not everyone see, in a minute, how this exchanging of fairs and markets for shops created idlers and traffickers; created those locusts, called middlemen, who added to the value of nothing, who improved nothing, but who lived well out of the labour of the producer and the consumer.

There was that numerous sect, the Quakers, engendered by the Jewish system of usury. Till excises and loan-mongering began, these vermin were never heard of in England. They seemed to have been hatched by that fraudulent system, as maggots are bred by putrid meat. All they talked about was dealing; and the government, in place of making laws that should have put them in the stocks, really seemed anxious to encourage them. But, everything tended the same way: all the regulations, all the laws that were adopted, had a tendency to give encouragement to the trickster and the trafficker.

There was something new in the manner and shape of manufacturing. Formerly the business was carried on in all parts of the country: now it had been so managed; the taxing and paper-money system had created such a mass of mono-

polies; had drawn the wealth of the country into
such great heaps, as to cause the manufacturing
work-people to be collected into enormous masses,
and that, too, in those parts of the country least
productive of food. This was a most unnatural
state of things; it robbed the land of all that which
would have been earned by the wives and the
small children of the agricultural labourers; and,
in case of any fluctuations in the manufacturing
business, all the horrors attendant upon ruin and
poverty [were to] be witnessed, in the parts of the
country in which great numbers of people were collected together. For years I had been endeavouring to call the attention of the country to this
great evil. I stood alone; and was, indeed opposed
by the whole of the press, and by every speech
that I ever heard of, that ever uttered a word upon
the subject.

The editor of the "Morning Chronicle", [Dr
Black,] invariably advised [the farming labourers]
to go North, and there to become manufacturers.
That was, according to him, the only possible way
of obtaining for themselves and their families a
sufficiency of food. He had, indeed, suggested
another mode of lessening their wants: namely,
that of abstaining from breeding, which mode, if
it had been recommended to people of threescore
years and ten, might have had some chance of
success; but, as the recommendation had addressed itself to bouncing girls of eighteen or
twenty, with the blood ready to burst through

their skins, and to young fellows that valued life
itself only because it afforded them the gratifica-
tion of their tastes and passions, the recommendation dropped dead.

The truth was, that these men were mere
writers: they were writers by trade: they understood that trade pretty well; but, they knew
nothing of the real situation of the people of this
or of any other country. Such men knew a great
deal about words, but, what the devil could they
know of men or of things; they were extremely
enlightened; but they had no knowledge. Hence
all this stupid stuff in praise of manufacturing
establishments: hence all their exaltations at the
prosperity of Manchester and Paisley: hence all
their everlasting clamour in praise of paper
money.

The villages down [the] Valley of the Avon,
[near Salisbury,] and, indeed, it was the same in
almost every part of the country, used to have
great employment for the women and children in
the carding and spinning of wool for the making
of broad-cloth. It was now wholly gone; and this
made a vast change in the condition of the people,
and in the state of property and of manners and
morals. In 1816, I had written and published a
"Letter to the Luddites",[2] the object of which
had been to combat their hostility to the use of
machinery. The arguments I there had made use
of were general. I had taken the matter in the
abstract. The principles had all been correct

[234]

enough; but their application could not be uni-
versal; and, we had a case here before us, which,
in my opinion, showed, that the mechanic in-
ventions, pushed to the extent that they were,
were productive of great calamity to this country.
The greater part of manufacturing consisted of
clothing and bedding. Now, if by using a machine,
we could get our coat with less labour than we got
it before, the machine was a desirable thing. But,
then, mind, we had to have the machine at home
and we ourselves had to have the profit of it; if it
was worked by other hands; if other persons had
the profit of it; and if, in consequence of the
existence of the machine, we had hands at home,
who had nothing to do, and whom we had to keep,
then the machine was an injury to us, however
advantageous it might have been to those who
used it, and whatever traffic it might occasion
with foreign states.

[Not all] manufacturing was like that of cottons,
a mere gambling concern, making Baronets to-day
and Bankrupts to-morrow, and making those who
did the work slaves. [In many] there were no
masses of people, called together by a bell, and
"kept to it" by a driver; no "patriots", who,
while they kept Englishmen to it by fines, and almost by the scourge, in a heat of 84 degrees, were
petitioning the Parliament to give freedom to the
South Americans, who, as these "patriots" had
been informed, used a great quantity of cottons!
A considerable part of the decay and misery of

1825
to
1830

[the country side] was owing to the use of machinery and to the monopolizing; to that system of gambling and fictitious money, which conveyed property from the hands of the many into the hands of the few.

[And worst of all] how many greedy gambling [people] were there in England; not only in and about the Wen [of London]; but in every country town, in every village you found them, [eager] to gamble in Funds or shares of some sort or other; and who could not sit with you five minutes without your hearing some of their slang about fives and fours and threes and consols and reduceds and India and Greek and so on. A woman asked me my opinion one day, about *investing*, as she called it, some money that she had. I made free, as to giving men advice, now and then; but, experience had taught me to be very careful how I presumed in this way, with petticoat speculators. Being pressed, however, with some degree of earnestness, I advised the getting rid of all the securities of every sort, and took an opportunity of showing, very clearly, as I thought, how much more secure, as well as more honourable, the possession of land or house, or security on land or house, would be than the possession of a thing that might become of no value at all to-morrow; adding some observations on the lowness, the meanness, the filthiness of these sort of usurious transactions, appealing, by a side wind, to her religion. In short, I, before I concluded, had

made, as I thought, great impression upon her 1825
mind, if I had not already converted her. After *to*
this, a short pause ensued, while we were looking 1830
out of the window, and I was admiring some very
pretty rose trees. And she, all at once, as if I had
never said a word to her on the subject of funds
and bonds, asked me, with great seeming earnestness: "Mr Cobbett, what do you think of Colum-
bians?"

I knew what I thought of her, though I did not
tell her; and that was, that she was a nasty,
gambling, grovelling, mercenary, sordid, merciless
devil in petticoats, who did not care if the whole
people of the village in which she lived, perished
of hunger, provided the cause of that perishing
were also the cause of making her gain a few additional pounds a year. Were it not for the system
that created them, there could be no such wretches
who, being too lazy to work, wished to make fortunes out of the sweat; and, if necessary, the blood
of the people; and who, therefore, might be, with
justice, called muckworms. But, this was no
justification of the wretches themselves; the
system merely presented the temptation; that
was the greater crime of the two, certainly; but
the wretches who yielded to the temptation were
criminal also.

[Whenever I] sallied forth to see the farmers,
to view the state of the crops, and to philosophize,
unchoked by smoke and unstunned by the rattle
of the infernal coaches and drays, [I met evidences

1825
to
1830

of change]. I went, [one of these times,] to a sale at a farm, which the farmer was quitting. Here I had a view of what had long been going on all over the country. The farm, which belonged to Christ's Hospital, had been held by a man by the name of Charrington, in whose family the lease had been a great number of years. The house was hidden by trees. It stood in the weald of Surrey, close by the River Mole, which was here a mere rivulet, though just below this house the rivulet supplied the very prettiest flour mill I ever saw in my life.

Everything about this farm-house was formerly the scene of plain manners and plentiful living. Oak clothes-chests, oak bedsteads, oak chest of drawers, and oak tables to eat on, long, strong, and well supplied with joint stools. Some of the things were many hundreds of years old. But all appeared to be in a state of decay and nearly of disuse. There appeared to have been hardly any family in that house, where formerly there had been, in all probability, from ten to fifteen men, boys, and maids: and, which was the worst of all, there was a parlour! Aye, and a carpet and bell-pull too! One end of the front of this once plain and substantial house had been moulded into a "parlour"; and there was a mahogany table, and the fine chairs, and the fine glass, and all as bare-faced upstart as any stock-jobber in the kingdom could boast of. And I daresay it had been *'Squire* Charrington and the *Miss* Charringtons; and not

plain Master Charrington and his son Hodge and 1825
his daughter Betty Charrington, all of whom the *to*
accursed system had, in all likelihood, transmuted 1830
into a species of mock gentlefolk.

This 'Squire Charrington's father used, I daresay, to sit at the head of the oak table along with
his men, say a grace to them, and cut up the meat
and the pudding. He might have taken a cup of
strong beer to himself, when they had none; but,
that was pretty nearly all the difference in their
manner of living. So that all lived well. But, the
'Squire had many wine-decanters and wine-glasses
and a "dinner-set", and a "breakfast-set", and
"desert knives"; and these implied carryings-on
and a consumption that must of necessity have
greatly robbed the long oak table. That long table
could not share in the work of the decanters and
the dinner-set. Therefore, it became almost un-
tenanted; and the labourers retreated to hovels,
called cottages; and, instead of board and lodging,
they got money; so little of it as would enable the
employer to drink wine; but, then, that he might
not reduce them to quite starvation, they were
enabled to come to him in the King's name, and
demand food as paupers.

I could not quit this farm-house without reflecting on the thousands of scores of bacon and
thousands of bushels of bread that had been eaten
from the long oak table which, I said to myself,
is now perhaps, going, at least, to the bottom of
some bridge that some stock-jobber will stick up

1825
to
1830

over an artificial river in his cockney-garden. "By—, it shan't", said I, almost in a real passion: and so I requested a friend to buy it for me, and kept it for the good it had done in the world. When the old farm-houses were down, what a miserable thing [for] the country! Those that were erected were mere painted shells, with a Mistress within, who was stuck up in a place which she called a parlour, with, if she had children, the "young ladies and gentlemen" about her: some showy chairs and a sofa (a *sofa* by all means): half a dozen prints in gilt frames hanging up: some swinging book-shelves with novels and tracts upon them: a dinner brought in by a girl that was perhaps better "educated" than she: two or three nicknacks to eat instead of a piece of bacon and a pudding: the house too neat for a dirty-shoed carter to be allowed to come into; and everything proclaiming to every sensible beholder, that there was a constant anxiety to make a *show* not warranted by the reality. The children (which was the worst part of it) were all too clever to work: they were all to be *gentlefolks*. Go to plough! Good God! What, "young gentlemen" go to plough! They became *clerks*, or some skimmy-dish thing or other. What misery was all this!

Strange were the workings of Peel's Bill [among such men; it left] no vestige of the fine spirit that had been floating about in [earlier] years. The yeomanry cavalry we never heard mentioned, except cited as the cause of heavy expense. The bang, bang from their pistols, and the rattle of the feet of their horses, that charming music, really appeared to be gone forever. No paradings in parks; no dinnerings and toastings at taverns, or at Lord's houses; no votes of thanks and stupid correspondence in the newspapers, between troops and their commanders; no boastings about gallant exploits in sallies on old women and boys. All was gone; and the rusty sword, the furred-up pistol, and helmet cap, and uniform jacket were all thrown aside. They did not hang these up now in the "parlour" for everybody to see them: they hung them up in their bedrooms, or in a cockloft; and when they met their eye, they looked at them as a bridegroom does at a girl that the overseers are about to compel him to marry. When any of them complained of those acts of the Government which stripped them, [they should have recollected] their own base and malignant conduct towards those persecuted reformers, who, if they had not been suppressed by these very yeomen, would have put an end to the cause of that ruin of which these yeomen now complained. [They should have remembered] the toasts which they had drunk in anti-jacobin times; their base and insulting exultations of the 16th of August at Manchester;[3] their cowardly abuse of the men, who had been endeavouring to free their country from that horrible scourge which they themselves now felt.

[It was] the sound and consistent and faithful

1825
to
1830
Peel. [He] brought in [his] Bill, to "restore the currency of our ancestors"! The Parliament was delighted, the drunkards and gluttons of the city were charmed, the old debauched annuitants were bewitched by this fine young man who was giving them gold instead of flimsy paper.

In spite of all this, however, the stupid hogs of landlords soon found that their estates were slipping from under them. They had looked upon their buildings and their stock as being worth, from time to time, certain sums; but, whenever they came to the sale, they always found themselves deceived; they found their fortunes and their possessions diminished. No man, however careful, and of how solid a nature soever his means, knew what he would be worth [one] day month. One convulsion ended only to make way for another; one class of the community was crushed [one] three months; another next three months; a general and terrible convulsion was always threatening. To pay the interest of [the] Debt in gold, of the full weight and fineness, was impossible; that was, without taking away the estates of the present possessors, and transferring them directly or indirectly to those who owned the securities on the debt.

The world never beheld a triumph more complete and more honourable than that which time and events awarded me. In the city of Bath, the people, amidst the crash of Banks, shouted in the streets, "COBBETT IS RIGHT! COBBETT IS

A TRUE PROPHET!" It was my anxious wish 1825
to put a stop to the fatal progress of hideous re- *to*
volution. I was well aware that it was no easy 1830
task to effect an object like this. No small part
of every twenty-four hours, whether on sea or on
land, on my pillow, in my garden, on my horse, or
on my feet, was spent in thinking of the means
necessary, when the danger should have become
clear to all eyes, to the rescuing of England from
the natural and inevitable consequences of all-
corrupting, all-enfeebling, all-degrading curse of
paper money.

The measures I proposed, subverted nothing
that was acknowledged by the laws and constitution of England; tended not to pull down, but
to uphold, the government of King, Lords, and
Commons; took away no lawful privilege or im-
munity; tended to destroy no lawful establish-
ment; and they would have restored a fixedness
as to property, and that harmony and good will
between the rich and the poor, which had so long
been banished from the land.

It, however, pleased God to [give me] numerous
faithful friends and adherents, and constantly to
give me that which was, perhaps, the best sort of
vengeance, namely, a constant fulfillment of my
predictions, and most severe punishments inflicted upon those who despised those predictions.
I had that species of vengeance, which truth always, at last, gains over falsehood.

[One of my adherents was Sir Thomas Beevor,

of Hargham Hall in Norfolk. He published the opinion that]⁴ "with regard to the present calamity, nothing was so likely to effect the purposes (of preventing the ruin that must fall upon trade, manufactures, and commerce) as the placing of Mr Cobbett in the Common's House of Parliament"; [and to this end he collected the necessary funds. For the attempt,] I hesitated some time between Westminster and Preston; yet when I think of the excellent people of the North, I can feel sorrow at nothing that tended to take me into their country. I went to the North a total stranger as to person. I had no friends. Yet, on my first entrance into Preston, I was met and accompanied by, at least, ten thousand people, and was received with marks of attention and respect surpassing those ever shown to any other man.

[The election failed, and] calumniators of mine began to comfort themselves with the thought that I was a "Poor Old Man"; and that I could not possibly last long. It was an "old man", recollect, who could travel five hundred miles, make speeches of half an hour long twice a day for a month; put down the saucy, the rich, the tyrannical; that could be jostled out of his majority at an election; and that could return towards his home through forty miles of huzzas from the lips of a hundred and fifty thousand people.

What of those landed gentlemen, who admired, who applauded the spirit of Sir Thomas Beevor, and yet were not found at his back? We are to

think not that they were corrupt, but we are to
think of them as of men trammelled by an accursed system, that took from the mind every
spark of conscious dignity, and that made him
that should have been the lord truckle to him that
should have been the lackey. It was impossible
to look, without indignation, at the group who
wielded the destinies of England; who, amidst a
mass of blunders that covered a country with
misery, sat, perked up like schoolmasters and
their ushers, while the owners of the soil, the
natural magistrates of the country, the guardians
of its happiness and its honour, stood before them
like a set of schoolboys, silently listening to their
pompous imbecility, and patiently waiting for
their fate at their hands.

[During these years, I made, at Kensington,]
a nursery ground, which had been, for the greater
part, a rough and sour meadow in 1823. [By
1827,] on about four acres of land, disposed in
about four hundred and fifty beds, there stood,
more than a million of seedling forest trees, and
shrubs, and about three thousand young apple
trees. Yet, as if this place were insufficient to
provide occupation for my leisure hours, I had
another nursery ground on the Surrey side of the
Thames, which also was a walled-in plot. There,
I made experiments. There, too, I was as safe
from the world as a monk of Latrappe. I positively shut all out, except the gardeners and one
gardener's wife, who kept the key of the door. I

1825
to
1830

did this, not for the sake of secrecy; but because I would be certain of being uninterrupted when I was in that place. [I got in time] at Barn Elm, a farm of nearly a hundred acres, the richest land I believe in this whole world, except those marshes which bring diseases along with their riches. My farm was taken care of by my only surviving brother, who had been either gardener or farmer all his life time. He, from the fruit of his own labour, raised a family of ten able children, who brought him a score of grandchildren.

I never could go out "to take a walk" in the whole course of my life; nor to take a ride: there had to be something to make me take either one or the other, and, though it would be pretty difficult to make me lie abed late in the morning, without actually tying me down with ropes, I might, I daresay, have degenerated in time into that disgraceful thing called a sluggard, if I [had not had my work] to call me out into the gardens or the fields.

I derived the greatest of pleasures from the reflection, that I caused millions of trees and shrubs to be planted in England, that would never have been planted in England, for ages yet to come, had it not been for me. [Years later, when in Scotland, I saw in an orchard] some American [apple] trees, sent by me, which were beginning to bear. "Cast your bread upon the waters", says the precept, "and have patience to wait to see it return." I had sent from England to Long Island

[for] some cuttings of apple trees; they had come 1825
to me at Kensington; Mr M'Gavin, at Hamilton *to*
(four hundred miles from Kensington), had got 1830
some of the cuttings after they came from Long
Island; he had put some of them upon some of the
branches of his trees: and he showed me a bough
which had proceeded from this cutting, from which
he had gathered forty pounds weight of fine apples !
What a deal I did in my lifetime to produce real
and solid good to my country ! and how different
was the tendency of my pursuits to that of the
pursuits of the noisy, canting, jawing, popularity-
hunting, newspaper-puffing fellows !

[In June, 1829, I began to publish my famous
"Advice to Young Men".] The work was intended
to contain twelve Numbers, and the price of each
Number was Sixpence. So that, for six shillings,
expended in one year of his life, any youth or
young man might acquire that knowledge, which
would enable him to pass the rest of his life with
as little as possible of those troubles and incon-
veniences which arise from want of being warned
of danger in time. At any rate, I, who had passed
safely through as many dangers as any man that
ever lived, gave my young countrymen the means
of acquiring all the knowledge which my experience had given me.

[As the agitation for Reform began to grow
again, I began to lecture, first in London, and then
about the country.]⁵ I gave above one hundred
and fifty in number, one or more in every con-

1825
to
1830

siderable town in twenty-one of the counties of England, during two journeys of about three thousand miles, and all between December 1829 and July 1830. If you could have heard one of these, you could not wonder that the nation was roused, that all spoke as one man, and that we now have that Reform which the nation owes to those lectures more than to all other causes put together. I cannot lay down my pen here without expressing my gratitude to the public who gave me their countenance at the first lecture [in London]. The assembly was, in numbers and of a character, so far beyond my expectation, that, for the first time in my life I felt my voice falter; for which, however, I was not sorry; for it would have been a shame indeed, if, under the then circumstances, I had discovered a want of sensibility. I had only just arrived from Barn Elm; I had no idea of meeting more than three or four hundred friends; and, therefore, when all of a sudden, I found myself before such an audience, the twenty years of calumnies on me, my long and cruel persecutions, the merciless and degrading and ruinous imprisonment, the exile, the bonds, my sufferings of all sorts, only for inculcating the very principles which I was then about to enforce, all these rushed into my mind in a moment; and seeing in this audience my just countrymen assembled, to wipe away the thousands of indignities that had been heaped upon me, I was overpowered with feelings of joy, of just pride, and of gratitude.

CHAPTER XIV

1830–1834

*   *   *   *   *

[BY THE YEAR 1830,] AS THE WORKING 1830
people went on getting poorer and poorer, they *to*
became more and more immoral, in innumerable 1834
instances men committed crimes for the purpose
of getting into jail; because the felons in jail were
better fed and better clad than the honest working
people. As the working people became poor, the
laws relating to them were made more and more
severe; and the Poor-Law, that famous law of
Elizabeth, which was the greatest glory of England for ages, had by degrees been so much muti-
lated and nullified, that, at last, it was so far from
being a protection for the working people, that it
had, by its perversions, been made the means of
reducing them to a state of wretchedness not to
be described. The sole food of the greater part of
them had been, for many years, bread, or potatoes, and not half enough of these. They had eaten
sheep or cattle that had died from illness; children
had been seen stealing food out of hog-troughs;
men were found dead, [in] May [of that] year,
lying under a hedge, and when opened by the
surgeons nothing but sour sorrel was found in
their stomachs. The spot on which these poor

creatures expired was surrounded with villas of
Jews, and fund-jobbers, living in luxury, and in
the midst of pleasure-gardens, all the means of
which living they had derived from the burdens
laid on the working people.

Besides suffering from want, the working people
were made to endure insults and indignities such
as even Negroes were never exposed to. They were
harnessed like horses or asses and made to draw
carts and wagons; they were shut up in pounds
made to hold stray cattle; they were made to
work with bells round their necks; and they had
drivers set over them, just as if they had been
galley slaves; they were sold by auction for certain
times, as the Negroes were sold in the West Indies;
the married men were kept separated from their
wives, by force, to prevent them from breeding;
and, in short, no human beings were ever before
treated so unjustly, with so much insolence, and
with such damnable barbarity, as the working
people of England had been. Such were the fruits
of public debts and funds! Without them, this industrious and moral and brave nation never could
have been brought into this degraded state.

[For some years,] I had seen the cause of Reform fast gaining ground; but, it was not until
the month of October, 1830, when the chopsticks
set about the work, that I really expected it to
come in any reasonable time. Every event must
have a beginning; and the greatest events have
frequently had their beginnings in trifling causes.

I had often used to tell [my] friends, in Long Is- **1830**
land and at New York, that no change would ever *to*
take place, unless it were begun amongst the **1834**
hedgers and ditchers and the ploughmen and the
thrashers; how often had I told them that people
were not formidable when assembled together in
great towns. What, then, was it not the meetings
and petitions of the great towns that produced
Parliamentary Reform? They did good, particularly by the speeches they brought forth, but, the
great and efficient cause was, the movements of
the chopsticks. I had had my eye upon all the
movements of the great bodies. I had, in the two
preceding years, been about lecturing in person
over the far greater part of England; [but, until
I found] the working people in almost all of the
counties of England in a state of commotion [my
hopes did not grow fixed].

All across the South, from Kent to Cornwall,
and from Sussex to Lincolnshire, the commotion
extended. It began by the labourers in Kent
entering the buildings of the great farmers and
breaking their thrashing machines; for, please to
observe, one effect of heavy taxation was the invention of machinery. The farmer or manufacturer
was so pressed for money by the government, that
he resorted to all possible means of saving the
expense of labour; and as machines would work
cheaper than men, the machines were preferred.
The labourers saw, at any rate, that the thrashing
machines robbed them of the wages that they

1830
to
1834

should have received. They, therefore, began by demolishing these machines. This was a crime; the magistrates and jailers were ready with punishments; soldiers, well fed and well clothed out of the taxes, were ready to shoot or cut down the offenders. Unable to resist these united forces, the labourers resorted to the use *of fire*, secretly put to the barns and stacks of those who had the machines, or whom they deemed the cause of their poverty and misery. The mischief and alarm that they caused by this means were beyond all calculation. They went in bands of from 100 to 1000, and summoned the farmers to come forth, and then they demanded that they should agree to pay them such wages as they thought right.

The farmers, in their defence, said that they could not pay the wages, that were demanded, because they had so much to pay in rent, taxes, and in tithes. The labourers, therefore, in many instances, went to the parsons; and in one parish, in Sussex, they ordered the collector of the taxes not to take the money out of the parish, as it was, they said, wanted there. These proceedings would have been put an end to had it not been for the fires. The military forces, backed by all the great farmers, the land-owners, and especially the parsons, would have subdued these half-starved machine-breakers; but the Fires! No power on earth could have prevented them, if the millions of labourers resolved to resort to them.

The fires, after spreading westward along the

county of Kent, soon stretched through Sussex, **1830**
and thence through Hampshire, Wiltshire, Dor- *to*
setshire, Berkshire, and all the most fertile corn- **1834**
growing counties. A Special Commission, sent
into the West and Southwest, transported about
four hundred men, and left a fearful number for
execution. This mass of punishment did not,
however, destroy the effects of these risings of the
labourers. The trials, the publications making
observations of the trials, the endless discussions,
in all shapes and sizes, relative to the poor-laws;
and, I may say, my "Protestant Reformation"
and "Poor Man's Friend", made the *Swing* men,
these thrashers, hedgers, ditchers, plough-men,
mowers, and reapers understand [a great deal].

Such was the state of England. Here you saw
a people, inhabiting the most productive land in
the world, a people to whom God had given a
large portion of all his choicest blessings, safety
from foreign foes, climate, soil, mines, woods,
downs, flocks and herds, and, above all, *industry*
perfectly unparalleled; a people, too, whose forefathers gave them the best laws that ever existed
in the world; here you saw this people, who were
famed for their willing obedience to the laws, and
whose forefathers had scorned the thought of maintaining even a single soldier except in case of war;
here you saw this people, whose laws said that no
man should be taxed without his own consent;
first reduced to a state of half-starvation; next
setting the laws at defiance; and then attacked by

1830
to
1834

a standing army sent against them to capture them and put them in prison. Such were the effects of heavy taxes, and particularly when raised for the purpose of upholding a funding system, which was a system of usury and monopoly added to that of grinding taxation.

[I was accused by the Government of being engaged in inciting these labourers in their work of destruction, and I was indicted by the Whigs.] According to our laws and usages, a man by whom a woman is in a family way is, in certain cases, compelled to marry her, and then he is said to be led to the church by a halter. Yet he, when in the church, promises and vows that he will love and cherish the bride to the end of their days! Just such a marriage took place between the Whig-Ministry and Reform; I had very kindly, [by my activities], furnished the halter for the happy occasion: and they showed their gratitude by this prosecution.

When the news of the indictment was brought to my house in Bolt Court, by a reporter of "The Star" newspaper, about eight o'clock in the evening, and when the servant came up and told me of it, after I was in bed, I prayed to God to protect me, turned myself round, and fell fast asleep. The next morning I went home to Kensington, and set down with my family whom I found at breakfast; the whole group heard my resolution with delight. They had made up their minds to the same thing before my arrival. Not a tear, not a sigh, not a sorrowful look did this dreadful menace produce, if I except one little mark of anxiety which discovered itself in my wife on the morning of the trial. She had got me a pair of new silk stockings to wear on that day; and when I put them on, I found them too short, and spoke rather hastily about it, whereupon she made a little bit of a cry. As to my two sons John and James, it would have been worth years of imprisonment to witness their conduct. They instantly set to work to prepare the defence, as soon as we found that the Whigs were in real earnest; my son John undertook the preparing my case, assisted by his brother in the evenings, the latter being engaged in the daytime with his master in town.

On the day of my trial,[1] [the 7th of July 1831], I, having had seven hours sound, unbroken sleep, got up at four o'clock, went into the garden and gave instructions for the day, came off for Bolt Court at six, arrived there [and] found breakfast ready for me and a good many friends; and now, mind, ate about half a pound of good fat leg of mutton, roasted the day before, ate no bread or anything else with it, and no salt, and never drank one drop of anything that whole day until after the conclusion of my speech, when I drank two stone bottles of milk, out of a horn, given me [the] summer [before] by a pretty little American lady, the wife of Mr Cooke, the portrait painter.

When I went into the Court, which was about ten minutes before the Judge entered it, I found

The Progress of a Plough-boy

the whole of the Court crowded in every part, so
as to find great difficulty in getting in; and indeed,
a body of doorkeepers made a desperate effort to
keep out my three sons and three other gentlemen
who accompanied me. The moment I entered,
there was a great and general clapping and cheering for some time. When I got to my station I, in
order to produce silence, turned round, and, addressing myself to the audience, said, "Be patient,
gentlemen, for, if truth prevail, we shall beat
them". Soon after this the Chief-Justice entered
the court and took his seat. Soon after him, came
in the Attorney-General; and he, in opening his
address to the Jury, told them that I had come
into court with a great mob at my heels; and, that
a shouting had taken place, which showed the
spirit in which the defence was to be conducted.
This was an abominable falsehood. I had come
from Kensington in a close-carriage, hired at
Kensington. At Bolt Court I had taken into the
carriage Sir Thomas Beevor, Mr Palmer, Mr
Blount, and my attorney, Mr Edward Faithful,
of Staple's Inn, and one of my sons rode on the
box with the coachman.

I had forced the [Whig Ministers] to come by
subpoena; and I intended to question them every
one, if the Judge permitted me, with regard to the
grounds on which they had advised his Majesty
[to proceed in the agricultural commotion]. For
this purpose, I brought together, to sit upon the
bench in front of me, Lords Grey, Brougham,

Melbourne, Durham, Goderich, and Palmerston. **1830** There they sat, ranged in a row, to hear my de- *to* fence; and there sat between two and three thou- **1834** sand intelligent men to witness the scene. From every county in England, I believe, some one man or more was present. Well might I say that it was a day of joy to me! it was a reward going ten thousand times beyond all that I had ever merited.

[The cry for Reform reached its loudest at this time. Its history and its success are now well known. I might say, that] if the Lords had been wise [then, and were wise now], they would see, that their danger arises from the very class that sets up an outcry against the Radicals. The further men are removed from them, the less envy they have of them; that it was not the artisan and the labourer that looked with an eye of envy on the Lord's town-house, and on his country-mansion and park; but the money-monger in the town, and the great swelled-up bull-frog farmer in the country. I have known for many years, and have been a strict observer of all classes of men in this country; and I never heard amongst common tradesmen, little farmers, artisans or labourers, anything indicating a wish to see the nobility pulled down; but, amongst those; amongst the *parvenus*, as the French call them, I have seen one portion aiming at getting to the height of the nobility, and have seen those who despair of ever doing that, always trying to pull them down. The

1830
to
1834

Liberals, or those that the French call *Doctrinaires*, a race, whom I hate (oh, God, how I hate them!) were always talking in the same strain; one of their sayings being, "that men are not born legislators". Why to be sure they are not: but that is not the question: the question is, whether [our institutions] be, taking the defects along with the advantages, for the good of the people amongst whom they exist?

The working people, the common tradesmen, and the farmers, had, [and have,] none of the envies that bother the brains of this monied tribe: the change that they wanted was a change from bad living to good living: a single thought about the change of the constituent parts of the state, never, even by accident, came athwart their minds: they took the country as they found it; and if they had had the means of leading those happy lives, to which their virtues and their industry entitled them, I would have defied all the *feelosofers* and *liberals* that the devil ever sent upon the earth, to have persuaded them that there ought not to be Lords, or that there ought to be any change at all in the government.

So early as June, 1803, I had begun to predict that this nation must be brought to ruin, if [the] system of squandering were persevered in. I was actuated by no party or factious motives: I never was; and am not now, any more than I was then. I never in my life did that which ought to offend any nobleman or person in authority, unless I had been ill-treated by that person. I never showed any mark of disrespect to any person of rank or station. I never was amongst those who ridiculed titles of nobility; not that I thought persons in that station wiser or better than men in general; but because long experience had shown to this nation, that the greatest degree of freedom and of happiness, of which communities were capable, had been enjoyed, and for centuries too, under a government, in which hereditary honours and hereditary rights had formed so large a part.

I had had too much opportunity of studying men and things to be led astray by any wild theories about liberty. I knew, that there must be a government, and that there must be law, without which there could be no such thing as property, nor any safety even for our own persons. I wanted to see no innovation in England. All I wished and all I strove for, was the Constitution of England, undefiled by corruption.

It had always been my wish, that the institutions of England and her fundamental laws should remain unchanged. There was so much of good in the institutions which we had inherited from our fathers, that I always looked at any change in them with great apprehension. But, with regard to the *innovations* in these institutions; with regard to the monstrous encroachments of the aristocracy and the usurers, within the last fifty years especially, it was impossible for me not to wish for a change. It was impossible for me to

17-2

1830
to
1834
look at the new treason laws, new felony laws, Bourbon-police laws, laws violating the compact between the people and the clergy, new and multiplied laws hostile to the freedom of the press, hundreds of acts of parliament, subjecting men's persons and property to be disposed of, to a certain extent, without trial by jury; the monstrous partiality in taxation; a standing army in time of peace, greater than was ever before needed in time of war; new crimes in abundance, created by act of Parliament; new punishments for old crimes; employment of spies justified in the Houses of Parliament; or, at least, no punishment inflicted on anyone for being a spy, or for having employed spies.

It was impossible for me to behold these things, and not exert myself in an endeavour to put a stop to these encroachments, and to bring my country back to something like the government that had existed when I was born. I was in hopes that the "Reformed Parliament" would, at once, set to work to sweep away these innovations. [As events turned out], not only did it not do this, but it set itself to work to add to them in number, and to enlarge those that already existed.

[Near the end of 1832, I visited the North and Scotland, and was] upon the most interesting [spots] of earth that I ever set foot upon in the course of my long and rambling life. It is hard to say which part of [England] is the most valuable gift of God; but everyone must see how perverse

and injurious it is to endeavour to produce in the
one that which nature has intended to confine to
the other. [In the North, there were] unnatural
efforts made to ape the farming of Norfolk and
Suffolk; it was only playing at farming, as stupid
and "loyal" parents used to set their children to
play at soldiers during the last war. It was a most
lamentable thing that the paper-money price of
corn tempted so many men to break up [their]
fine pastures; the turf thus destroyed could not
be restored, probably in a whole century; the land
did not yield a clear profit, anything like what
it would have yielded as pasture; and thus was
destroyed the goose with the golden eggs. The
accursed paper money caused even the fruitful
qualities of the earth to be anticipated, and thus
was the soil made worth less than it was before
the accursed invention appeared !

[In Scotland, it was] very fine: cornfields,
woods, pastures, villages; a church every four
miles, or thereabouts; cows and sheep beautiful;
oak trees, though none very large; and, in short,
a fertile and beautiful country, wanting only the
gardens and vine-covered cottages that so beautify
the South and West. All the buildings were of
stone. Here were coal-works and railways every
now and then. The farms were all large; and the
people who worked on them either lived in the
farm-house, or in the buildings appertaining to
the farm-house; and they were well fed, and had
no temptation to acts like those which sprang up

1830
to
1834

out of the ill-treatment of the labourers in the South. Such stack-yards, and such a total absence of dwelling-houses, as never were before seen in any country. You very frequently saw more than a hundred stacks in one yard; all built in the neatest manner; thatched extremely well, the thatch bound down by exterior bands, spars not being in use owing to the scarcity of wood. In some of these yards the thrashing machine was worked by horses, but in the greater part by steam; and where the coals were at a distance, by wind and water; so that in this country of the finest land that ever was seen, all the elements seemed to have been pressed into the amiable service of sweeping the people from the face of the earth, in order that the whole amount of the produce might go into the hands of a small number of persons, that they might squander it at London, at Paris, or at Rome. A man who had lived here all his lifetime, could form no judgement at all with regard to the situation, the wants, and the treatment of the working people in the counties of the South. Yet Scott Eldon and Dr Black used to prate away about the poor-rates not being excessive in the North. A man who had been paid as a statesman for pretty nearly fifty years, and another who had been a professed enlightener of the people for twenty years, ought to have known that there was no such thing as a village purely agricultural to the north of Leeds, while the southern, eastern, and western counties consisted

of very little else. Such men ought to have known
this; but they did not know it, therefore, they
spread about error.

[I was shown much of manufacturing during my journey.] I never liked to see machines, lest I should be tempted to endeavour to understand them. I constantly resisted all the natural desire which people had to explain them to me. As in the case of the sun and the moon and the stars, I was quite satisfied with witnessing the effects. [These] things afforded nothing interesting to me, who thought a great deal more about the condition of the people, than I did about the cause of the movement, or about the mechanical effects of the machines.

Being at New Lanark, however, I was rather curious to know whether there was any reality in what we had heard about the effects of the Owen "feelosofy". The building which Owen had erected was used as a schoolroom; and here I saw boys in one place and girls in another, carrying on what was called "education". There was one boy pointing with a stick to something stuck up upon the wall, and then all the rest of the boys bawling out what that was. In one large room they were all singing out something at the word of command. In another great apartment there were eighteen boys and eighteen girls, the boys dressed in Highland dresses, without shoes on, naked from three inches above the knee, down to the foot, a tartan plaid close round the body, in their shirt

1830
to
1834
sleeves, each having a girl by the arm, duly pro-
portioned in point of size, the girls without caps,
and without shoes and stockings; and there were
these eighteen couples marching, arm in arm, in
regular files, slow march, to the sound of a fiddle,
which a fellow, big enough to carry a quarter of
wheat, was playing in a corner of the room. They
seemed to perform with great regularity and ele-
gance; and, it was quite impossible to see the half-
naked lads and girls, without clearly perceiving
the manifest tendency of this mode of education,
to prevent "premature marriage", and to "check
population".

It was difficult to determine, whether, when
people were huddled together in this unnatural
state, this sort of soldier-ship discipline might or
might not be necessary to effect the purposes of
schooling; but I thought it a very strange thing,
if a man, calculated to produce effect from his
learning, could ever come to perfection from a
beginning like this. It was altogether a thing that
I abhorred. I do not say that it might not be
useful when people were thus unnaturally congregated; and, above all things, I was not disposed
to bestow censure on the motives of the parties
promoting this mode of education; for the sacrifices which they made, in order to give success to
their schemes, clearly proved that their motives
were benevolent; but I was not the less convinced
that it was a melancholy thing to behold; that it
was the reverse of domestic life, that it reversed

the order of nature, that it made minds a fiction; and, which was among the greatest of its evils, it fashioned the rising generations to habits of implicit submission. However, the consolation was, that it was impossible that it ever should become anything like general in any nation. The order of the world demands that nine-tenths of the people should be employed on, and in the affairs of the land; being so employed, they must be scattered about widely: and there must be homes and domestic life for the far greater part of the rising generation. When men contract a fondness for anything which has a great deal of novelty and of strangeness in it; when they brood over the contemplation of some wonderful discovery which they think they have made; when they suffer it long to absorb all the powers of their minds; they really become mad, as far as relates to the matter which has thus absorbed all their mental faculties; and they think themselves more wise than all the rest of mankind.

[I do not say], that there should be no schools! Oh, no! Schools are very proper things in many cases: in large cities and towns they are very necessary for many reasons. But, because it is indeniably true, that there are many professions and pursuits in life, which require book-learning; because it is equally true that book-learning is very frequently not to be acquired without schools, does it follow, that all boys and girls, nine-tenths of whom must live by manual labour, or become thieves and strumpets, are to be crammed up in schools, instead of being employed from their infancy in those little labours and cares which make them valuable when they grow up to be men and women? But, "they can go to school before they are old enough to work". [Some time] ago, I had a string of diggers at work in a field at Barn Elm. In this string an awkward big boy from the country happened to have his station cast between two gardeners of Felham, the name of one of whom was John Ives. The young chap, though very tall, was only about sixteen; and though he would have beaten Ives at plough, there he was with both his feet close up·to the trench, toiling and sweating, while Ives and his companion were going on, leaving him upon a narrow causeway, and laughing to themselves all the while. "Come", said I, "Ives, why don't you show that young fellow how to dig? You were young yourself once, recollect." "Aye, Sir", said he, "and *very* young, too, when I did not know how to dig." [I do not know] how soon the doctrinaires would take them from school and put them to work; but I do know, that I myself was at work in the fields before I was six. And this was "education", properly so called. Education means *rearing-up*, not teaching to read and write. He is a learned man, who has great knowledge in his profession or calling; and not he who can read about the knowledge of others.

Why, I, who wrote the Grammar, was a plough-boy myself, and a real and good and true plough-

boy, too, and so early was I such, that I was
compelled to get up upon a gate, to put the bit-
halter upon a cart-horse's head. And, observe,
never did I acknowledge schoolmaster to be my
master; and long after I could mow short grass
in the Bishop of Winchester's garden, I could no
more have read this paragraph and understood
the sense of it, than I could have driven the Bishop
out of his palace.

Being a plough-boy and having had resort to
grammars to teach myself, when I took a fancy
to book-learning; having experienced the want
of a grammar at once simple and profound, I
wrote one myself for the use of other plough-boys,
and to commemorate my attachment to that class
of society, amongst whom I was born, and to live
and die amongst whom impediments raised up by
hell itself shall not prevent me.

On my own personal account, I set not the
value of a straw upon a seat in Parliament. I had,
for a long while, wished to be in the Common's
House; but never for the sake of any advantage
or personal pleasure of my own. From a very early
age, I had imbibed the opinion, that it was every
man's duty to do all that lay in his power to leave
his country as good as he had found it. I knew
that my country presented a scene of wretchedness and disgrace, compared with the scene it had
presented at the time that I was born. I hated
the life of the great cities: I hated their everlasting
noise and bustle: my taste, all my own personal

1830
to
1834

enjoyments would have led me far away from them for ever. I could, if I had been so minded, have secured out of my own earnings, much greater possessions and in a state of tranquillity, much greater than I ever had a desire to be master of. But, feeling that I possessed the mind to enable me to assist in restoring my country to the state in which I found it, a sense of duty to that country restrained me from consulting my own ease and my own private enjoyments. Nothing [other than duty] could have induced me to sit by candle light. It was impossible that an assembly keeping such hours, even if it consisted of wise and upright men, could produce good works. All the world knows, that the morning is the time for all matters of importance; that the mind is then serene, if it ever be; that it is then unclouded by heavy food and muddling drink; that it is then, if ever, fit to be employed in the making of laws; that is to say, in the performance of things affecting the happiness of millions.

The invitation to become a candidate [for Parliament] came first from Manchester. The people of Oldham, about eight miles distant from Manchester, knowing how difficult it would be to carry an election for Manchester, by mere voluntary support, came to the resolution to secure my return for Oldham, which, though inferior to Manchester, in point of population, was still a very large and opulent town. Had the invitation come first from Oldham, I should certainly have de-

clined that from Manchester, because my object
was not to disturb any place, but to take the seat
with as much quietness as possible.

I was at the opening of the elections at Manchester; where, having obtained an immense
majority upon the *view*; having obtained the
decision of the public at Manchester; having,
upon these hustings, seen hooted off that very
Mr Sharpe, who was the boroughreeve that forbade me to enter Manchester on my return from
America in 1819; having done this, I went off to
Oldham, there to remain until I should come back
to Manchester a member of Parliament. The election at Manchester was, doubtless, greatly in-
fluenced by the election at Oldham, which was
known at the former place by twelve o'clock of
the first polling-day. So that, after that it was
naturally to be expected that the electors of
Manchester who had intended to vote for me,
would either transfer their votes, or that they
would not vote at all. Yet, in spite of this, the
state of the poll, at its close, was as follows:

Phillips ...	2923
Thompson	2069
Loyd ...	1823
Hope ...	1560
Cobbett ...	1305

This result was sufficiently honourable to me. Not
one single pint of beer, or glass of gin, had been
given to any human being on my part; no at-

1830
to
1834

torney, and no attorney's clerk had been employed, and not a single person hired, I believe, to do any one thing connected with my election. All, except the mere printing, and the hire of a few carriages, was the effect of voluntary exertion, chiefly by young men in the middle rank of life, whose zeal and activity I never can sufficiently applaud.

So much for the election at Manchester. [At Oldham] the polling was over on the 13th [of December], when the numbers stood as follows:

Fielden	...	670
Cobbett	...	642
Bright	...	153
Burge	...	101
Stephen	...	3

At this election not one single farthing's worth of victuals or drink was given to anybody, for any services whatsoever. The committee, composed of sensible and sober manufacturers and tradesmen, paid for the printing that they had done, and paid all the expenses of the hustings, polling-places, clerks, etc. They paid also for the entertainment of the candidates at the hotel: and even the carriages to and from Manchester that I went in, I found paid for; and not a man nor woman in this excellent town, attempted to obtain from [me] either money, drink, or any promise to do anything for them in their private concerns. This was *purity of election* indeed. It was an honour, indeed,

to represent a people like this. Neither [Mr Fielden
nor myself] ever canvassed in any shape or form,
either individually or collectively; neither of us
ever asked the people to give us a vote; but we
contented ourselves with saying, that, if they
chose us to represent them, we would be their true
representatives to the best of our power.

Of one thing we were both of us particularly
proud; and that was, that the people had the good
sense; that sense of their own worth and our rights,
as to scorn to attempt to *chair* us, or to drag us
through the streets. In my address to them, I be-
sought them not to think of imitating the slaves
of the borough-mongers. "Now", said I, "my
friends, I shall come down from the hustings, and
the first handloom weaver I meet with, I shall
take by the arm and walk with him up to the hotel
from which I came." I did this, Mr Fielden did
the same; and thus, in this appropriate manner,
we closed this election, which should be an example to every borough and every county in the
kingdom. Not a disturbance of any sort; not a
blow given in anger; scarcely an abusive word
from one person to another; not a single drunken
man to be seen about the streets; much singing,
much playing music, much joy, much triumph;
but all was peace and decorum, from the beginning to the end. As a mark of victory over the
combined malignity of factions, I set a very high
value upon this seat in Parliament. But I set a
higher value upon it, as vindicating the character

1830
to
1834

of the Commons, or common people of England. I always stood firmly up in defence, not only of the rights, but of the character of the common people, who, of late years, were looked upon by both the political factions, and by all the hordes that lived upon the taxes, as not being of the same flesh and blood with themselves.

[As I have said before,] I was in hope that the "Reformed Parliament" would set itself to work to sweep away innovations [and encroachments]. [Lord Grey could have proceeded] at once to make great changes. I do not say have proceeded to make them in a hurry; but, to have shown an intention to make them. He was sure that he would have the people at his back. He could have done what he liked for the people, who now knew the extent of their power. For many, many years they had not known it. They were patient, they were not unreasonable; they were full of knowledge; they desired to overthrow nothing that ought to have remained; to assert of them, that they sought anarchy and a scramble, was the most atrocious slander that ever was uttered by mortal man. There never was a working people in the whole world, so reasonable, so just, and so easily satisfied. These were the materials with which Lord Grey had to work; [and worse than nothing was done, for the new Poor-Law was passed]. Having got parliamentary reform, in name, at any rate, my resentment was becoming blunted. But, the Poor-Law Bill I could not

stomach! That revived all that was dying in my 1830
breast. I had no direct power; but I had great *to*
indirect power; and that I used to the utmost 1834
of that capacity which it pleased God to give
me, always remembering His promise to be
the protector of him "who considereth the
poor".

[I wrote much,] the object of which was to induce [the labourers] resolutely to maintain the
rights which, agreeably to the laws of our country,
we all had inherited from our forefathers. Amongst
these rights was, the right to live in the country
of our birth; the right to have a living out of the
land of our birth in exchange for our labour duly
and honestly performed; the right, in case we fell
into distress, to have our wants sufficiently relieved out of the produce of the land, whether that
distress arose from sickness, from decrepitude,
from old age, or from inability to find employment; because there were laws, and those laws
were just, to punish us if we were idle or dissolute.
For a thousand years, necessity was relieved out
of the produce of the Tithes. When the Tithes
were taken away by the aristocracy, and by them
kept to themselves, or given wholly to the parsons,
provision was made out of the land, as compensation for what had been taken away. That compensation was given in the rates as settled by the
poor-law. The taking away those rates [by the
new poor-law] was to violate the agreement,
which gave as much right to receive, in case of

need, relief out of the land, as it left the land-owner a right to his rent.

[It was easy, after this, to see] in what the present Lords differed from the Lords of former times. In everything; except in the shape of their bodies. It had been the business of the Lords, each one to protect his people from wrong; to see that they had fair play; they were their advocates in courts of justice. The bishops and abbots were in Parliament to take care that the the poor were not plundered out of their patrimony; and thus nobility was "the cheap defence of the realm". What do we behold now? a prodigious band of spungers, living upon the labour of the industrious part of the community.

For many years there existed a fashion of looking upon the working people, and particularly the labourers in husbandry, as an inferior race of human beings, and of treating them as such. [It still goes on.] They are the contrary of this; they are the superior race, and they have always been so; they are content as to their station in life; they are unpresuming; they are honest; they are sincere; and he who says the contrary is a base and infamous slanderer. It has been among the greatest delights of my life to see them happy, and amongst my most ardent desires to contribute to that happiness. I have admired their character and their conduct ever since I was able to estimate them; and I would willingly strike dead at my feet the insolent brutes who speak contemptuously of them.

I was born and bred a farmer, or a sort of **1830** labourer; and I have never desired to have any *to* rank, station, or name, or calling, more and other **1834** than that of a farmer. [Everyone had known] that I wanted nothing for myself, but they knew that I wanted to take [away] the power of oppressing and pillaging the order to which I belonged; admire my industry, my perseverance, my wonderful exertions; but there was at the bottom, to balance against all these, my strong and implacable hatred of oppression of all sorts; and particularly the partiality of taxation; the stripping of the working people of their earnings, and the heaping of these earnings upon idlers. This has been the constant ground of hostility to me; and I must say, that I trust in God that I shall so conduct myself as to cause the hostility to continue until the last hour of my life.

CHAPTER XV

1835

*　　*　　*　　*　　*

1835 THE STATE OF MY HEALTH [NOW] IS THIS:
[a] cough reduces me pretty nearly to hoarseness,
[and it] will not quit me until the wind shift from
the east to the west and the south-west. The experience of fifty years assures me this. When I was
young and cared less about the matter, I was
hoarse, and it did not signify whether I was or not.
I beat my way through it, and had more strength
in proportion, to bear up against the attack. It is
a curious thing; it has nothing at all to do with the
lungs; never affects the breast; its great symptom
is, and I know nothing else about it, that there is
a tickling in the throat, just below the chin, producing a very constant inclination to cough. It
was just the same in New Brunswick; just the
same in Pennsylvania; just the same in Long
Island. I have very seldom missed it in any year;
but I should have missed it now, if I and my
secretary had not been so busy, as not to attend to
the circumstance that the careless wench had been
heaping on coals in an American fireplace, till we
were both pretty nearly suffocated. I cannot go
to sleep for fear that the cough will come. I dare
not go out of doors, though I want to be out from

morning till night. However, I have been able 1835
to-day to think about dining upon a sucking pig
on Sunday next; and to think about it without
loathing. [And now I must go on.]

To communicate to others the knowledge that
I possess has always been my taste and my delight; and few will be disposed to question my
fitness for the task. Talk of rocks and breakers and
quagmires and quicksands, who has ever escaped
from amidst so many as I have! Thrown (by my
own will indeed) on the wide world at a very early
age, without money to support, without friends to
advise, and without book-learning to assist me;
passing a few years dependent solely on my own
labour for subsistence; then becoming a common
soldier, and leading a military life, chiefly in foreign
parts, for eight years; quitting that life after really,
for me, high promotion, and with, for me, a large
sum of money; marrying at an early age, going at
once to France to acquire the French language,
then to America; passing eight years there, becoming bookseller and author, and taking a pro-
minent part in all the important discussions of the
interesting period from 1793 to 1799, during which
there was, in that country, a continued struggle
between the English and French parties; conducting myself, in the ever-active part which I took in
that struggle, in such a way as to call forth marks
of unequivocal approbation from the government
at home; returning to England in 1800, resuming
my labours here, suffering two years' imprison-

The Progress of a Plough-boy

1835 ment, heavy fines, three years' self-banishment to
the other side of the Atlantic, and a total breaking
of fortune, so as to be left without a bed to lie on,
and, during these years of troubles and punishments, writing and publishing every week of my
life, whether in exile or not, eleven weeks only
excepted, a periodical paper, containing more or
less matter worthy of public attention.

Writing and publishing during the same years,
a grammar of the French and another of the
English language, a work on the "Economy of the
Cottage", a work on "Forest Trees and Woodlands", a work on "Gardening", "An Account of
America", a book of "Sermons", a work on the
"Corn-Plant", a "History of the Protestant Reformation"; all books of great and continued sale,
and the last unquestionably the book of greatest
circulation in the whole world, the Bible only
excepted.

During these same years of troubles and embarrassments without number, [I] introduced into
England the manufacture of straw-plat; also
several valuable trees; the cultivation of the corn-
plant, so manifestly valuable as a source of food;
and always (whether in exile or not) sustained a
shop of some size in London; and during these
years, bred up a family of seven children to man's
and woman's estate.

Not all the genius in the world could, without
something more, have conducted me through these
perils. There must be something more than genius:

there must be industry: there must be perse- 1835
verance: there must be, before the eyes of the
nation, proofs of extraordinary exertion: people
must say to themselves, "What wise conduct must
there have been in the employing of the time of
this man! How sober, how sparing in diet, how
early a riser, how little expensive he must have
been!" These were the things, and not genius,
which caused my labours to be so incessant and
so successful.

I am sure that everyone will say, without any
hesitation, that a fourth part of the labours I have
performed never would have been performed if I
had not been a married man. In the first place,
they could not; for I should, all the early part of
my life, have been rambling and roving about as
most bachelors are. I should have had no home
that I cared a straw about, and should have wasted
the far greater part of my time. The great affair of
home being settled, having the home secured, I
had leisure to employ my mind on things which it
delighted in. I got rid at once of all cares, all
anxieties, and had only to provide for the very
moderate wants of that home. But the children
began to come. They sharpened my industry: they
spurred me on. To be sure, I had other and strong
motives: I wrote for fame, and was urged forward
by ill-treatment, and by the desire to triumph
over my enemies; but, after all, a very large part
of my nearly a hundred volumes may be fairly
ascribed to the wife and children.

[279]

1835   I might have done something; but, not a
thousandth part of what I have done; for the
chances are, that I being fond of military life,
should have ended my days ten or twenty years
ago in consequence of wounds or fatigues, or,
more likely, in consequence of the persecutions
of some haughty and insolent fool whom a
system of corruption had made my commander.
Love came and rescued me from this state of
horrible slavery; placed the whole of my time at
my disposal; made me free as air; removed every
restraint upon the operations of my mind, naturally disposed to communicate its thought to
others; and gave me a companion, who, deprived
of all opportunities of acquiring what is called
learning, had so much good sense, so much useful
knowledge, was so innocent, so just in all her
ways, so pure in thought, word, and deed, so dis-
interested, so generous, so devoted to me and her
children, so free from all disguise, and, withal, so
beautiful, so talkative, and in a voice so sweet, so
cheering, that I must, seeing that health and
capacity which it has pleased God to give me,
have been a criminal, if I had done much less than
that which I have done: and I have always said,
that if my country feel any gratitude for my
labours, that gratitude is due to her as full as
much as to me.

Care! What care have I known! I have been
buffetted about by a powerful and vindictive
government; I have repeatedly had the fruit of

my labour snatched 'away from me by it; but I 1835
had a partner that never frowned, that was never
melancholy, that was never subdued in spirit,
that never abated a smile on these occasions, that
fortified me, and sustained me by her courageous
example, and that was just as busy and as zealous
in taking care of the remnant as she had been in
taking care of the whole; just as cheerful, and just
as full of caresses, when brought down to a mean
hired lodging, as when the mistress of a fine
country house with all its accompaniments; and,
whether from her words or her looks, no one could
gather that she regretted the change. What have
I had worthy of the name of cares?

And, how is it now? How is it when the [end]
has come [near]? And how should I have been
without this wife and these children? I might
have amassed a tolerable heap of money; but
what would that have done for me? It might have
bought me plenty of professions of attachments;
plenty of people impatient for my exit from the
world; but not one single grain of sorrow for any
anguish that might have attended my approaching end. To me, no being in the world appears so
wretched as an old bachelor.

What do I want in the world but the things that
I have. I have a house in Fleet Street, I have
another in Kensington, I have another at [Nor-
mandy Farm, near the place of my birth]. These
are all good houses, too; they are furnished with
every necessary. What more than this can I want?

1835 I have horses at my will: always not less than half a dozen men to start at my call: God has blessed me with health and strength very rare at my age. Has ambition its calls upon me? What can it suggest beyond the farm that I have? Beyond the real power which I possess of upholding my friends and beating down my enemies?

An old Quaker, at Philadelphia, when I was writing away at a famous rate, used to send me a letter about once a week, containing these words, and no more: "Friend William, keep thyself cool". In the rigid sense of the term, I am certainly very far from being a Christian: I feel the dominion of the turbulent passions: when my coat is taken from me, I cannot give my cloak; nor does a buffet on the one cheek incline me patiently to turn the other. How many well-meaning people have exclaimed, "It is a pity that Cobbett is so *violent*"; such persons never asked themselves whether they would think a man too violent who should knock down a ruffian. This has been my state: when I began to write, I was as modest as a maid, and dealt in qualifications, and modifications, and mitigations to the best of my poor powers in the line of palavering; [but,] when I was first unprovokedly assaulted, I instantly resolved to proceed in the very same way, giving three, four, or ten blows for one.

It is a curious thing how the government of England has worked along with regard to me. Since about the year 1797 it has grown into a new

sort of government; and I do verily believe, that 1835
the history of my life will be the history of its life;
for we have been at war from the day of its birth;
or, at least, from its very infancy. It has, in its
march, destroyed, or silenced every formidable
assailant except myself; and the war between me
and it is certainly as curious a matter as ever
attracted the attention of mankind. The irre-
sistibleness of its power had been confirmed by
the melancholy fate of so many victims, that it
laid hold of me, expecting that one good sharp
bite would be enough. It did bite sharply, to be
sure. As the French say, it carried away the piece.
It regarded surviving as impossible; it was deceived for once; it had never had to do with a
plough-boy before. It is truly curious, that I, at
[this] time, who had always hated cities, and
London in particular, was actually entering into
arrangements for getting rid of everything in
London, publications and all; was sowing seeds
of trees, and plants of trees, and making all my
calculations for bringing up my family as farmers.
Some time in 1809 I had brought me a copy of the
ex-officio information [against me]. I was leaning
over a gate, and looking at the turnips in the field.
I saw at once the hell-born intention, and I saw
the consequences. The beautiful field disappeared,
and, in my imagination, I saw the walls of a prison.
My blood boiled with resentment and, cramming
the paper into my pocket, I made an oath never
to cease to oppose, never cease to annoy, as far

[283]

1835 as I legally could, [this] body of men. Which [oath] I have kept, with a little more fidelity than Tories keep their pledges. God is just; and as man is said to be made in the image of God, man should be just too; and to forget or not to punish as far as we are able, and legally can punish, is a neglect of sacred duty.

For now more than twenty-five long years, I was the great and constant and only really sharp and efficient thorn in the side of that system which, at last, brought this great country to the edge of convulsive ruin. I was the evening and the day star, the moon and the sun and the aurora of the press; all other parts of it have come twinkling behind me, shining now and then, indeed, but shining with a borrowed light. I always led the way at a great distance forward; I foresaw, foretold every event, every effect; my predictions in due succession became history; I was the teacher of the nation; the great source of political knowledge, and of all those powerful arguments by which so many hundreds of thousands were able to combat [the] nefarious and desolating system of sway.

It was, [not long ago,] my intention to close the "Register", and then I intended to publish, as the work of another year, "The History of My Life";[1] and then I intended to go into Hampshire, there to cultivate a garden and a few fields to the end of my life, the close of which I hoped to pass amongst that class of society that I have always most loved and cherished, the people employed in 1835 the cultivation of the land. I have it rooted in me, that happiness and riches are seldom companions; I have seen too much of the misery and opprobrium attending the living upon the public money not to have long ago resolved never to pocket a single farthing of it; and as to what are called honours, they have always been with me objects of contempt.

Born amongst husbandmen, bred to husbandry, delighting in its pursuits even to the minutest details, never having, in all my range of life, lost sight of the English farm-house and of those scenes in which my mind took its first spring, it is natural that I should have a strong partiality for country life, and that I should enter more in detail into the feelings of labourers in husbandry than into those of other labourers.

If the cultivators of the land be not, generally speaking, the most virtuous and most happy of mankind, there must be something at work in the community to counteract the operations of nature. This way of life gives the best security for health and strength of body. It does not teach, it necessarily produces early rising; constant forethought; constant attention; and constant care of dumb animals. The nature and qualities of all living things are known to country boys better than to philosophers. The seasons, the weather, the causes and effects of propagation, in cultivation, in tillage, are all known from habit, from incessant

1835 repetition of observation. The nature, the properties, the various uses, of different soils and
woods are familiar to the mind of country boys.
Riding, climbing, swimming, nothing comes a-
miss, and they are come, and are not sought.
Rural affairs leave not a day, not an hour, un-
occupied and without its cares, its promises, and
its fruitions. The seasons, which wait for no man;
the weather, which is no respecter of person, and
which will be what it will be, produce an habitual
looking forward, and make the farmer provident,
whatever might have been his natural disposition.
The farmer's cares are pleasing cares. His mis-
fortunes can seldom be more than lessons. His
produce consists of things wanted by all mankind.
His market-day is a ready-money one. No day-
books, bills, and ledgers haunt his mind. Envy
can, in the natural state of things, find no place
in his breast; for, the seasons and the weather are
the same to all; and the demand for his produce
has no other measure than the extent of his crops.

I [repeat], I intended to drop "The Register";
but I could not do [it]. It was so efficient! People
got into the habit of taking it in in clubs and
societies so nicely. Like the sun, it shed its beams
so truly all over the kingdom, that I could not
cease to publish it.

[But now,] I am once more in a farm. I might
have been, I am aware of it, possessed of bags of
public gold or of landed domains, purchased with
that gold. I trudge through the dirt, and I might

have ridden in the ring at Hyde Park, with four 1835
horses to draw me along in a gilded carriage, with
a coachman before me and footmen behind me.
What I might have been, it is hard to say; what
I have been and what I am, all the world knows;
I was a plough-boy and a private soldier, and I
am a Member of the House of Commons, sent
thither by the free voice of a great community.
I started at the same age, or thereabouts, with
Canning, Liverpool, and Huskisson. I always told
them that it was judgement as well as taste, that
led me into a path different from theirs. Time has
shown that my judgement was as sound as my
taste; for, if we are to estimate the future as well
as the past: they are already rotten; and the kingdom hardly recollects that there were such men.
Whereas, some generations, at least, will pass
away before the name of William Cobbett will
cease to be familiar in the mouths of the people
of England; and, for the rest of the world, I care
not a straw.

If I have one wish more ardent than all other,
it is this; that I, enjoying my garden and few
fields, may see England as great in the world, and
her industrious, laborious, kind and virtuous
people as happy as they were when I was born;
and that I may at last have a few years of calm
at the close of a long life of storms and of tempests.

This morning, long before four o'clock, I heard
the blackbirds making the fields echo with their
whistle; and a few minutes after four I, for the

1835 first time this year, heard the cuckoo, which I never before heard earlier than May-day. And now, this cuckoo will, on Midsummer day, cease to call us up in the morning, and cease its work of sucking the hedge-sparrow's eggs, depositing its own in the nest, making the poor hedge-sparrow bring it up, until it be big enough and strong enough to kill and eat the hedge-sparrow; in all which respects it so exactly resembles the at once lazy and greedy and ungrateful and cruel vagabonds, who devour the fruit of our labour. But, my friends, I do verily believe that, before we shall hear this harbinger of summer again, the vagabonds, of whom it is the type, will have received a souse, such as they never received before.

* * * * *

[These concluding paragraphs were written by Cobbett's sons.]

A great inclination to inflammation of the throat caused him annoyance from time to time, for several years, and, as he got older, it enfeebled him more. He was suffering from one of these attacks during the late spring, and it will be recollected, that when the Marquis of Chandos brought on his motion for the repeal of the malt-tax, my father attempted to speak, but could not make his voice audible beyond the few members who sat around him. He remained to vote on that motion, and increased his ailment; but on the voting of Supplies on the nights of Friday the

15th and Monday the 18th of May, he exerted himself so much, and sat so late, that he laid himself up. He determined, nevertheless, to attend the House again on the evening of the Marquis of Chandos' motion on Agricultural Distress on the 25th of May, and the exertion of speaking and remaining late to vote on that occasion were too much for one already severely unwell.

He went down to his farm early on the morning after this last debate, and had resolved to rest himself thoroughly and get rid of his hoarseness and inflammation. On Thursday night, last, he felt unusually well, and imprudently drank tea in the open air; but he went to bed apparently in better health. In the early part of the night he was taken violently ill, and on Friday and Saturday was considered in a dangerous state by the medical attendant. On Sunday he revived again, and on Monday gave us hope that he could yet be well. He talked feebly, but in the most collected and sprightly manner upon politics and farming; wished for "four days' rain" for the Cobbett-corn and the root-crop; and, on Wednesday, he could no longer remain shut up from the fields, but desired to be carried round the farm; which being done, he criticised the work that had been going on in his absence, and detected some little deviation from his orders, with all the quickness that was so remarkable in him. As he was carried to see the fields, a little boy in a blue smockfrock happened to come by us, to whom my father

1835 gave a laughing look, at which I thought I should
have dropped, I knowing what was passing in his
mind. He seemed refreshed at the sight of the little
creature, which he had once precisely resembled,
though now at such an immeasurable distance.

On Wednesday night he grew more and more
feeble, and was evidently sinking; but he continued to answer with perfect clearness every
question that was put to him. In the last half-
hour, his eyes became dim; and at ten minutes
after one P.M., he leaned back, closed them as if
to sleep, and died without a gasp.

THE END

NOTES

CHAPTER I

1. *page* 3. Cobbett's Age.
The facts are confusing. Cobbett himself said that he was born in March 1766. His son, John Morgan, wrote in 1835 (*Pol. Reg.* 26 June 1835), that the date was 9 March 1762. E. I. Carlyle, after examining the parish register at Farnham, concluded that the date was 9 March 1763. (See Carlyle, *William Cobbett*, Appendix A.) The reader must keep in mind these variations, for Cobbett consistently makes himself younger than is the fact.

2. *page* 5. Long Island was taken by the British in August 1776.

3. *page* 14. George the Fourth, who was Prince of Wales at the time of this incident.

CHAPTER II

1. *page* 20. Cobbett's Regiment was the 54th, Major Lord Edward Fitzgerald commanding. (See Note 3, p. 45, Chap. III.)

2. *page* 22. Lowth's Grammar.
A Short Introduction to English Grammar. London, 1762. By John Lowth. He was later Bishop of London. There were numerous editions.

CHAPTER III

1. *page* 30. The "new discipline"
This probably refers to the *Principles of Military*

[293]

Notes

Movements, chiefly applied to Infantry, etc., by Sir David Dundas, Field-Marshal. London, 1788.

2. *page* 35. The Reid Family.

Cobbett's father-in-law was Serg. Thomas Reid of the Royal Artillery. The following brothers and sisters-in-law were closely connected with Cobbett:

Thomas: b. Woolwich, 31 March 1777.

Eleanor: b. Woolwich, 2 August 1781.

Frederick: b. Gibraltar, 11 February 1785.

Cobbett's wife, Anne, was born at Chatham, 28 March 1774.

(See *Cobbett Papers.*)

3. *page* 45. Lord Edward Fitzgerald (1763–1798).

After an excellent military career, he joined his regiment, the 54th, in New Brunswick. Under the influence of Rousseau, he carried his admiration for the "noble savage" to the extent of living in the American wilderness, joining the Bear Tribe at Detroit, and journeying down the Mississippi River to New Orleans. He returned to Ireland, and, becoming involved in the circulation of revolutionary propaganda, was cashiered from the army. In 1796, he was deeply concerned in the conspiracy of the United Irishmen against England, and when the conspiracy was betrayed, he was shot in the arm and died in Newgate in consequence of his wound.

(See *Dict. of Nat. Biog.*)

CHAPTER IV

1. *page* 47. The Campaign of 1793 is referred to. The Duke of York was sent to the Low Countries to reinforce the Allies against the republican armies of France. The campaign was so disastrous that Wellington, who served in it, thought it a marvel that any of the English escaped.

Notes

2. *page 56. The Soldier's Friend; or, Considerations on the late pretended Augmentation of the Subsistence of the Private Soldier.* Ridgway, London, 1792 (July).

Cobbett both denied authorship (in 1805) and claimed it (in 1832). All his biographers accept his claim. The editor has here used the account which best suits the story Cobbett is telling.

(See Carlyle, pp. 33 ff.)
(See Cole, *Life of William Cobbett*, pp. 43 ff.)

3. *page 56.* The volume of Paine referred to is *The Rights of Man.* London, 1791.

4. *page 57.* The marriage certificate of William Cobbett and Anne Reid is dated 5 February 1792, at the parish church Woolwich. Cobbett is described as of the Parish of Portsmouth.

(See *Cobbett Papers.*)

5. *page 57.* The Works of Raynal.

Guillaume-Thomas-François, Abbé Raynal (1713–1796). Cobbett may be referring to one of two books:

1. *Histoire philosophique et politique des Établissements et des Européens dans les deux Indes.* Amsterdam, 1770.
2. *Tableau et Révolutions des colonies anglaises de l'Amerique Septentrionale.* Amsterdam, 1781.

For an analysis of the significance of the work of the Abbé Raynal, see Fay, *L'Esprit Révolutionnaire en France et aux États-Unis. . . .* Paris, 1926.

6. *page 57.* Lisle and Brissac.

Efforts to trace Lisle and Brissac as personal names have been unsuccessful. Captain Liddell Hart suggests that as Cobbett has just been speaking of fortified towns, and as he is not above taking liberties with his spelling, he is referring to Lille and Neu-Breisach, for the fortification of the latter place by Vauban (1698) was always regarded as the perfected example of Vauban's method, and is commonly referred to as his "third system", being a development of the method which he had employed in his still more celebrated fortification of Landau.

CHAPTER V

1. *page* 62. The following is a list of Cobbett's children. Those surviving infancy are in italics.
    1. A boy: b. ?, d. 3 June 1794.
    2. Child: Still-born 15 March 1794.
    3. *Anne: b. 11 July 1795, d. 22 October 1877.*
    4. *William: b. 26 November 1798, d. 12 January 1878.*
    5. *John Morgan: b. 13 November 1800, d. 13 February 1877.*
    6. Child: Still-born 1 May 1802.
    7. *James Paul: b. 23 June 1803, d. 11 March 1881.*
    8. A boy: b. 9 December 1804, d. 27 December 1804.
    9. *Eleanor: b. 6 December 1805, d. 11 January 1900.*
    10. *Susan: b. 24 April 1807, d. 2 February 1880.*
    11. ?
    12. Child: Still-born 27 August 1809.
    13. Child: (Still-born during his imprisonment).
    14. *Richard: b. 18 March 1814, d. 3 June 1875.*

There is a difficulty about the eleventh child. Cobbett writes (*Pol. Reg.* 13 July 1810): "I have acquired the means of making provision for a family of six children (the remains of thirteen)...".

2. *page* 65. *Le Maître Anglois.*

This first appeared with the title *Le Tuteur Anglais ou Grammaire régulière de la langue Anglaise.* Bradford, Philadelphia, 1795.

(See E. Smith, *William Cobbett*, I, 102, for details of later editions.)

Notes

3. *page* 67. *The Law of Nations.*
First published in Philadelphia, 1794. There are also, 2nd ed., London, 1802, with a dedication to John Penn, Esq.; 3rd ed., which the editor has not seen; 4th ed., London, 1829.

4. *page* 68. On the Political State of America, 1794–1800.
When Cobbett entered American politics, differences of opinion were clearly defined. There were two parties, calling themselves Federalists and Democrats. The former, which had the mercantile, industrial, and banking interests as its chief supporters, maintained the policy of a strong central government soundly financed, of friendliness to England as an important factor in American commercial life, and of aloofness to the overtures of the new French republic. The latter party, consisting of land-owners, the dwellers on the American frontier, and the urban proletariat, advocated strong local government, the perpetuation of revolutionary hatred of England, and assistance to the French in their struggles against "outworn" monarchies.

Philadelphia was the capital of the United States, and was the scene of the most frank intrigues between the Democrats and the agents of France. As far as Cobbett can be said to have fought on any side, it was on the side of the Federalists; but, more exactly, he was fighting for England against the ideas and practices of French republicans, as these showed themselves in America. This was his interest, and that he became involved in American affairs was largely an accident of the times and of his character.

His sympathy with the Federalist position was, at most, an abstract sympathy, and any services he rendered to their cause was by the way. His difficulties in Philadelphia came from the fact that, although the government of the United States was Federalist

in tone, the local government of Philadelphia and of
the State of Pennsylvania was Democratic. It was
with the law, dubiously administered by democratic
judges, that he had his troubles.

After 1798, when President Washington retired and
President Adams was elected, Cobbett seems to have
become the even more outspoken supporter of England
and so laid himself open to the charge of being a
dangerous alien. He says that President Adams had
listed him for deportation under the Alien and Sedition Act of 1798. Although there is no evidence in
support of this statement, it is correct to say that the
tension of American politics had so increased that
Cobbett could no longer occupy his unstable position
among local contentions.

The circulation of his once-popular *Porcupine's
Gazette* dropped by the end of 1799; his point of view
no longer fitted with that of the Federalists; and when
the blow of his lawsuit with Dr Rush fell (see Note 6,
p. 82, Chap. vi), he found that his wisest course was
to remove to England.

(See Fay, *op. cit.*, Chap. v, for a detailed discussion.)

CHAPTER VI

1. *page* 74. M'Kean and Ankerstrom.
Thomas M'Kean: Chief Justice of the Supreme
Court of Pennsylvania and later Governor. Cobbett
met him judicially on two occasions.
Ankerstrom: Swedish gentleman who assassinated
Gustavus Adolphus III of Sweden in March 1792.

2. *page* 74. Admiral Earl Howe defeated the French
fleet under Villaret de Joyeuse in a battle off the
northern coast of France 28 May to 1 June 1794.

3. *page* 76. Benjamin Franklin Bache (1769–1798) was
a Philadelphia journalist, founder of *The Aurora*, a

leading democratic newspaper. William Duane (1760–1835) was its editor after Bache's death.

Matthew Carey (1760–1839) was an Irish economist, pamphleteer, and publisher in Philadelphia. Being Irish, his anti-English feelings brought him into conflict with Cobbett.

4. *page* 79. Talleyrand was in Philadelphia from 22 May 1794 to 11 June 1796.

5. *page* 81. Moreau de St Méry (1750–1819).

Born in Martinique, went to Paris and was president of the *électeurs* when the Bastille fell, receiving the key of the fortress in the name of the city. Fled to America at the beginning of the Terror and became a bookseller in Philadelphia, 1794 to 1798. He was the author of: *Description topographique...de la partie espagnole de l'île Saint-Domingue.* (English translation by Cobbett, 1796.)

(See *Voyage aux États-Unis de l'Amérique*, 1793–1798, ed. S. L. Mims, New Haven, 1913.)

6. *page* 82. The Rush Libel Suit.

In 1798, in *Porcupine's Gazette*, Cobbett began to attack Dr Benjamin Rush of Philadelphia for advocating copious bleeding followed by a violent purge as a cure for the Yellow Fever. The abuse resulted in a libel suit. The occasion was improved by Cobbett's democratic opponents, who used every device to delay the cause, and who inconveniently brought it on in 1800 after Cobbett had moved his business to New York. Cobbett's only consolation was the knowledge that, when General Washington died, the use of Rush's treatment to reduce fever probably hastened his end. A full account is found in a pamphlet called *Farewell Number, Porcupine's Gazette*, published in New York, 13 June 1800; and in a brief periodical of seven issues, *The Rushlight*, New York and London; February to October 1800.

Notes

1. *page* 89. Windham's Speech. (See *Hansard Parliamentary History*, XXXVI (1801–1803), 1679.)

2. *page* 92. The Pitt Pamphleteers.
Bowles, John.
Reflections on the Political and Moral State of Society at the Close of the Eighteenth Century. London, 1800.
Brand, John, d. 1808. Presented by Lord-Chancellor Loughborough to rectory of St. George's, Southwark.
Historical Essay on the Principles of Political Associations in a State. . . . London, 1796.
D'Ivernois, Sir Francis.
Histoire . . . des finances de la République Française. 1796.
Immense préparatifs de guerre . . . après le Traité d'Amiens. London, 1804.
Eden, Sir Frederick (1766–1809).
The State of the Poor. . . . London, 1797, 3 vols.
Eight Letters on the Peace. . . . London, 1802. Originally addressed to Cobbett's *Porcupine* over the signature "Philanglus". The opinion of Karl Marx can be placed beside Cobbett's: "the only disciple of Adam Smith during the eighteenth century that produced any work of importance".
Gifford, John (1758–1818), properly John Richards Green. Prefixed an essay to the English reprint of Cobbett's *Bone to Gnaw for the Democrats*, London, 1797. He was also concerned in *The Porcupine*. Edited the *Anti-Jacobin Review*.
Gifford, William (1756–1826).
Baviad, London, 1794.
Maeviad, London, 1795.
These were republished in Philadelphia by Cobbett in the year 1799. Edited *Anti-Jacobin, or Weekly*

Notes

Examiner, 20 November 1797 to 9 July 1798. Edited
Quarterly Review which began February 1809.

Ireland, John (1761–1842).
Close friend of William Gifford.
Letters of Fabius to William Pitt.... London, 1801.
First addressed to the *Porcupine*.

Marsh, Herbert (1757–1839).
*History of Great Britain and France, from the time of
the conference of Pilnitz to the Declaration of War
against Great Britain.* Originally written in German,
it had great influence on the continent.

du Pan, Mallet (1749–1800).
Edited the *Mercure Britannique*, a fortnightly paper,
distributed on the continent.

Reeves, John (1752–1829).
Appointed King's Printer in 1800 by William Pitt.

Vansittart, Nicholas (1766–1851), first Baron Bex-
ley. His pamphleteering consisted chiefly of defences
of Pitt's system of finance. He was Chancellor of the
Exchequer 1812 to 1824.

3. *page* 96. "The accursed thing in the camp of the
Israelites." (See Joshua vii.)

4. *page* 98. Mr John Morgan.
After Morgan's return to America, his close connection with Cobbett was maintained. He distributed
Cobbett's writings in America and owned the American copyrights of many of his books. In 1817, he
acted as Cobbett's banker, and assisted him in the
seed business which the latter started in New York.

5. *page* 100. The news of the Preliminaries of the Peace
was announced in London on 10 October 1801, and
Cobbett's shop in Pall Mall was attacked the same
evening.
The Treaty itself was signed at Amiens 27 March
1802. Cobbett's house was again attacked when the
news reached London a day or two later.

6. *page* 102. *The Porcupine* was sold to John Gifford, one of the Pitt pamphleteers, on 21 November 1801. Gifford immediately transferred it to Mr Redhead Yorke, who had "an allowance from the Ministry"; and it disappeared, by a merger with *The True Briton*, a ministerial sheet.

(See Cobbett to Windham: 24 November 1801. Add. mss. 37,853.)

7. *page* 103. The New Opposition.

This was a small parliamentary group that broke with Pitt at the time of the Peace with Napoleon, and maintained its antagonism to Bonaparte. The group looked upon *The Political Register* as its mouthpiece. Windham was its leader and represented it in the Ministry of All-Talents.

8. *page* 106. Single-stick at Botley.

A match took place at Botley 11 October 1805. It was part of the campaign against those who would destroy old English sports and tastes; a campaign in which Windham's speech in favour of bull-baiting and a series of articles in *The Political Register* also played a part.

(See Add. mss. 37,853, fol. 186, for a copy of the "Advertisement"; and also Cobbett to Windham, 6 October 1805. Add. mss. 37,853.)

CHAPTER VIII

1. *page* 132. The following is a list of the anti-Cobbett publications during the great outburst of 1807–1809.

Cobbett Against Himself	1807
The Camelon	1807
A Refutation of the present Political Sentiments of Himself	1808
Blagdon's Political Register	1809
Cobbett's Oppression !	1809

Notes

CHAPTER IX

1. *page* 139. Cobbett's Debts in 1810.

A great deal of correspondence is extant covering this matter. It can be found in *Cobbett Papers*.

Mss. Eng. Hist. C. 33 in Bodleian Library, contains correspondence between the Swanns, who were papermakers, Cobbett, and John Wright.

Add. mss. 22,906, 22,907, 31,126 contain correspondence with John Wright.

2. *page* 140. James Paull, or Paul.

A Quaker farmer, living at Bustleton, in Lower Dublin Township, Bucks County, to the north of Philadelphia. Cobbett first met him when he removed his family to Bustleton to avoid the Yellow Fever of 1793. Several open letters in *The Political Register* were addressed to him. In 1818, Cobbett visited James Paull and found him, then an old man, near his death.

(See *A Year's Residence.*)

3. *page* 144. Farming Correspondence.

This has been in great part preserved in *Cobbett Papers*.

4. *page* 151. Paine's *Decline and Fall of the English System of Finance.*

Published in Philadelphia and London, 1796. This pamphlet had some of the same delusive simplicity that made Malthus' work so attractive. Paine found that the National Debt of England had increased through the eighteenth century in a fixed mathematical progression—a series in which a given number was produced by taking the preceding number and adding to it one-half of itself, thus, 8, 12, 18, 27, etc. Paine confidently, therefore, predicted the end of the English financial system about 1805–1815. The work is not as delusive in its details as in its fundamental assumption.

5. *page* 155. Charles James Fox to Windham: 24 November 1804.

"I suggest he (Cobbett) pushes his notions concerning the depreciation of money too far, though they are by no means without foundation.... I mention this subject the rather, because I am informed Cobbett has rather fatigued his readers by dwelling too much upon it."

(See *Windham Papers*, II, 242.)

CHAPTER X

1. *page* 167. The Riots of 1816.

These outbursts, the consequence largely of industrial misery, were marked by episodes of machine-breaking and food riots. The rioters acted under the feigned leadership of Capt. Ludd. Attempts were made to link these sporadic incidents to an agitation for the reform of Parliament. The movement collapsed in the following year, with results to himself that Cobbett records in Chap. XI.

(See *The Last Hundred Days of English Freedom*, extracted from *Pol. Reg.*, ed. J. L. Hammond, London, 1921.)

Notes

2. *page* 168. *A Letter to the Journeymen and Labourers of England, Scotland and Ireland. On the Causes of their present miseries....* Published in *Pol. Reg.* xxxi, 2 November, 1816.

3. *page* 169. Samuel Bamford writes:
"At this time the writings of William Cobbett suddenly became of great authority; they were read on nearly every cottage hearth in the manufacturing districts....This influence was speedily visible; he directed his readers to the true cause of their sufferings—misgovernment; and to its proper corrective— parliamentary reform. Riots soon became scarce, and from that time they have never obtained their ancient vogue with the labourers of this country."
(See *Life of a Radical,* 1859, p. 6.)

4. *page* 172. Sidmouth's Bill.
Seditious Meetings Bill and Suspension of Habeas Corpus.
(See *Hansard,* 1st Series, xxxv, 554.)

5. *page* 176. Mr Astor.
This apparently is William Backhouse Astor, the second son of John Jacob Astor of New York, the famous fur merchant. This son, who had been studying in European universities, was returning to enter his father's business. The date is incorrectly given in *Dict. of American Biog.*

CHAPTER XI

1. *page* 185. The Harrisburg Petition.
This petition was for the restitution of recognizances in connection with a suit for libel brought against Cobbett in 1797 by Count Yrujo, Spanish Envoy to the United States. The Grand Jury had dismissed the case. An account of the incident is to

be found in *The Democratic Judge*, for M'Kean, the
hero of that pamphlet was the Count's father-in-law.

The petition, in Cobbett's hand, is in the collection of
the Pennsylvania Historical Society at Philadelphia.

2. *page* 187. The "Pennsylvania wagons" described by
Cobbett are better known by the name of "Conestoga
wagons". They should be familiar to English readers
from such films as *The Covered Wagon*.

3. *page* 197. The Life of Paine.

A full account can be found in Moncrieff-Conway's
Life of Paine, ii, Appendix A.

In 1818, Cobbett negotiated with Madame Bonne-
ville, then living in New York, agreeing to give her
$1000 for the ms. of a Life on which she was
working, and which contained important letters. She
stipulated that it should be published in England
without additions, and that it should be separate
from all other writings. The bargain fell through.

Cobbett worked on another Life, although he never
published it. Moncrieff-Conway saw this latter ms.
through the courtesy of Eleanor Cobbett and her
nephew Sir William Cobbett of Manchester. The
present editor, however, could not find it among the
Cobbett Papers.

4. *page* 202. Cobbett in agreeing not to enter the city
of Manchester was making capital of the notorious
"Peterloo massacre", which had taken place the
16th of August previous.

(See Note 3, p. 241, Chap. XIII.)

CHAPTER XII

1. *page* 204. Cobbett's paper was *The Evening Post*;
his son William was printer and publisher. It began
29 January 1820, and ran for about two months.

Notes

Public taste apparently found *The Political Register* a more satisfactory vehicle for Cobbett's abilities.

2. *page* 211. The ill-judged letter from America about his debts received a good deal of attention from pamphlet-writers.

This is a single-sheet folio, in which Cobbett is elected to the Club with applause, after passages have been read from his letter.

(See ms. Montagu d. 17, in the Bodleian Library.)

3. *page* 214. My "Trash".

The name of "Two-penny Trash" was given by Cobbett's opponents to the cheap *Political Register* of 1816. He kept the name in his mind and, when the later agitation for reform was under way, he used the title for a cheap publication which ran monthly from July 1830 to July 1832. *Cobbett's Two-penny Trash; or, Politics for the Poor* consisted of reprints of articles from *The Political Register*. There was no number for March 1832.

4. *page* 217. "Peel's Bill" for the resumption of cash payments, i.e. return to the gold standard, was passed April–May, 1819. The nature of the distress occasioned by the consequent deflation of money value is amply indicated by Cobbett.

5. *page* 225. *Cottage Economy: containing Information ...relative to...matters deemed useful in the conducting of the Affairs of a Labourer's Family.* London, 1822.

This was first issued in seven parts, from 28 July 1821 to 1 March 1822.

Notes

CHAPTER XIII

1. *page* 227. Baring Brothers and Co., the London financial house, consisted of Alexander, Baron Ashburton; Francis, Lord Northbrook; and Thomas Baring, during this period. They were all active in political life.

2. *page* 234. *Letter to the Luddites* was one of the cheap *Registers*, published in XXXI, 30 November 1816.

3. *page* 241. "The 16th of August at Manchester" refers to the Peterloo Riot, when an assembly of workers, meeting in St. Peter's Fields, were ridden down by the yeomanry under the direction of the local magistrates.

4. *page* 244. Sir Thomas Beevor, 3rd Bart. (1798–1879).
   This baronet, whose seat was Hargham Hall, near Attleborough, Norfolk, first became acquainted with Cobbett through his interest in timber growing. He stocked his plantations from Cobbett's nursery, and Cobbett conducted experiments in setting-out, grafting, etc. with his help. Sir Thomas was the bearer of a letter of congratulation from the English Reformers to the French republicans at the conclusion of the Revolution of 1830.

5. *page* 247. Readers wishing to judge the character of these lectures will find some of them in a series of pamphlets published in 1830, and entitled *Eleven Lectures on the French and Belgian Revolutions, and English Borough-mongering....* They were delivered in the Theatre of the Rotunda, Blackfriars Bridge, between 2 September and 7 October 1830. Another collection is *Cobbett's Manchester Lectures, in Support of his Fourteen Reform Propositions....* These were given at the end of December 1831. For the most part Cobbett spoke from brief notes, several sets of which

[308]

have been preserved in the *Cobbett Papers*. The itinerary of the lectures can easily be traced in G. D. H. Cole's edition of the *Rural Rides*.

CHAPTER XIV

1. *page 255.* Cobbett's Trial.

   The Political Register contains only a brief article of comment. The detailed report is to be found in a pamphlet, *A Full and Accurate Account of Mr. Cobbett's Trial, etc.*, London, 1831. The contemporary importance of the occasion can be judged from the description given of it in *The Examiner*, where it is called "a trial of the Government more than of Cobbett".

CHAPTER XV

1. *page 284.* "History of My Life."

   Cobbett writes: " ...my chief object in writing it, or, at least, one of my chief objects, being to assert the natural rights of the working people; to assert the superiority which nature frequently gives them over birth, title, and wealth. I shall entitle my book 'The Progress of a Plough-boy to a seat in Parliament, as exemplified in the History of the Life of William Cobbett, Member for Oldham'; and, I intend that the frontispiece to the book shall represent me, first in a smock-frock, driving the rooks from the corn; and, in the lower compartment of the picture, standing in the House of Commons, addressing the Speaker".

   (See *Pol. Reg.* LXXXIII, 15 February 1834, p. 409.)

THE SOURCES OF THE TEXT

The paragraph numbers at the left refer to the preceding text; the page numbers at the right refer to the various sources

CHAPTER I

Sources of the Text

CHAPTER II

CHAPTER III

CHAPTER IV

¶14 ⎰ *Political Reg.*, VIII, 5 Oct. 1805 p. 522 ⎱
    ⎱ ,,   ,,   XV, 17 June 1809 p. 915 ⎰
15   ,,   ,,   VIII, 5 Oct. 1805 p. 522
16   ,,   ,,   VIII, 5 Oct. 1805 p. 522, 523
17   ,,   ,,   VIII, 5 Oct. 1805 p. 523
18 ⎰ ,,   ,,   XV, 17 June 1809 p. 903 ⎱
   ⎱ ,,   ,,   VIII, 5 Oct. 1805 p. 524 ⎰

CHAPTER V

1 *Life and Adventures of Peter Porcupine* p. 32
2   ,,   ,,   ,,   ,,   ,, p. 33, 34
3 Letter to Rachel Smithers. Phila., 6
     July 1794. (Printed in Melville, *Life
     and Letters*, I, 85 ff.)
4 Letter to Rachel Smithers. Phila., 6
     July 1794
5 *Advice to Young Men* p. 145, ¶166,
                           p. 146, ¶167
6 ⎰ ,,   ,, p. 169, ¶192 ⎱
  ⎱ ,,   ,, p. 102, ¶100 ⎰
  ⎰ *Emigrant's Guide* (London, 1830) p. 139, ¶101 ⎰
7 *Advice to Young Men* p. 169, ¶192
8   ,,   ,, p. 89, ¶90,
                p. 92, 93, ¶92
9 ⎰ ,,   ,, p. 142, ¶161 ⎱
  ⎱ ,,   ,, p. 220, ¶259 ⎰
      ,,   ,, p. 143, ¶162
10 ⎰ Letter to Rachel Smithers. Phila., 6
   ⎱ July 1794
     Political Reg., XXXII, 6 Dec. 1817 p. 1094
11 *Advice to Young Men* p. 145, ¶166,
                           p. 146, ¶167
12 *Political Reg.*, LXVIII, 22 Aug. 1829 p. 229
13 *Advice to Young Men* p. 143, ¶162
14 ⎰ *The Democratic Judge* (Phila., 1798) p. 7 ⎱
   ⎱ *Political Reg.*, VI, 29 Sep. 1804 p. 450 ⎰
15   ,,   ,,   29 Sep. 1804 p. 450

¶16   *Political Reg.*, VI,   29 Sep. 1804   p. 450
17   ,,   ,,   VI,   29 Sep. 1804   p. 451
18   ,,   ,,   LXIX, 10 April 1830   p. 453, 454

CHAPTER VI

1 *Porcupine's Works* (London, 1801) iv, p. 3
2   ,,   ,,   iv, p. 3
3   ,,   ,,   iv, p. 3, 4
4   ,,   ,,   iv, p. 4
5   ,,   ,,   iv, p. 4
6 { ,,   ,,   iv, p. 4
   { *Political Reg.*, VIII, 5 Oct. 1805   p. 519
7   ,,   ,,   VIII,   5 Oct. 1805   p. 519
   { *The Democratic Judge*   p. 9
8 { *Political Reg.*, LIII, 29 Jan. 1825   p. 264, 261,
   {   p. 280
9   ,,   ,,   LXIX, 10 April 1830   p. 455
10 { ,,   ,,   VIII,   12 Oct. 1805   p. 549
    { ,,   ,,   VIII,   12 Oct. 1805   p. 547
11 { ,,   ,,   LXIX, 10 April 1830   p. 454
    { ,,   ,,   VIII,   12 Oct. 1805   p. 547, 548
12 { ,,   ,,   LXIX, 10 April 1830   p. 455
    { ,,   ,,   LXXII, 4 June 1831   p. 545
13 *Porcupine's Works*   v, p. 361, 362
14   ,,   ,,   v, p. 362, 363
15 *The Porcupine* (London, 1801). 26 Aug.
     1801
16 *Porcupine's Gazette.* No. 799, 13 Jan.
     1800   p. 50, 51
17 *The Rushlight*, I, 1, 15 Feb. 1800   p. 1, 2
18   ,,   I, 1, 15 Feb. 1800   p. 2
19 *Political Reg.*, LXIX,   10 April 1830   p. 454
20   ,,   ,,   XIII,   26 March 1808   p. 486
21   ,,   ,,   XIII,   26 March 1808   p. 489
22   ,,   ,,   XLIX,   31 Jan. 1824   p. 284, 285
23   ,,   ,,   LXXXII, 2 Nov. 1833   p. 258
24   ,,   ,,   LXXXII, 2 Nov. 1833   p. 259

CHAPTER VII

(Add. mss. 37,853, f. 17.

" . . . Mr. Gifford has lost about £300, and I about £450, which is enough, in all conscience, to reward me

for all my exertions, dangers and losses in America.
The light is now extinguished completely. One half of
the papers are devoted to France, and the other half
to the Ministry.... I have done all I could do without
exposing my family to beggary.")

¶22	*Political Reg.*,	VIII,	12 Oct. 1805	p. 551
	,, ,,	LXIX,	10 April 1830	p. 457
	,, ,,	VIII,	12 Oct. 1805	p. 552, 553, p. 554
	,, ,,	III,	8 Jan. 1803	p. 1
23	,, ,,	IX,	4 Jan. 1806	p. 22
	,, ,,	VII,	26 Jan. 1805	p. 120
24	,, ,,	III,	29 Jan. 1803	p. 99
	,, ,,	XI,	28 Feb. 1807	p. 324
	,, ,,	I,	27 Feb. 1801	p. 176
25	,, ,,	III,	15 Jan. 1803	p. 34
	,, ,,	VII,	9 Feb. 1805	p. 220
	,, ,,	XIX,	25 May 1811	p. 1283, 1284
26	,, ,,	IX,	8 Feb. 1806	p. 169
27	,, ,,	VI,	1 Sep. 1805	p. 340
28	,, ,,	IV,	31 Dec. 1803	p. 930, 931
	,, ,,	XV,	17 June 1809	p. 898, 899
29	,, ,,	X,	20 Sep. 1806	p. 451
30	,, ,,	IX,	28 June 1806	p. 968, 969
31	,, ,,	IX,	28 June 1806	p. 970
32	,, ,,	IX,	28 June 1806	p. 971
33	,, ,,	IX,	28 June 1806	p. 972
34	,, ,,	IX,	28 June 1806	p. 972, 970

CHAPTER VIII

1 *Advice to Young Men* p. 241, ¶ 283
  Letter to Windham, 12 Aug. 1805
  (Add. mss. 37,853, f. 177.

"...Botley is the most delightful village in the
world. It has everything in a village, that I love; and
none of the things I hate. It is in a valley. The soil is

rich, thick set with wood; the farms are small the cottages neat; it has neither workhouse, nor barber, nor attorney, nor justice of the peace...there is no justice within six miles of us, and the barber comes three miles once a week to shave and cut hair! 'Would I were poetical', I would write a poem in praise of Botley.")

"...My intention is to make the boys fit to fight their way through life, for, who can be so weak as to imagine, that we shall, or, that they will, ever see many days of tranquillity! To write English; to speak French; to read a little Latin, perhaps; to ride, to play at single-stick, and, above all things, *to work at husbandry*, it is my intention to teach them, in all by precept and in the most instances, if. please God to spare me, by example. I have seen too many proofs of the insufficiency of riches to the obtaining of happiness and too many instances of the misery to which a dependance upon patronage leads....I shall do nothing to stifle genius; but, if it be not of a stamp to rise of itself, there is no raising it."

Sources of the Text

CHAPTER IX

Sources of the Text

CHAPTER X

CHAPTER XI

Sources of the Text

CHAPTER XII

¶ 1 { Letter to his Wife, 2 Feb. 1820. (See Melville, II, 128) }
{ Letter to his Wife, 4 Jan. 1820. (See Melville, II, 125) }

2 *Political Reg.*, XXXVI, 25 March 1820   p. 86, 87

3   ,,   ,,   XXXVI, 25 March 1820   p. 87, 88

4   ,,   ,,   XXXVI, 25 March 1820   p. 88, 89

5   ,,   ,,   XXXVI, 25 March 1820   p. 90, 91

6   ,,   ,,   XXXVI, 25 March 1820   p. 92, 99, 100, p. 101

7   ,,   ,,   XXXVI, 25 March 1820   p. 101, 102, p. 103

8   ,,   ,,   XXXVI, 25 March 1820   p. 104, 105, p. 106

9   ,,   ,,   XXXVI, 25 March 1820   p. 106, 107

10   ,,   ,,   XXXVI, 25 March 1820   p. 109, 110, p. 119, 120

11   ,,   ,,   XXXVI, 25 March 1820   p. 113, 114

12   ,,   ,,   XXXVI, 25 March 1820   p. 114, 116, p. 125

13   ,,   ,,   LXIX,   10 April 1830   p. 472, 473, p. 474

14   ,,   ,,   LXIX,   10 April 1830   p. 473

15 { ,,   ,,   LXIX,   10 April 1830   p. 473 }
   { ,,   ,,   LXXIX, 26 Jan. 1833   p. 194 }

16 { ,,   ,,   LXXIX, 26 Jan. 1833   p. 195 }
   { ,,   ,,   LXIX,   10 April 1830   p. 473 }

17   ,,   ,,   LXIX,   10 April 1830   p. 473

18 *Rural Rides* (Ed. G. D. H. Cole, London, 1930), i, p. 8

19   ,,   ,,   (Cole)   i, p. 50, 51

20 Letter to J. P. Cobbett, 25 May 1821. (See *Cobbett Papers*)

"...I am here most delightfully situated. We keep five fine cows. We have a pigeon-house to hold a hundred pair; and Dick is the grand pigeon-master. Pigs in stye; and a most abundant and fruitful garden. Our publications, particularly the Sermons, more famous than ever...and no villains to cheat us any more."

¶21 *Rural Rides* (London, 1830)   p. 665, 547

22 {   ,,   ,,   p. 665 }
   {   ,,   ,,   p. 335, 336 }

23   ,,   ,,   p. 99, 100,
                                                      p. 101

24   ,,   ,,   p. 76, 77

25   ,,   ,,   p. 18, 19

26   ,,   ,,   p. 417

27   ,,   ,,   p. 303

28   ,,   ,,   p. 303

29 {   ,,   ,,   p. 381 }
   { *Paper Against Gold*   p. 28 }

30 *Political Reg.*, LXVIII, 17 Oct. 1829   p. 495, 496

31   ,,   ,,   XLVI, 31 May 1823   p. 513, 514

32 {   ,,   ,,   XLVI, 31 May 1823   p. 514 }
   {   ,,   ,, XXXIX, 7 April 1821   p. 9, 10 }

33 *Rural Rides*   p. 498

34   ,,   ,,   p. 167, 168

35 { *Political Reg.*, XLIII,   17 Aug. 1822   p. 441 }
   {   ,,   ,, LXXXII, 28 Dec. 1833   p. 777, 778 }

36 *Rural Rides*   p. 94, 95

37   ,,   ,, (Cole)   i, p. 29

CHAPTER XIII

1 *Rural Rides*   p. 312

2 {   ,,   ,,   p. 312 }
  { *Political Reg.*, XL,   29 Sep. 1821   p. 709, 710 }
  {   ,,   ,, XXIX, 16 Dec. 1815   p. 331 }

3   ,,   ,, XXIX, 16 Dec. 1815   p. 331

4 {   ,,   ,,   XL,   29 Sep. 1821   p. 710 }
  { *Rural Rides*   p. 124 }

5 { *Political Reg.*, XXIX, 16 Dec. 1815   p. 312 }
  { *Rural Rides*   p. 331 }
  {   p. 209 }

Sources of the Text

Sources of the Text

¶25 *Political Reg.*, LXXXI,   21 Sep. 1833   p. 729
26   „   „   LXXXI,   21 Sep. 1833   p. 729, 730
27 { „   „   LXXVIII, 22 Dec. 1832   p. 713, 714 }
     „   „   LXXV,   31 Dec. 1831
28   „   „   LXXVIII, 22 Dec. 1832   p. 714, 715
29   „   „   LXXVIII, 22 Dec. 1832   p. 715, 716
30   „   „   LXXVIII, 22 Dec. 1832   p. 720, 722,
                                                p. 723
31 { „   „   LXXVIII, 22 Dec. 1832   p. 723, 724 }
     „   „   LXXVIII, 22 Dec. 1832   p. 708, 709, }
                                                p. 710
32 { *Tour of Scotland*   p. 53 }
     Political Reg., LXXXVIII, 18 April 1835 p. 145
33   *Tour of Scotland*   p. 101, 108
34   *Life of Andrew Jackson* (London, 1834), Dedication
35   *Political Reg.*, LXX,   25 Dec. 1830   p. 1099
36   „   „   LXXXV, 30 Aug. 1834   p. 529, 530

CHAPTER XV

1 { *Political Reg.*, LXXXIV, 26 April 1834   p. 193, 194 }
     „   „   LXXXIV, 3 May 1834   p. 258
2   *Advice to Young Men*   p. 4, ¶4
3   „   „   p. 5, ¶4
4   „   „   p. 5, ¶4
5   „   „   p. 6, ¶5;
                                                p. 6, 7, ¶6
6   „   „   p. 186, 187,
                                                ¶215
7   „   „   p. 187, ¶217
8   „   „   p. 188, ¶217
9   „   „   p. 188, 189,
                                                ¶218
10 *Political Reg.*, LXIV,   20 Oct. 1827   p. 205, 206
11 { „   „   XXXIX, 16 June 1821   p. 721 }
     Porcupine's Works, V   p. 25
     Political Reg., LXV,   26 Jan. 1826   p. 114
12   „   „   LXXXVIII, 4 April 1835 p. 143, 144

¶13	*Political Reg.,*	LXIX,	10 April 1830	p. 452
14	,,	,,	LXXI,	8 Jan. 1831	p. 65, 66
15	,,	,,	XXXIX,	5 May 1821	p. 343
16	,,	,,	XXXVIII,	17 March 1821	p. 731, 732
17	,,	,,	LXXVIII,	17 Nov. 1832	p. 422
18 {	,,	,,	LXXXVIII,	4 April 1835	}
	,,	,,	LXXXII,	5 Oct. 1833	p. 28 }
19	,,	,,	LXXI,	8 Jan. 1831	p. 66
20	,,	,,	LXXXVIII,	18 April 1835	p. 146
21	,,	,,	LXXXVIII,	20 June 1835	p. 705, 706
22 {	,,	,,	LXXXVIII,	20 June 1835	p. 706 }
	,,	,,	LXXXVIII,	27 June 1835	p. 775 }
23	,,	,,	LXXXVIII,	20 June 1835	p. 706, 707

INDEX

Index

Index